Face The Bear

Tales of Laugh'n, Cry'n & Learn'n

By

Roger Geiger

Printed in the United States of America, First Printing, 2017

ISBN 1546927263
EAN 978-1546927266

https://sites.google.com/site/taidyftb/

Scripture quotations taken from the New American Standard Bible® (NASB), Copyright © 1960, 1962, 1963, 1968, 1971, 1972, 1973, 1975, 1977, 1995 by The Lockman Foundation
Used by permission. www.Lockman.org

Image by Don Pugh, licensed under following terms:
https://creativecommons.org/licenses/by-nd/2.0/legalcode

Image ID 1996-022-0001 from Missouri History Museum, St. Louis, used by permission.

Image IMG-0032 by Theresa Westaby, Rootstock Coop, used by permission.

Special thanks to:

Kate Finlayson - cover image
Addison McElveen - cover design

Beta Readers / Editors
Amy Cousineau
Carly Geiger
Jerre Geiger
Jeff Goodman

Neil Melillo - Writing Coach

Mary Holmes – Proof reader

The Sachse Wylie Authors Group
Firewheel Fiction Writers' Workshop

Images contributed by:
Jeff Cunkelman, Howard Geiger, Al Judd

Introduction

This book is a life travelogue. My life. The stories are as true as failing memory and good sense allow them to be. Most of these tales relate experiences gained after an opportunity presented itself. Others are the tragic consequence of living.

I never set out to be an adventurer, yet I experienced many adventures. I'm more often foolish than wise, but I've learned truth along my road. Throughout the course of my life I've been known by several names: Sport, Rog, Hodji, Daddy, Brother Roger, and now Taidy (pronounced Tidy), which is an adaptation of the Welsh name for grandfather. Each of these characters has a story to tell and a lesson to share.

It is unfortunate that my younger self paid little heed to needs waiting in his future. I wish I had written letters to my older self when I was young. My efforts to recall life's experiences would have met with more success had I thought to write letters to Taidy, as I am known today, when the incidents occurred. I did not. The letters related at the beginning of the following chapters accurately represent what I might have written to myself had I shown more foresight.

May you find my stories compelling, humorous and insightful. Whether around the lunch table or campfire, telling these stories has proved interesting to all. Those listeners often suggested I write a book, so here I go. An opportunity has presented itself; I haven't had an adventure in a while, and I suspect I'm overdue.

1

November 1975

Dear Tidy,

Today, morning light illuminated waterspouts as they tickled our horizon. A sperm whale breached to consider the intruders invading her world. Tonight I sat on the bow plate, my legs straddling a small flag pole, to watch dolphins ride our bow wake below. Luminous plankton sparkled off their dancing backs like meteors streaming star-dust as they led us to harbor. Above, millions of stars, hidden from those moored to the land, reflected the wonder I saw below. I feel blessed to be here. These make it all worthwhile. These are the good times.

Rog

For as long as I live you could blindfold me, toss me on a plane, throw me out in that town and I'd know I'm in Dakar. It's the smell. Like burnt peanuts with shell rot. With the North Sea getting too rough for seismic work, our ship made its way through the Canary Islands then on to the armpit of Africa's western hump. There lies the country of Senegal. All sea traffic to Senegal puts in at the port city of Dakar. After four months in the grey days and high seas of the North, cruising south under sunny skies for a couple of weeks was almost a pleasure. Maybe I got cheered by the sun, maybe by extra space due to our skeleton crew, or maybe I needed a break from too many twelve hour shifts. Whatever the reason, once we arrived in Africa, I felt whole again.

My story is starting in Africa because this first tale is so exciting I can't wait to tell it. Beginnings can be set straight later. Tragedy and happy endings are still far away. Today, we begin with adventure.

Much as I enjoyed the trip from Middlesbrough to Dakar, seeing the guys I'd left in England also brought joy to my heart. As our ship idled upstream toward the dock, I saw Martin Hodge, a six-foot plus Englishman with flaming red hair and beard. "Bushfire" danced at dockside in his shorts, unlaced boots and bright plaid shirt while he waited for us to arrive. Our small ship had barely touched the quay when he jumped up on an empty shipping crate to hail those of us leaning on the deck rail to watch. "And how are all the fine lads on board this morning? Had a lovely cruise have we? Well, if you like, I'll be the first to welcome you to sunny Africa. I've got the place all sussed out for you." Martin, one of our geophysical engineers, saw no reason to take life too seriously.

As usual when we arrived in port, fresh supplies and bosses were lined up waiting at dockside. The supervisors never seemed comfortable with wasted time. Labor began before the skipper had cut the engines and didn't quit until there was nothing left to do or it got too dark to do it. Around dusk, I finally managed to hunt up Martin. "Let's go. You've been here for a day already. Where's the bar?"

"Right then. Follow me. There's a fine pub just down the way if you don't mind a few bugs and such."

In Dakar, local port authorities provided token protection for ships at dock. As soon as we exited the security fence, heading down a rubble filled street, we got swarmed by junk sellers and shine boys of all sizes. Hawkers usually lost interest if you ignored them. The kids kept after us like mosquitos.

"Shine m'sieur. Shine?"

"You give me money?"

"Vous voulez femme?"

About a dozen of the little guys gathered all around me pushing and shoving for a chance to get in close. In frustration I stopped to yell, "I don't want a damn shine. I'm wearing sneakers for Christ sake. No, NO. ARRET!" The pesky urchins ignored my distress.

From ten yards ahead Martin yelled back, "Don't stop Rog. They'll tear you apart! Almost there." I made a move to follow after him as the vicious little buggers pulled on my arms, pockets, belt, whatever offered itself to be latched on to. "GET THE HELL OFFA ME." I'd really started to lose it so I grabbed one of the boys and swung him into as many more as I could reach, gaining myself a bit of space. That let me build up enough speed to catch Martin who waited in the door of a seedy little bar. As I went in, the barman came out swinging a long stick and laid into the boys who mostly managed to dodge his strokes and take off down the street.

While I watched the man drive off the mob, Martin handed me a beer and raised his glass in a toast. "Cheers mate. Welcome to Dakar." That evening the crew had an early curfew, and we were out to sea before midnight.

While in port, sightseeing pretty much took a backseat to alcohol in all its wonderful forms. We'd hit the bars as soon as our party manager released us from work and not return till the wee hours. Even for a young fellow like myself, this wore on my energy reserves. God knows how the older guys would have managed if our employer hadn't seen fit to provide each of us with a medical kit. In that kit I found all kinds of prescription medications including the beloved Doc Walker's Patented Hangover Pills. No kidding, they actually issued these wonder drugs. A little yellow pill filled with painkillers, vitamins and amphetamines guaranteed to cure any hangover in fifteen minutes. Now this was a company that understood its employees.

Still, the workday routine, while offshore, remained about the same as it had been in the North. The weather was better, but the same guys worked the same jobs, twenty-four seven, hunting up likely places for oil companies to drill. Only when we put into port did we see the difference three thousand miles had made. Dakar proved to be as third world as it gets. Lepers sticking rotting fingers in my face as they begged for money; a deadly knife fight on the quay below as I stood deck guard; men beaten for pilfering a little food. Life was hard in West Africa. Some men became predators. Rich foreigners were fat prey.

Shore time became a luxury. Most of our days passed at sea, then every few weeks we'd make it to port for a quick stop and resupply. I liked those days. We got time off to explore, buy souvenirs or relax in a local tavern. Sadly, West African port towns seemed contaminated with thugs. Young men who followed outsiders, staying out of reach while looking for a weak spot to exploit. A few members of the crew had to stand guard on board every night as the rest ventured out on the town in a pack. Gangs of young toughs would hang out in alleys, watching for one of us they could cut out of the group like lions stalking zebras. The bad guys were always hunting for a loner who got separated from the herd. Even a mixed herd sticks together when lions are around. In ours, most of my shipmates were British plus a few Americans and a French Canadian from Nova Scotia thrown in to liven things up. Unlike the herd, it wasn't every man for himself. We tended to look out for each other.

During my third port call, as a bunch of us enjoyed an afternoon at a beach resort down the coast, one of the locals snatched Chris Taylor's watch right off his arm. The young man threw it to an accomplice who tried to take off in another direction. Chris grabbed the second teenager by the wrists and pulled the boy's arms wide, twisting one till he dropped the watch. The kid's eyes bugged out, a disturbing moan escaped his mouth and muscular limbs shook as he feebly struggled to break away. His partner gone, our thief begged for mercy in incoherent French. Whether from fear or malnutrition, he had no strength. His muscles were a charade. Chris let him go. Now we had a new puzzle. We usually walked around in big groups to protect ourselves from these guys. Were they as intimidated by us?

I can be a slow learner, but after several port calls two important truths about Dakar finally hit home. The big hotels were too expensive, and the little bars were too sleazy. That left only one good option in the way of a pleasant tavern, the local house of ill repute. That's right, the brothel. Please understand that this place did not resemble what you see in the movies. No half-naked girls running around for our viewing pleasure; no fat pimp waiting to sell his virgin sister; no drug dealer holding court in the back room. Clearly separated from the "business" side, the bar seemed clean by West African standards, and the atmosphere was... interesting. Their friendly staff never pressured us to partake in other activities, yet those services could be purchased if you happened to be so inclined.

One evening, my French Canadian buddy Pat Lantaine, Martin and I visited this fine establishment to enjoy a few beers. I'd gotten to know Pat well enough by this point, so I had to ask a question. The puzzle had bothered me since I was a kid in the heart of English Canada. "Hey Pat, when we were kids in Toronto we called you guys frogs. What did you call us?"

With a big smile Pat replied "Nussing, mostly we juss threw rocks at you."

I thought that was one of the best lines ever and so did the true Englishman at the table. "Well that calls for another round," Martin said, "I'm buying."

Pat wasn't much of a drinker so after finishing his beer he joined a bunch of crewmates eager for a quiet night and headed back to the ship. Martin and I should have departed as well. The two of us stayed in the bar drinking Carlsberg while re-telling one-liners from Monty Python TV shows. "Oh, oh, did you see their Holy Grail movie?" I asked Martin.

"Of course. The daft knights didn't even have real horses. Just skipped on down the road, banging coconuts together for the sound of hooves."

"NO, they had horses! You just couldn't see 'em."

"Rog, old son, they were pure make believe. Only a bloody yank would pretend to see them."

"But that's what made the thing hilarious. Total, obvious, rubbish!"

"Right Rog. Total rubbish."

Once all but the hard core drinkers had gone home, we called it a night as well. We would have taken a cab if such a thing could be found at two a.m. If Dakar had taxis in the nicer part of town, they didn't visit this neighborhood. Feeling rather bulletproof, Martin and I convinced ourselves that a walk back to the harbor would be fine. Neither good sense nor fear ever got the upper hand, and we left secure in the notion we were wise men of the world.

Outside, the streets looked deserted so off we went in the direction of our ship. Setting a fast pace, we made several blocks before the first of our worries showed up. Stark light from a rare streetlamp outlined a handful of thugs leaning against mud brick walls in a side street a block ahead.

A slight breeze ruffled their torn t-shirts as they watched us. "Just ignore them and keep going," I told Martin, "maybe we can bluff 'em out." As we drew nearer, the bunch to our side didn't move. Their coal black eyes followed our progress as a second small group appeared to block the road before us. With a quick glance back for a way of escape, I saw two more thugs coming up behind us at a slow walk. The group on our left came out of their alley to surround us completely. We stopped.

"Do you reckon we can break through and outrun them?" Martin asked.

"Not a chance." I looked him in the eyes while my heart pounded toward panic. "I'm slower'n Christmas."

"That's it then. We'll have a go at 'em." He looked back with wide eyes. "It's been fun boyo."

I glanced at Martin, studied the gang around us and got an idea. It was a really dumb idea but better than fighting a horde, so I thought, *what the hell, why not?* With a grin on my face and my heart abandoning terror in favor of absurdity, I turned to Martin. "We can't outrun the bastards, but with our horses they'll never catch us. LET'S RIDE!" Off I went, skipping up the street clapping my hands together for the hoofbeats of my pretend horse. Martin never missed a beat, riding at my side as we approached the thugs blocking our way. Our would-be attackers just stared at us, their stunned inaction turning into something like fear. As we skipped forward, they looked at each other and just faded away, back to whatever hole they'd come from. Martin and I *rode* all the way back to our ship with only tired legs in consequence for our foolishness. Some days the zebra gets away.

What did those stalkers in the night think when they saw Martin and me riding phantom horses up their street without a care in the world? Did they take us for men with twisted minds? If so, it may have made us bad juju and untouchable. While talking over the escapades various crew members had experienced in Dakar, one of them put forth a theory about predators, prey and the herd mentality. As long as we showed fear, the toughs would continue to be aggressive. If we didn't show fear, we became a potential threat and a creature they should avoid. Many of us tested his speculation by walking the streets alone and found it worked. We'd learned to face our predators with a steady heart.

The port of Dakar is an international hub with vessels coming in from all over the world. Sometimes, if the docks are full, they have to stack smaller ships, like ours, side by side to give them a place to tie off. When getting to shore involved climbing over several decks, I would meet crews from almost anywhere. Russians were interesting to watch and seemed as curious about us as we were about them but they always acted nervous if we'd attempt to communicate. The Korean fishermen had no such issues. Every time I'd cross over their decks they'd try to trade for things we had on board. That's fine for guys with a boat full of fish, but I struggled to come up with anything good for my end of the deal. I happened to be sitting in our ship's lounge one evening, contemplating my lack of trade supplies, when Martin came in holding a tattered old *Penthouse.* "These things are knackered. Not a decent picture left in the lot."

As he held it out to show me holes where all the pictures used to be, I looked about the room thinking. *Stacks of old magazines everywhere. We do have a lot of old girly magazines lying around. That's it! Barter goods.*

The next morning I clambered over to a Korean trawler and offered all our used *Playboys, Penthouses* and *Mayfairs* for a big frozen fish. They were delighted, handshakes sealed the deal, and I'd bought myself a large problem. My frozen tuna weighed a few hundred pounds. It took five of us to shift it onto the floor of the ship's walk-in freezer, but we managed. Keeping our eyes open for our cook to return from shopping, we sat topside to wait. As he came up the gangway, I hailed him. "Hey Cookie. We got a fish we want you to fix for dinner. It's in the freezer." None of us had the fortitude to follow him inside so we listened from the doorways as he made his way to the galley. Cooks must have lots of time to work on vocabulary. It took ours ten full minutes before he ran out of names for the rotten crew fate had forced him to serve.

Our fish stayed in the freezer until we sailed well out to sea again and then went over the side to feed the sharks. Extravagant fish food off a coast where people were starving.

During a port call several weeks later, we'd moored the Arctic Seal alongside a staging area where a shipper had offloaded his cargo of food. As we unloaded boxes of data tapes, my eyes were drawn to thirty desperate men engaged in something like a ritualized game that might let them take home a meal. I called it potato tag.

The center of the playing field was a pile of potato sacks twenty feet across and four feet high. On top of the pile stood two defenders, each with a four-foot wooden stick. The rest of the men played offense and formed a loose circle around the pile from which they could dart in and out of range of the defenders. The goal, it seemed, was to cut a sack then grab some potatoes before a defender hit the runner with a stick. If one took a solid hit, the rules were clear. The prize had to be dropped, and the runner got a beating. The players had different strategies for reaching their prize. Some would go it alone and others would work in pairs with one taking some glancing blows so his partner could dash and grab. The defenders never left their pile, allowing a successful runner to keep his prize if he made it out of range of the stick. All captured potatoes were placed in small stacks on the outskirts of the field of play and never touched by other runners, defenders or casual fans. I watched the potato ritual for an hour during which many of the runners took injuries for want of a little food. Their price for a chance at life.

A group preparing for a dangerous game with potatoes

In West Africa, those lives stood in stark contrast to the secure world I'd known as a child. In my world, everyone I knew had a good home and took three meals a day for granted. In Africa I discovered gratitude for the plenty I'd always known. The experience changed my perceptions if not my actions.

Viewed from the vantage point of seasoned age, my

whole life has been a journey of discovery. Given that all lives are a journey of discovery, I am not unique, though I find my days have been filled with far more commotion than I had expected. I was a normal guy trying to get by, not an adventurer searching for celebrity. What began as my quest for self-gratification gave way to a search for deeper fulfillment, then crashed in the despair of grief. Yet I have survived. Escaping a few thugs by acting crazy was not the first of my life's adventures nor the last. It's the commotion of our individual journeys that becomes stories worth telling. A story untold is just a memory. The following chapters recount many of the stories of my life, starting with my first independent adventure at age twelve. Some may lead to laughter; others will make you cry; a few could cause you to stop and think.

2

Summer of '65

Dear Taidy,

I'm so tired I can't feel my legs. I wobbled all over the road for the last ten miles while cars honked at me to get the heck out of their way. Don't know where Rick is. He left me about noon because I peddle too slow and kept having to stop to tie all my stuff back on my bike. I don't think I'll do this again real soon.

My adventure started a couple of weeks ago when Rick and I got this great idea to go camping on our own. I'm not talking about going up to the Finch woods where we used to build lean-tos, but a real trip to a real provincial park with tents and stuff. It would be easy, just find one close enough to reach by bike, get our parents to let us go, get some food and stuff and be off. Simple. "First, we have to get permission," was my opinion.

Rick said "No, we gotta figure out where we're go'n, what we're gonna do an' everything. They'll never let us go if we don't have a good plan."

"Yeah, ok," I said. "That sounds like the way it oughta work."

We found this place on the map called Bruce's Mill Conservation Area. It looked like it was about twenty-five miles away, and it had camping and, well, it was the only place we found. I've been camping lots of times with Dad so I knew we had a pup tent and some pots and pans and sleeping bags and axes and ropes and water cans and probably anything else we'd need. "What about food?" I asked. I'm always pretty concerned about food.

"We can get some cans of stew and spaghetti outta my Mom's cupboard," was Rick's idea. It sounded good to me.

With map in hand and our minds set to counter any objection they'd come up with, we set off to ask our parents. Now according to them, there's a firm set of rules as to who asks whose parents when. Usually it goes like this. "Can Rick spend the night?"

"What did his parents say?"

"Nothing. We didn't ask them yet."

"Well no then, you should have asked them first."

Later, "Can I go to the smoke shop with Rick?"

"I don't know. What did Rick's Mom say?"

"She said it's OK."

"Well you should have asked me first. NO." Get things out of order and you're sunk for sure. Trouble is, I can never get it straight, so we decided to ask at the same time. That way we'd have both ends covered no matter what they said. On my way to find Dad (he's always better for these sort of questions) I thought, "There's only one possible catch, the dreaded I'll call his parents and we'll discuss it." Better than a flat out no, but man, the waiting can kill you. I guess I've got ESP 'cause that's what we got from both sides. We had suffered a couple days of guesses and worry before we got our answers. They said YES. No kidding, they agreed to let two twelve-year-olds ride twenty-five miles and camp for three days. What a hoot!

The day before we were supposed to leave we got all our camping gear together and figured out right off that two bikes don't hold as much as a station wagon. In fact they don't hold much at all. You don't suppose our parents thought we'd give up do you? Ha, no way. We just got rid of everything but our tent, sleeping bags, a few clothes and some food. Oh, and my Scout canteen for water. We had a bit of rope and some pretty good strings so we got everything tied on OK and were ready to take off as soon as the sun came up.

Next morning we woke up at about 6:00 and got ready to go by 6:30. The route was all planned out, and we each had a map. Before we left, Mom gave me two dimes and said "Now don't spend these. The first is so you can call when you get there. The other is for emergencies. If you have any real problems, find a phone and call." Then we were off. The ride seemed fine for the first mile or two but soon things started getting loose. We must have used stretchy string or something 'cause first the tent came half off my handlebars and got caught in the spokes. Next my sleeping bag slid off the crossbar and my backpack hung lopsided off the rat trap and rubbed on my rear tire. Rick's gear was in no better shape than mine so finally we had to quit shoving things back where they belonged and stop for a big rethink.

"Did you bring the string?" I asked.

"Yeah, it's here in my pack and we've got plenty."

"OK. Let's use lots more this time and tie it really tight."

We helped each other hold our gear in place, got everything as tight as we could and used gobs of string with lots of knots. It seemed to work. Pretty quick we got on our way again with hardly any more stops. Getting away from houses and into the farms doesn't take long if you can keep at it, and before long the countryside was real nice to look at but the hills started getting awfully big. With only 3 speeds on our bikes sometimes we had to climb off and push. Downhill riding was way more fun as long as we didn't get go'n too fast. That could be a little dangerous if you hit a rock or a hole or something. As we rode along, I noticed we kept passing the strangest woods I've ever seen. The pine trees were pretty big, but they were all in perfect straight lines. Just like they'd been planted in a garden. Who plants trees when they grow wild everywhere?

I started getting really tired around lunchtime so we stopped and ate our sandwiches, a little squished but good, and took a look at the map to see how far we still had to go. We were only about half way! "We're gonna hafta go faster," Rick said. "At this rate we won't get there in time to cook dinner."

I thought "Easy for him to say, he's like the field day star of school. I'm the fat kid. Crap, I can't keep going as fast as we've been going, how am I going to speed up?"

"Ok," I said, "you lead and I'll be right behind you." Too embarrassed to fall way back, I managed to keep Rick in sight, then every once in a while he'd stop to let me catch up. We finally got to the campground at around 4:00. I called my mom and off we rode to find a good camp site.

Rick and I camped in the backyard plenty of times. We liked to stay up half the night so we could sneak into Mr. Kennedy's garden to sneak peas. Fresh raw peas are really good, especially when stolen from a garden at midnight. I think that might have been all the camping Rick ever did 'cause when it came to setting up our camp and cooking, I was definitely the chief. It kind of helped me look good after being a slowpoke on our ride. After cutting off all our strings, Rick unloaded our gear while I got the tent up. A nasty can of stew for dinner, a bit of a campfire and off to bed. Staying up half the night was not gonna happen. Too tired. I don't think I moved until late the next morning.

Now let me tell you a funny thing about camping when you're on your own. You don't have a canoe, no fishing gear, no hammock, no car for going to go get ice cream… there's not much to do. We played with the fire for a while, that's always fun, then we got more fire wood. Lots more firewood. It's kind of a Geiger tradition. Finally we decided to walk around the campground a bit to find something to do. We'd only gone a little ways when we came across three boys about our age camping on their own just like us. They saw us and started waving us over, all excited. "Guys, come here. Come on. Take a gander at what we found." Their faces were lit up like Christmas morning as they crowded around a picnic table looking at something. As we got closer, I saw every boy's dream, a vision, the ultimate… They had a PLAYBOY magazine.

"Holy crap, let me see."

"Move."

"Turn the page." We looked at every picture until we wore it out and finally got bored.

Having found some new friends, Rick and I spent the rest of the day with them, exploring the park, eating some of our food and just doing guy stuff. Late in the afternoon one of the boys named Eric said he was going to teach us something. "My uncle showed me," he said. "It's called a cedar bark cigar. You can smoke 'em." Rick and I looked at each other 'cause we'd never smoked before but it sounded like a pretty good idea, so we were all for it. "First you gotta scrape some cedar bark off the tree so it's all fluffy. Not in strips, but like cotton." He rubbed his knife up and down the bark over his cupped palm until he got a handful of fluffed-up bark. "Now you need some paper and just roll the bark up inside it. You gotta lick it pretty good to get it to stick together and sometimes twist it up a bit." He did all that and ended up with something that looked a little like one of Dad's cigarettes, but not much. "Who's got a match?" Eric lit his cigar, sucked on it and blew out some white smoke. He coughed a few times but had to keep puffing pretty steady or the darn thing would go out.

"Heck, I can do that." I said. "Lend me a piece of paper." Then we were all scraping, rolling, lighting and puffing away like we were grown. I gotta tell ya, you really can smoke that stuff but it'll make you cough up a lung if you really breathe it in. You gotta hold it in your mouth and blow it out again before any goes down.

Not long after, it started to get dark, so Rick and I headed back to our tent and made a campfire. We sat beside it and shot the breeze for a while but were too tired to do much else. As we talked about the stuff we'd done that day, we decided it was one of our best days ever. It seemed so exciting to be on our own doing things that were against the rules at home. Rick said we were just like the gear on our bikes. "At home, our parents have us all tied up with strings so we can't fall off and get lost. I think here we've cut the string."

"Yeah," I replied "but my mom's got plenty more when I get home."

The next morning was about the same as the last. Our new friends' parents had shown up and they were packing to leave. That left just the two of us again so the day got sort of slow and boring. We ate most of the rest of our food and organized our campsite a little so it would be easier to get stuff packed when we got up. Morning came pretty early 'cause we were ready to go home. I liked being on my own and all but I was missing good meals, a comfy chair in front of the TV and my real bed. We didn't have as much as we came with, but we'd used up a lot of our string so we couldn't do as good a job of tying things on our bikes. It worked OK but not great. Anyway, we headed out and I found out real quick my legs hadn't recovered from our first ride. After about five miles I was winded. After ten I was beat. At fifteen, Rick said he had to be home and left me to get home on my own.

That last ten miles is sort of a blur. My legs ached so bad I wasn't able to ride up the hills so I had to get off and walk. When I could ride, I was so tired my balance was all messed up, and I wandered off into the road when I should have stayed to the side. I remember cars honking, people yelling at me to get off the road and I think I almost got hit once. I just kept going. My water was gone. My friend was gone. My strength was gone. The only thing I had left was a goal... home.

When I was five, I went horseback riding with my Uncle Ward. The horse they put me on didn't want to do anything but get *back to the barn and thought throwing the kid off his back would be a good way to get there. Uncle Ward, a large man not known for putting up with rude animals, used his fist to "explain" the importance of manners to the horse, then made me get right back on again. When I did, my horse raced off for the barn anyway, with me screaming the whole way. He had a goal and good sense didn't enter his thinking. I guess I take after that horse 'cause nothing entered my mind but the road I could see in front of me. "Just push over this hill. Come on, keep going around this next corner. See, houses... can't be long now. I know I'll make it if I Just - Keep - Going."*

When I finally rolled off our street and onto the driveway, Mom stood waiting for me in front of our house. She told me Rick had stopped by to let her know I would be along later. I don't guess she was too happy with him. Like I said, I won't be taking another ride real soon. Never did use that second dime.

Rog

Looking back on my schoolboy days, I can't help cherishing the start I got in life. I know the realities of suburban Toronto included plenty of sorrow in the late '50s and early '60s, but the idyllic world in which I lived was rarely intruded upon. Although we suffered many of the growing pains of childhood, in general, homes were stable, death was a stranger and children were safe. I now understand it to have been a wonderful place and time to be a kid. Mine was a world full of innocent security. Well before Rick and I took off on our first solo adventure, my home life was often enriched by journeys to visit relatives who seemed to live so far away.

One yearly trip took us to the city of Rutland, nestled in the mountains of Vermont, where every fall my family would travel to see my mother's father. We called him Taid (pronounced Tide), the Welsh name for grandfather, because he came from a full-blooded Welsh family. Mom had called her grandfather Taid, so we called ours Taid as well. Everyone else called him Newt. As a young boy, I'd shadow Taid around town as he attended to important tasks reserved for important men. A stop at the bank for some high finance, "Good morning Newt. I see you have your assistant today." Then off to the Post Office to pick up mail for his coal company. "You're a little late this morning Newt. You and the boy must be very busy today." Later we'd check in at the best place of all, the Elks Club, where we'd greet all the men playing cards, shooting billiards or hanging out in the bar. "Afternoon Newt, would the young man like a drink? How 'bout a root beer?" Storybook days whose only sorrow came from the long separation until I got to return the next year.

Although distance often conspired against our spending time together, Taid and I remained great buddies throughout his life of ninety-three years. When my wife, Jerre, and I married, I still considered Taid to be one of my best friends and asked him to be in the wedding. Taid didn't hesitate a second, even though it meant traveling all the way to Texas. There's just something about an eighty-six year old gentleman in a tux. All the ladies loved him.

"Taid" circa 1958

Another more frequent journey led to a land of woods, meadows, wondrous animals and characters larger than life. This was the home of Aunt Edna and Uncle Ward. Located in the farm country of upstate New York, the Davis farm became my destination of choice for extended summer vacations. What child would not want to visit a place so different from his home in the city? With both my father's parents having died before I knew them, Aunt Edna and Uncle Ward often acted as my surrogate grandparents. I find splendid continuity in a similar situation today. The early passing of my wife's parents has left us to act as surrogate grandparents to her brother's three young children.

When a place has fifty acres, a big red barn, horses, dogs and cats, it's a farm, right? Never mind that they didn't raise any crops, except the Christmas trees Uncle Ward planted one year, I know it was a farm. The house looked like what farm houses are supposed to look like and my aunt served great big farm meals every time we gathered in the kitchen to eat. My uncle rode horses, drank hard cider from a barrel he had laid up in the cellar and kept guns in the kitchen as well. Right there beside the best homemade cookies known to exist, stood a gun cabinet full of deer rifles, shotguns and handguns. Now don't misunderstand. Uncle Ward was serious about his weapons, so children did not play with guns. They might, however, get to use a gun once he taught the child to do so properly. If an older child proved he was also serious about weapons, that child might be allowed to use small caliber guns without supervision. In this Uncle Ward had a unique perspective and I thank him for his trust.

Edna and Ward didn't live alone in their country home. With them were my cousins Jack, Bill and Penny, along with the greatest dog who ever lived. I rarely saw Jack, and because of our age difference, my fellowship with Bill and Penny mostly resulted from occasions when Aunt Edna made them include me. Two happy exceptions to this grew out of long hours Penny and I spent with their horses, and any time Bill and I went trout fishing. As I understand it, grooming, feeding and caring for horses did not qualify as "hanging out" with your little cousin and was, therefore, acceptable behavior for teenage girls of the day. Trout fishing is a calling in life. Age has little to do with the matter.

Ward and Edna Davis. Circa 1954

The dog, a boxer named King, would play catch as long as I did, follow me on treks to the far corners of our little world and perform all his best tricks at my command. He even let me ride on his back until I got too big. King was smarter than me, but allowed me to be his best friend anyway.

If stability, kindness and opportunities to grow are

foundations for a happy childhood, mine was built on bedrock. So many advantages, yet I remained oblivious to my abundance. Fortunately we don't stay children forever, so by the summer of 1965 I began taking a few tentative steps toward independence. As Rick discovered during our bike ride, we had started to cut some strings.

Part of independence means being free to make your own choices. Freedom is great but the price of our decisions can be high. At Bruce's Mill, I tried smoking for the first time. I liked it and enjoyed the habit off and on for the next forty years. When I reached my early fifties, my doctor told me I had chronic bronchitis, probably from smoking, so I quit for good.

Similar to smoking, seeing my first *Playboy* magazine at age twelve left me greatly impressed. So much so that by the time I left for college in Florida, I'd chosen to gather a collection of similar magazines and had hidden them in our attic. I thought leaving them there might be foolish, and remembering the joy one such bit of contraband brought to a group of boys back at the park, I made a plan. I am not proud of my plan, but I suppose it gave the lads at North Agincourt Public School the thrill of their young lives. On a Sunday night in September, the night before I left for Florida, I drove to my old elementary school. On the seat beside me, a large stack of magazines, bound up in string, sat like an offering to the temple of trouble. With the car parked away from the glare of streetlights, I carried my treasure up the sidewalk into the schoolyard and left it under the first bushy tree that presented itself. I don't know what happened the next morning, but leaving the country seemed a good idea at the time.

As with becoming a surrogate grandparent, my life has occasionally followed a cyclical path that seems to cover ground I've trodden before. When that path offered the opportunity to atone for the misdeed of corrupting young minds, I considered myself fortunate. Forty years after leaving adult magazines at an elementary school, I found myself in the role of internet porn police for a Texas school district. Given the chance to identify and speak with students who had gotten involved with explicit material, I tried my best to assure them their interest was normal, yet educate them as to its dangers. I hope I made a difference in a few lives. When looking at poor choices, perspective changes everything.

One final result of my adventurous ride proved to be a little more positive. I developed a habit for stowing gear properly. You could say I gained a compulsion for bungees, straps and ropes tied with good knots. If you remember nothing else I write, remember this: The most useful knot known to man is called a trucker's hitch. If you learn it and use it, your world will be a better place.

3

May 1965

Dear Taidy,

Guess what I learned? A kid can figure out almost anything from the World Book Encyclopedia. No joke, you can. I figured out how to make gunpowder. I looked in the G book and there it was with diagrams and everything. A couple of chemicals and some charcoal, and you're good to go.

Ya gotta understand I didn't wake up one morning and think, "I wonder what I'll do today? I know, I'm going to make some gunpowder." No way. At first I was only curious about what's inside those bullets Dad has, so I pulled the lead out of one and emptied it out on a piece of paper. Hum... gunpowder. Touch a match to the powder and pssst, just like that it's gone. Pulling the lead outta bullets works great, but pretty quick I ran into a few hitches. Dad's not much for hunting, so he's only got one box of ammo, and seeing as he's really smart, one day he's bound to notice there's some missing. Besides that, you never know what the darn things might do.

Harry, a kid in my class at school, was playing with his dad's bullets last month. He'd laid some on the ground and was throwing rocks at them, then shot himself in the leg. Harry had to go to the hospital. I figured I was safe with no lead in them but then I almost messed up big time. I wanted to flatten out one of the empty brass things, so I laid it on on top of Dad's workbench vice down in the basement. Then I got his big hammer and gave the brass a good whack. BAM! It went off like a firecracker and knocked the hammer out of my hand. Scared the snot out'a me. Before I even picked up the hammer, Mom was at the top of the stairs. "ROGER? WHAT ARE YOU DOING DOWN THERE?"

"Nothing. I just dropped a hammer."

"Are you sure?"

"Yes, everything's fine Mom."

The worst problem with using bullets is there's just not much in the little things. I'd had all kinds of good ideas about what to do with gunpowder if I got my hands on a bunch of the stuff. After wondering about my problem for a couple more days the answer came to me in a flash. "If I want lots of gunpowder, I'll just have to make it myself."

Now, as a reasonable person, I'm sure you'll think walking into a local store to buy bags of potassium nitrate and sulphur might be hard. Plus, who'd sell it to a twelve year old anyway? What do I know? In my ignorance, I rode my bike to the plaza at the end of our street and looked for a store that would sell chemicals. "Probably not the milk store or the smoke shop, but maybe the hardware store? Ah, the drug store. They sell lots of weird stuff." I went in and then up to the counter where a tall guy in a white lab coat was standing.

"Do you sell potassium nitrate here?" I asked.

"Why, yes we do."

"How about sulphur? Do you have any of that?"

"Yeess."

"Well how much is it? I've got money and I want to buy some."

Mr. Lab Coat sold me a bag of each without even asking why I wanted it. I was in business.

Mixing up gunpowder is just like making Kraft Dinner. You have to follow the recipe. One part this, two parts that, plus two parts of the other, combine in a good container and you're done. The one part this and two parts that were easy. Those parts were already powder. The hard part is grinding two parts of the other, charcoal, down to a powder. In fact, it's a real pain in the bum, but after an hour of work I had the right amount to go with my other ingredients. Once I got them mixed together I had a couple of quarts of the stuff. Sure, my powder didn't look much like what came out of the bullets, it smelt bad and I'd made a big mess, but I was confident. Enough so that I decided some things are best done outside.

A little pile of powder on an old piece of wood; a match; light the match and touch it to the pile... WIZZLE, FIZZLE, BUBBLE AND SMOKE, I'd reached a whole new level of playing with matches. "Holy crap," I thought "this stuff works! Now what can I make with it?" At first I mostly just let piles of gunpowder burn up so they'd make lots of sparks and smoke, but that got kind of boring pretty quick. Then I started wrapping it in paper for smoke bombs, so I could stick them in odd places or throw them. Tying one to a homemade arrow and shooting it at night looked really cool, kind of like a giant American bottle rocket without the bang.

You know, all this trial and error can really go through a guy's supply of gunpowder, especially when a spark goes sailing into his storage can and sets off the whole thing. That'll make some smoke! I got real tired of grinding up all that charcoal. I guess I'm a thoughtful kind of fellow, 'cause I started thinking about a way to get charcoal that's already ground up. "So what's in charcoal that makes this work anyway? Carbon?" I checked the encyclopedia. "Yep, carbon. What else is made of carbon?" It took a little more thought, but after a while, I had an idea. "I bet sugar's mostly carbon. I wonder if I should try sugar?" Back to the encyclopedia and sure enough, lots of carbon in sugar. "Even better, I'll use powdered sugar." It worked great, no grinding. My black powder turned white and left no mess to clean up when I was done.

Dad's usually not all that worried about how our lawn looks, but pretty soon he started noticing black burn marks all over the back yard. "Roger? What's all this business in the yard? Why all the burnt spots, young man?"

"Well I guess that's where my smoke bombs landed."

"Your what!? Where'd you get smoke bombs?"

"Um, I made them."

"You did?" he asked, looking at me like I'd claimed the ability to fly. "How'd you do that?"

"Well, remember the chemistry set you got me last Christmas? I got to doing some of the experiments like you showed me in the book and got interested. I'm trying to learn to be a chemist like you Dad."

"Sport, never try to kid a kidder. What's going on?"

"Ok, I learned to make gunpowder from the encyclopedia."

"No kidding?" he smiled. "Oh. Well that's very dangerous son," he continued sternly. "Don't burn any more holes in the lawn, and be careful you don't burn down the house or yourself. You can experiment out in the garden until I plant this year. And you're cutting the grass till the holes grow over."

Can you believe it? Even when I got caught, Dad wasn't all bent outta shape about the gunpowder. Could be he was really kind of glad to see me interested in something he did besides fishin'. Shoot, who knows? I'd rather be a secret agent spy anyway. Yeah, I wanna be cool just like the guys on "Man From Uncle." They use all kinds of crazy spy tricks to get by their enemies, so I've worked out a few tricks of my own. You know the one where they use some fancy powder to melt the lock on a door and then sneak in anywhere they want? I can do the same thing with my gunpowder. It didn't work on the lock for our wood door 'cause the keyhole was too small to get any powder inside, but it worked great on a storm door. I tried their trick a couple of weeks ago. Just use some paper to funnel the powder down the hole and light it. Everything smokes and melts just like on TV. The black marks took a while to clean up, and the lock doesn't work anymore, but Dad never locks that door anyway.

With only four screen doors in our house, I figured melting one was my limit. "Well that was pretty nifty but I guess I better quit while I'm ahead. I wonder why none of this stuff ever blows up like on in the movies? What I gotta do is learn how to make things go boom." I was sure a little more thought would get to an answer. "Firecrackers explode. Cannons explode. Bombs explode. What

33

makes them different than what I've got?" I couldn't work it out and the encyclopedia didn't explain anything, so I had to sacrifice a firecracker. Real slow and careful, I pulled one apart layer by layer and found... nothing. It was just lots of paper wrapped around a little powder and sealed up tight.

"OK," I thought, "I'll just do the same thing," except after several tries all I got were good smoke bombs that would burn through all my paper. "Forget paper," I decided, "I'm gonna use a pipe." Pulling a short pipe from Dad's junk box, I screwed on an end piece real tight. After drilling a little hole near the covered end and sticking in a wick from another firecracker, I filled the pipe part way up with powder, then mashed it in real tight with a railroad bolt that fit inside just perfect. So far so good!

By this time I understood that I'd have to seal the open end if I was going to get an explosion. "Let's see, I've got paper, plasticine, some styrofoam." The plan worked like this. First put in a layer of paper, then a layer of putty, more paper, hammer it down with the giant bolt. Now a layer of styrofoam; some more putty; a little more paper; hammer it down. Another layer, more hammering, on and on till I filled her up just about all the way. "There. I guess it's as sealed as it's gonna get. Now let's light the fuse."

Dad said to do my experiments in the garden, so with he and Mom away for a few hours that's where I went. If you've never been in Ontario in the spring, let me tell you the ground is hard as a rock. I could take a pick ax to our garden and not sink the tip in a half inch. Here I had a short debate with myself. "If you point the pipe this way, it will go off like a rocket and land who knows where. If you point the opening that way, it might work more like a cannon. Then again, it might just blow up like a bomb. Better go with the cannon." I put my pipe bottom side down, propped up by a forked stick. With one last look around to be sure no neighbors were out, I lit the fuse and ran like crazy for the big tree holding our tire swing.

Just as I got crouched down behind the tree, KA-BOOOOMMMM, the loudest blast I've ever heard. It was at least three times as loud as Uncle Ward's big shotgun, then dirt started falling out of the sky all over me. My brains got a bit scrambled, so it took a minute to get moving, but before I got up to go see what happened, back doors started opening all along our street. Mrs. Robinson, Mrs. Smith, old lady Hunt, even Mrs. White, three doors down, came out and started calling to each other. "Did you hear that?"

"Yes. What was it?"

"It sounded like an explosion to me."

"Maybe it was one of those sonic booms." They looked like a bunch of giraffes with their necks craning this way and that to see what was going on. I decided it would be best to stay down on the ground, hoping they wouldn't notice me.

Pretty soon they decided the explosion was a neighborhood mystery and gave up talking to go back to doing laundry or whatever. "Now Rog," I said to myself, "You can't be too careful with moms, they'll try to fake you out, and then watch out the window. You better lie low a few minutes before you get up." I gave them a little more time, then went running back over to the garden. Son of a biscuit, it was gone! No bull. Nothing left but a big ol' two foot crater. I was thinking "Dang it's a good thing I ran for it. That might have blown me to bits. I wonder how deep the hole is?" Kneeling by the edge I scooped a bunch of loose dirt out of the bottom. When my finger felt something hard, I scraped a bit more packed dirt away with a sick and found the top of my pipe.

"Alright," I started thinking, "I bet if I get Dad's big shovel I can dig that thing outta there. Yeah, I'll have to wait a few weeks, and I should probably use less powder, but next time I'm flippin' it over. I'm gonna make a rocket."

Rog

The rocket worked, in an unguided, highly dangerous sort of way. Predictably, my second blast left a crater in our garden, and once again covered me in dirt. It sent my pipe soaring a hundred feet up, then down range into the high school parking lot behind our house. Another "sonic boom" in our neighborhood increased the level of parental investigation, but no suspicion ever came my way. Not being considered an overly bright young fellow can have its advantages. Even Dad, who had found evidence that I'd been playing with gunpowder, never mentioned the explosions. He wasn't the type to keep things quiet for the sake of the family name, so I presume it never came up in his presence. It's possible that because blowing things up runs in the family, he didn't feel safe in mentioning my misdeeds to my mother.

Once, while camping in the Adirondack Mountains, he and I were sitting around the campfire at night. Well after dark, Dad, who had been drinking a couple of beers, said "Watch this" and threw an unopened beer can into the fire. This was not the easy open aluminum we enjoy today, but a heavy gauge tin can that had to be opened with a "church key". After a few minutes, enough that I'd started to get bored, he said "I think we better go in now." We headed inside our travel trailer. "Watch the fire out the front window," he instructed. Another minute and BOOOM. Sparks, coals and ash shot all over the campsite and into the woods. Thankfully, earlier rains had left our forest pretty damp, with little chance of spreading a fire. I suspect he'd considered that.

Having survived two significant detonations of my own creation, I decided the odds were against me for more attempts and gave up trying. I retired my demolition career at twelve, apparently several years ahead of my peers. During my freshman year in college, guys in our dorm started entertaining themselves with minor munitions. As they flushed M-80s down the commode and made rockets out of match heads, I'd walk away shaking my head, never being tempted to teach them a better way. I had matured before my time through experimental explosives. I wonder how that would go over with today's safety-minded parents?

Obviously, my parents were not overprotective. Nor were they prone to discuss their philosophies and decisions with their young son. I'm not sure why they chose the summer of 1965 to start letting me experience the world on my own. They may have been thinking about distancing me from the consequences of explosive endeavors. Probably they were looking for ways to get me out of the house because I'd become such a pest. My parents didn't let go completely. In several small ways they allowed me to cut a few more strings to see life beyond the protective umbrella of our family.

Fortunately for my neighborhood, that summer was my first to be sent off to canoe camp. Unlike Scout camp, where I'd spent an unsuccessful weekend the year before, canoe camp provided an experience that ranks high in my list of youthful memories. I'm sure the Boy Scouts are a fine organization in general, and great for most boys, especially those who spend little time out of doors. I hope other troops selected better leadership than mine. The bunch of bullies to whom I had been assigned were so out touch with my reality, we parted company as soon as I got my confiscated possessions back. I'm sure they appreciated our separation more than I did.

As I understood it, the whole purpose of Scouting was to teach boys to be prepared, help others and stay morally straight. Wasn't Scout camp supposed to be all about practicing to fend for yourself in the woods? When our leaders said the first order of business would be to cook food, I was all for it. *Great, I've cooked lots of meals over an open fire.* Dad had taught me how to build the fire, set it up for cooking, complete the task without getting burnt, and enjoy the result. This would be a no brainer. "First you boys go gather firewood," our Scout Master instructed. "You'll need enough for six fires, so get lots of it." No problem, I reached into my pack, got my hatchet and headed for the woods. "Woah Geiger. What have you got there?" he called with some alarm.

"Well it's my hatchet." I replied. "I'm gonna get some firewood for us."

"I think not young man. Hatchets are dangerous. Advanced Scouts only. Give it here."

"What? I know how to use it."

"No, we'll have to keep it for you until you get home. Just pick up dry sticks like the other boys." No more discussion, they impounded my hatchet. I started to question the wisdom of this organization, but figured we'd get cooking pretty quick, so who **cared?**.

With lots of wood piled by a circle of stones to mark the designated location of fires, our leader showed us how it's done. I watched him try to create a complicated teepee arrangement, with a windbreak backstop. When he failed to get it to light, I figured I should help him out and informed the man of his good fortune. "Sir, I know all about starting a fire and cooking on it. You want me to show the other kids? See, you have to start real small and work your way up.

Besides, the best fire for cooking is a crisscross, not that fancy thing." Was I allowed help out? NO. I didn't have the fire building merit badge and didn't stand much chance of getting it, given my ideas on how it should be done. Nor did I have the cooking badge. No badge, no demonstration. I felt lucky they didn't require an eating badge.

Ready for Scout Camp, summer 1964

About then I started to understand that I probably had more woodcraft skills at eleven than my leaders did as adults. They were reading everything right out of the manual and no deviation from the prescribed method would be tolerated. Then there was the knife incident. My father had given me my first knife when I was six so I could use it while trout fishing in the Adirondack Mountains. He taught me how to use it safely, insisted it be treated with respect, and never doubted I would comply. I always did. Well, mostly. During the same summer I was making gunpowder, I made a throwing knife. It worked well enough, but tended to bounce off trees. When it bounced off a black walnut and stuck in my ankle, I gave up knife throwing.

On my tenth birthday, Dad presented me with a high quality sheath knife to be used when we camped and fished. I sharpened it regularly, cared for it, and never used it when not in the woods. Naturally, on my first Scout camp weekend, the knife came with me. After dinner I got it out of my pack to whittle on a piece of wood. The Scout Masters had a fit! I didn't have the knife merit badge and could not be trusted to carry such a dangerous item. My knife got confiscated and impounded along with my hatchet.

The arrangements for sleeping at Scout camp dictate a "patrol" of six or seven boys be assigned to a tent under the watchful eye of a teenaged cadet leader and his helper. Apparently, our junior leader was not a happy young man. Fun didn't fit with his agenda and his desires equaled our law. When he decreed lights out, all lights had to go. When he said no more talking, that was it or else.

On Saturday night, one unfortunate Scout didn't quite understand the level of power our patrol leader had taken unto himself. He continued to joke around after being commanded to shut up and go to sleep. His punishment was to stand outside the tent for thirty minutes in his underpants while holding a Coleman lantern in each hand. Attracted by the light, mosquitoes and biting flies gathered for a feast. Inside the tent, the rest of us listened as the murmur of tiny wings grew to a roar. We then watched our friend's silhouette twitch over the walls of our tent. By the time our "morally straight" leader let him back in, the poor kid was a whimpering mass of bites. The next morning, none of us dared say anything about it. We were too scared and just glad to be going home. Besides, the adults couldn't have missed seeing him standing outside our tent. I suppose the insect torture had become an accepted practice in our troop. My parents did not find the practice acceptable. Soon after returning home, I said goodbye to the joys of Scouting.

Camp Comak proved to be nothing like my short lived acquaintance with the Boy Scouts. It was a rustic camp on Lake St. Nora where boys spent a month of summer fun in the heart of the Muskoka Lakes region of Ontario. There, I joined in the customary camp enterprises with great pleasure. Mess hall, crafts, riding, swimming and sailing, all provided a steady stream of amusement for our little gang of campers. Only on Sunday mornings did our leaders expect us to settle down and act like young gentlemen during the singing of hymns accompanied by a kind little man with an accordion. The rest of our time we spent on learning how to handle a canoe, the true focus of Camp Comak.

For a week, a dozen boys per outing got to head out on their wilderness canoe trip through a land of trees, streams and nature. Sleeping on the ground, cooking over a fire and paddling our days through scenery for which Ontario is still famous. I will forever love those clear water lakes surrounded by hills of granite and nestled in the middle of a forest.

To be fair to the Boy Scouts, I admit that I didn't even bring a hatchet and limited other blades to those found on a Swiss Army knife. On these trips, kids had an opportunity to gain knowledge about camping, but Camp Comak didn't try to make us woodsmen. The object here was canoeing. On a calm lake, we'd enjoy the view while cruising along to a gentle stroke. When the wind got up in our faces, we'd put our backs into it and paddle like voyageurs carrying furs to a trading post. When the wind got up in the right direction, we'd hold three canoes together, lash ground cloths to paddles and sail screaming down the wind at speeds beyond prudence. My memory of those rides is pure joy to recall.

Under the guidance of experienced young men known as "trippers", our expeditions ranged far from the shores of the island camp. All the gear had to be carried in a canoe.

Tents were scarce; luxuries were few and work was shared. If the sky dumped a little rain at night, we'd shelter under an old bridge, a big pine or just "sleep wet, you'll live." If a camper had the know-how to help with cooking, great, go for it. If not, help with the cleanup. On a portage, everyone carried his share. While in the canoe or on the shore, no lily dippers allowed.

Lily dipper: *A person who does not place their entire paddle in the water, or allows the momentum of the canoe to carry their paddle without adding any strength, is referred to as a lily dipper.*

Through it all, our trippers kept us motivated, tried to ensure nobody got hurt, then doctored those that did.

At the end of our adventure, we'd make a grand return to the home docks. While still far from the beach, the middleman in each canoe began banging his paddle across the frame to alert those on shore of our arrival. Six canoes picked up speed as we formed a line abreast. Our paddles churned the water as everyone chanted a camp song. A bunch of little survivors returning to the cheers of those standing on our docks. Dirty, tired and stinky, we arrived confident in the knowledge we could have fun under any conditions. A week of shared responsibility, rough living and accomplishment left most of us with a sense of camaraderie new to our suburban lives.

At Comak, they knew canoeing and made it their business to pass on mastery to the kids. Every camper started life as a middleman, then, with time and training, progressed to bowman. If you attended camp long enough and gave it a good effort, you could make sternman. A token worn around our necks on a lanyard proclaimed our rank, thereby ensuring an elevation in prestige with each advancement. Dad and I had fished from a canoe for years but these guys were serious.

A couple dozen different paddle strokes, competent steering, making way in rough weather, the list of required skills seemed endless. With a canoe, everything had to be done with balance, an eye to staying on top of the water and managing the unwieldy craft on land without damage. Even though the darn things were heavy as hell, we had to learn to carry them solo. At our camp, where the cedar strip canoes might as well have been seatless, everyone knelt all the time. It's safer and you get more power in your strokes. You also get two-inch ruts in your knees from the ribs of wood running across the hull. At canoe camp, kneeling was part of the rigor, so we all did it.

Dear God, just let me be a sternman and my life will be complete, I thought, as I stepped on shore to begin my second summer at camp. Apparently He didn't mind a silly prayer. A week after arriving I got my chance. Tripper Jim, the acknowledged expert of all things, finished his canoe class with an announcement. After saying a few words about hard work, he called out names of a handful of experienced bowmen who would be given the opportunity to test for advancement. "... Fredrick, VanStaubenzee, Geiger..." Two days later, during the cool hours of morning, a handful of boys were summoned to the docks.

One by one, trippers directed us to show mastery of skills and terminology, while judges observed, commenting on our delivery.

Tripper Jim demonstrating how to empty a swamped canoe. By Don Pugh.

"Good reverse skull Geiger."

"Try that draw stroke again Roger. See if you can bring 'er in parallel to the dock this time."

"On this sprint I want to see plenty of heeling, show us some power."

On it went until the judges nodded with satisfaction and Tripper Jim addressed our group. "Now lads, it's time for your final test. You will each take your canoe well out into open water, flip it, empty it of water, get back in and paddle back to the beach. When you get here, you will shoulder your canoe, carry it up to the mess hall and return it to this dock. Good luck. Now off you go."

As a thirteen year old wannabe, I had to have a talk with myself. *Oh jeez, how the heck am I gonna do that? Maybe I should twist my ankle or something?* It's not like I'd grown up as a junior athlete, searching for his next challenge. Other than fishing, my habits were more aligned with watching TV in the company of my good friends Mr. Potato Chip and Nestle's Quik. *Even if I do empty the water and get back to the beach, I'll be soaked. Then I'll have to hoist a ninety pound canoe onto my shoulders, carry it up the hill to the mess hall and back to the docks. That's gotta be a quarter mile. This is gonna kill me.* But standing in line, waiting my turn, what was I supposed to do? Fall on the ground and grab a leg? *Crap!* I thought. *All these trippers are look'n at me. The other guys are go'n for it. I can't quit now.*

In the end, gallant resolve proved less motivating than fear of failure. My turn came, so off I went. Well out from shore, but not too far from my friend VanStrawberry (Tony VanStaubenzee), I shipped my paddle, grabbed the right gunnel and leaned way left. Over we went. My canoe and I fell into water that felt cold enough to freeze a penguin. "BLOODY COLD, EH," yelled VanStrawberry. Only a grunted "YA" escaped my mouth in return. *Grab a gunnel, push down, now up and kick with all you've got!* Surprising myself, I managed to empty the canoe just like I knew what I was doing. It's a feat I cannot repeat today. I know, I've tried. The remainder of the test, as difficult as advertised, continued until all of us staggered back to the dock, carrying our canoes. We returned tired, cold, wet and proud. Everyone passed. My own sense of accomplishment filled me completely. I'd earned the blue token of a sternman. The leader's seat in a canoe for the rest of that summer. The leader's seat for the rest of my life.

As our summer at Comak came to an end, camp tradition took a dark turn. On the afternoon before our last day, everyone gathered for a haircut. Like the military, we all got the same look. Short. My friend VanStrawberry stood out as the coolest kid in camp. He had long hair, cut like the Beatles. Tony refused to get it cut. There must have been a clear agreement with parents because Comak's leaders didn't relent. They dragged him kicking and screaming to the chair. A small group held him down while the barber sheared his head. Tony fought to the end and beyond, but he lost.

Some activities are rewarding as a path to personal growth while others lead us away from paths we might otherwise have taken. I imagine my experience with the Boy Scouts and that last incident at Comak helped steer me away from a profession in the military. It's not that I don't respect military people, quite the contrary, I think they are heroes. My sense is that I'd never have succeeded within a military organization due to my independent nature. I'm glad I didn't get drafted.

Many pundits teach that the most valuable activities lead to material rewards. Rewards realized in the form of money. With the summer of '65 fading and no organized events on my agenda other than school, the discussion at the Geiger dinner table took a turn in the monetary direction. It was time for Roger to find a paying job. Although Dad was a strong proponent of the idea, I probably started the conversation because earning real money seemed like a fine notion to me. Heck, my friend Rick had a job, how hard could it be? At my first opportunity I intended to ask him.

On an early fall evening, Rick and I were skiing suicide boards in the high school parking lot behind our homes. All the cars were gone for the day, leaving the lot wide open. A suicide board is a makeshift skateboard made with the metal wheels from old clamp on roller-skates. Everyone had a few skates lying around, so we'd pull them apart and nail the wheels to the bottom of a board. Simple. Find a hill and go for a ride.

Without helmet or pads, our rides approached a condition of attempted suicide when we tried to turn. The darn things barely knew how, often forcing us to jump rather than crash. If lack of steering failed to kill us, the wheels surely would. Whenever those skinny metal wheels hit a small pebble, everything stopped dead, sending a rider flying. To ski a suicide board you tie a long rope to the seat post of a bike. The skier holds on while the tower rides the bike. Just like water skiing, only more painful. Real skateboards had not yet made their way from California to Canada.

As we rode, afternoon turned to dusk, and a heavy fog settled on the shoulders of nearby trees. Skiing ceased in favor of talking and our conversation veered off into life's big questions.

Skates for making suicide boards, from Missouri History Museum

"Hey Rick, do you make any money doing your paper route? Is it hard?"

"No," he said "it's easy. You pick up the papers where they drop them off, deliver them to houses on your route, and get paid." Rick then described details of his work while my mind dwelled on the money part.

Piece of cake really. Do a little work, make a bunch of money. Then I though, *of course it's still summer,* but Rick had already moved on to more important discussions like space, astronauts and aliens. The fog got thicker and our stories got spookier as we one-upped each other into a decent little frenzy.

Then "Rog, what's that light?" Rick asked pointing up.

"Yeah right, like I'm gonna buy that? I'll bet it's a flying saucer. Ooooh."

"No, honest, look. It's getting bigger."

I looked up into the low fog and sure enough, there was a light, bright like a car headlight. As we watched, it grew to the size of a softball and seemed to be moving fast. Real fast and in our direction. Now the size of a full moon but bright like the sun. Still coming right at us!

"AUUUGGGHHH" we both screamed with our eyes bugging out, but too paralyzed to move as it broke through the fog right over our heads. Still bright, but small like an arc welder, the light traveled a short distance past us and flickered out several feet before hitting the ground.

"IT WAS A METEORITE!" Rick yelled "Cool! Let's see if we can find it."

"WOW, we were almost killed by a meteorite," I replied. "It burned up right over top of us. We'll never find anything. Man, how bad would that be... smushed by a space rock. I'd like to see you explain that to my mom."

Rick, being from a fundamental Free Methodist family, suggested "Maybe it was a sign from God?"

I thought about that but said nothing. I was an Anglican, and Anglicans don't do well with God speaking through signs. *If it was a sign,* I reasoned, *it must be telling me life's kind of risky. I gotta get off my butt and do some stuff before somethin' else gets me.*

51

As a paperboy for the Toronto Globe and Mail, we did not "throw a paper" as folks do in the rest of North America. The company required us to place the paper neatly between the storm door and entry door of every home on our route, every morning, 365 days a year. Summer paper delivery is tolerable if somewhat boring. Winter delivery could be brutal. The newspaper company was just like the Board of Education. From kindergarten through high school, the Board never closed our schools a single day for bad weather. Nor did the Globe fail to be delivered. Even in a blizzard, snow was never an excuse. If you could make it, you went; so every morning, summer or winter, rain or shine, I delivered papers.

Throughout the kinder seasons, riding my bike helped get the job done a little faster. Once an inch or two of snow covers the ground, a bike makes for tough sledding. Then I walked while carrying fifty papers in a shoulder bag. On the worst mornings, when temperatures hovered around zero Fahrenheit, a good wind could cause my eyes to water and the lashes to freeze shut. I'd have to take off my mitts to pinch them long enough to let the lashes melt if I wanted to see again. On the bright side, I never got frostbite. That came years later.

As long as it wasn't raining or bitterly cold, I didn't mind my job so much. I kind of liked walking alone early in the morning. Besides, I'd made friends with a few family dogs, and since allergies meant I couldn't have one of my own, I really enjoyed daily visits with my canine buddies. As my first fall on the job turned to winter, it seemed this working business was pretty good. It was on a Saturday afternoon in December while putting up decorations with my Mom that an awful realization hit me. *Hey, the Globe delivers papers every day of the year. I'M GONNA HAVE TO WORK CHRISTMAS MORNING.* What a disaster! Christmas morning. The number one, best, magical morning of the year, and I would be the only kid out walking the streets. I fretted, whined, moaned and moped every time I thought about it.

"Dad," I asked "did you know I'm gonna be out working on Christmas? It's not right. It's not Christian. God don't want kids working on Christmas."

"Sport, I'm pretty sure God says lots of things about not being lazy when you should be doing your work. Besides, you made a commitment to do this job. You have no choice but to see it through."

Christmas morning came cold with a layer of new snow over everything. Hours before sunup, I got myself out of bed, pulled my clothes out from under the covers and got dressed. If you ever have to sleep in a really cold bedroom, remember to keep your clothes in the bed with you so they'll be warm when you put them on in the morning. As I made my way down to the kitchen, I smelled something. *Coffee? Who's making coffee this early?* Then I saw sure signs that someone was up and about in the house. *Must be getting presents ready.* My glum mood continued as I finished putting on winter gear and sat there lacing my boots. *Great. When I should be opening a stocking, I'll be opening a big bundle of papers.*

.With no alternative, I heaved myself up and out the door to get it over with. As I stepped into our garage to get my bag, I saw Dad, Mom and Amy. They were standing there, all dressed for winter with our station wagon warmed up and ready to go. "Need some help today Sport?" Dad drove while I sat with Amy on the lowered tailgate and gave directions. Mom doled out papers from the back seat. As we came to a cluster of houses, Amy and I jumped out and ran door to door. We finished in no time. It was a Christmas treat I've cherished for fifty years.

Throughout the years of 1964 to 1966, finding my life's path rarely crossed my mind. Potential rewards, fear of failure, cutting some strings, all of these were, at best, vague signposts pointing out paths I might take later in life. The desire that usually motivated my more adventurous exploits was a curiosity to learn new things that seemed useful. Knowledge allowed me to do what I wanted to do. I wanted to produce my own fireworks, so I learned to make gunpowder. I wanted to steer rather than paddle, so I became a sternman. I wanted to earn money, so I got a job. Through it all, I was blissfully unaware of any abstract thoughts concerning personal growth. Indifference, however, does not mean I failed to learn from those events. Ultimately, I learned this. My life became more rewarding when I took time to discover new things, involved myself in new experiences and practiced new skills. It is unfortunate this lesson, presented so early, met with understanding so late.

4

Summer of '67

Dear Taidy,

*Did you know a person can sleep standing up? It's true, and
I know it 'cause I did it today. I've fallen asleep standing up lots of
times this summer. Mostly it happens when I'm leaning on things,
but this morning I was just standing there in the middle of the barn,
leaned my head over on my shoulder and fell asleep. I didn't even fall
down. When I get the chance to sleep, I have to sleep fast. If Tom sees
me he'll make me fall down for sure. He'll knock me down. Dang I'm
tired. We work from before the sun comes up till way after it goes
down, seven days a week. Don't get me wrong, I showed 'em I'm no
jam tart and I'm not sorry I came, but this work is hard.*

*Cousin Penny called Mom and Dad back in May. She asked
if I could come to New York to work on their dairy farm for the
summer. I was beside myself. Nothing so wonderful had ever
happened to me. "Leave home for the whole summer and get paid?" I
told Mom working on the farm would be the best summer ever. I
promised Dad I'd be a perfect son. They only had to say yes. Sure,
I'm allergic to just about everything on the farm, and my asthma
might kick in, but "Mom, Penny's a nurse for Pete's sake. She can
give me my shots. Get some of whatever Dr. Walsh gives me, and I'll
take it with me. What else was I gonna do this summer?"*

They had to "talk about it" for a couple of days, but then

56

said OK. I could spend the summer working for Penny, and her husband Tom, on their dairy farm. Penny said I'd make $25.00 a week, plus room and board. As soon as school let out, Mom and Dad packed me up, drove to upstate New York, and dropped me off. Mom gave Penny my allergy shot serum, Dad told me to behave, they both wished me luck, and I was on my own. I figured it'd be pretty much like canoe camp or Uncle Ward's farm, but with a little more work and less swimming. Man was I wrong!

Dad used to talk about a school he went to when he was young. I know it's not a real school, but he sure believed he graduated from it. This place looks like a farm. This place smells like a farm. Really, it's that school. Mom and Dad shipped me off to the School of Hard Knocks!

The good news is, Saturday I start my week off. I'm getting on a bus, going home and doing nothing. Penny and Tom haven't said anything, but they've been acting a bit different the past couple of days. It's like they expect Saturday is the last they'll see of me this summer. They're wrong. I've already decided to come back for the second semester.

Rog

"RISE AND SHINE. TIME TO GET UP," Tom yelled as he passed my cot in the hall. He gave my leg a shake, then I heard work boots clunking down the stairs. "LET'S GO! IT'S FOUR O'CLOCK, TRUCK'S LEAVING IN 5 MINUTES."

I had arrived at Penny and Tom Canne's farmhouse apartment the day before. "Your bed's at the top of the stairs," Penny told me. "Put your bag under the cot so we don't trip over it."

From their kitchen, I saw stairs leading up from the only other room on the ground floor. At the top, I sidestepped an old foldup cot and followed the short hallway into a bedroom. *This looks like their bedroom, where am I gonna sleep? That cot in the hall?* I guess a proper bed didn't fit well in a hallway, nor, it seemed, did my new employers have an extra bedroom available. *I guess cots fit pretty well in the hallway. Geez, I've had my own room since I was born.* Then I figured a little hardship was necessary in an adventure. *Kinda like camping,* I thought. *Just keep your mouth shut and stick your duffle bag under the bed.* That night I went to sleep dreaming about horses, cows and cowboys roughing it like I'd seen on TV.

I knew Penny as a fun cousin, as long as you didn't get her temper up, but had only met Tom twice. Tom, who grew up on the farm, didn't seem to have had much interest in school. As he got older, he made his own way, running things for his father and taking life as it came. Penny helped when she wasn't working at her hospital. When Tom wasn't working, he ran model trains. With a nod to his hobby, Tom always wore a blue and grey train engineer's hat. He should have worked on the railroad.

After Tom woke me the first morning, I got dressed and made it to the kitchen faster than I'd ever moved in my life. Even my father didn't get up that early when we went fishing. I found Tom by the coffee pot, then learned his ideas of haste were somewhat flexible. He was leaning on the counter, drinking coffee, and looking through his mail. As I came through the door, he poured coffee into a second old cup. "Here, drink this. It'll wake you up and make you feel better." When he found a magazine about model trains, our urgency got sidetracked for several minutes. Dad used to give me coffee milk sometimes, but that was a tablespoon of coffee in a cup of milk. Tom gave me a cup of black coffee and nothing. Not wanting to appear like a kid, I took a sip from the cup. Not bad, in a hot, bitter, nasty sort of way. Coffee appeared to be the only thing on the menu, so I kept drinking. Soon I livened right up. Good thing because Tom had finished his puttering and started acting like it was time to go.

Outside, we climbed into a pickup that must have survived since the forties. Tom turned a key in the dash, hit a starter button on the floor, then off we went, down the road toward the barn. During the first part of that mile long ride, I was enjoying the pre-dawn view out the window. Then WHAM, Tom gave me a charley horse punch in the leg and yelled "YOU AWAKE NOW?" He laughed like it was all in a day's fun until we pulled into the barnyard. When he jumped out of the truck and went into an ancient barn, I hobbled in after him. *Good God what a smell. Dairy barns stink!* I stood there looking clueless and tried not to gag. *I wonder what they do with those metal collar things lined up along the sidewalks? Why so much stinky old straw?*

Alongside several cement walkways, I saw ditches half full of cow plop. Tom was running around the place turning things on, attaching hoses, getting buckets out and generally doing whatever farmers do. "Well don't just stand there like a Hunyak," he said "help me get ready to let the cows in."

"Ah, what do you want me to do?"

"Open all the stanchions so they'll be ready for the cows."

"Ah, what's a stanchion?"

Tom showed me that the metal collars were for holding a cow's head so she could be milked. As he worked, I went along the rows, opening stanchions. When I reached the last row, Tom went to the back of the barn and opened a big sliding door. "Here they come!" he yelled. I looked and saw that forty-three cows had been waiting at the door. They looked like customers waiting for the after Christmas sale at Walmart. The cows pushed and shoved their way through as each headed toward a stanchion and stuck her head in. Cows are big! I didn't want to be in the way as they bullied toward their place in line. They didn't slow down, and they didn't share the road very well. Cows don't look too smart, but each of these bovine ladies knew her own spot. We didn't have to help them at all. After they'd all stuck their heads in a collar, I walked down the middle of the row closing stanchions. I didn't feel too smart either, but I learned right away to walk in front of the critter or be real quick on my feet. Cows kick!

While Tom attached "pail at a time" milking machines to cows, I again stood there lost. "FILL THAT WHEELBARROW OVER THERE WITH GRAIN," he yelled over the sound of milking. "THEN GIVE EACH ONE A SCOOP BEFORE I LET 'EM GO." As soon as he'd finish milking a cow, Tom let it go. Straight away it exited the back door and returned to the pasture. These ladies were well trained. They'd push to get in, we milked them, then they trotted right out again. Tom poured each filled pail into a big milk can with a lid, the kind you see in old pictures and have painted for decoration. Once two cans had been filled, he'd carry both out to a different building and load them into the cooler. Each of those cans weighed a hundred pounds, so Tom's arms looked like Popeye's. On one of his trips he poured milk into a pitcher from the refrigerator. We worked for over an hour before all the cows left the barn. "How'd you like morning chores?" Tom laughed. "Let's get some breakfast." Before leaving, Tom grabbed the pitcher of milk.

My feet hurt, my clothes reeked of manure, and my mouth watered at the thought of a big farm breakfast. On the way back to the apartment something clicked in my mind, so I asked Tom, "Hey, where's Penny? Doesn't she help with milking?"

"Yeah, but she's working nights at the hospital. She'll be home in bed by now, so we have to be quiet. She can get a little cross if she gets woke up."

"Oh. Well who's gonna cook breakfast?"

"COOK? Cook what? Toast and Cheerios. That's our breakfast." Another dream shattered. Fortunately, I liked fresh, unpasteurized, un-homogenized, milk.

After a short meal, we headed back to the barn where Tom handed me a shovel while showing me where another wheelbarrow rested between jobs. "Now you get to clean the gutters," he proclaimed with a look I didn't like. "Just fill up the wheelbarrow, push it up the ramp out back, and dump it in the spreader."

"Ah, what's a gutter?"

Tom pointed to the cement ditches, which were now full of a brown soup of poop, piss, straw and who knows what, then said "That's a gutter." The stink had grown much worse than earlier that morning. Tom left me alone with my work and said he would be back to pick me up later.

Guess I'm on my own. Tentatively, I eased the shovel in for a big scoop of poop. *This is gross. And what... the heck... is that?* The soup was moving. I bent over to take a closer look and saw the whole mess with alive with... *Ah geez, maggots!*

I used the rest of the morning and took about thirty trips to the manure spreader, with a wheelbarrow full of poop, to get the gutters cleaned out. The sides of a spreader stand four feet off the ground, so I had to raise the wheelbarrow at least that high to dump it. The method of doing so at this wonderful operation was a narrow ramp, made of wood, laid on top of a pile of dry manure. Just get a good running start, push real hard... until you make it to the top of the ramp and dump it. Easy, right? I figured it out, but let me tell you, lots of soup splashed out and it never failed to land on me. By the time I'd finished, I was covered in crap and smelled as bad as the barn.

Have I mentioned Tom's flexible notion of getting places on time? I first noticed it that day. With Tom, a schedule was just a hunch. He wasn't into time and he never met a stranger. Tom couldn't resist talking to people, and he seldom arrived when I expected he should. The gutters looked good long before he returned, so I played with the cats.

I like cats. It's a good thing because on any given day, the farm had thirty to fifty barn cats, plus one house kitty named Boots. The total varied depending on how many new kittens arrived and how their luck was running. Barn cats live dangerous lives. They need all nine of them. House kitties usually fare a little better, but poor old Boots got run over by the corn cutter. She was our only indoor cat and belonged to Tom's mother who lived in an old farmhouse beside the barn. We found little stew sized pieces of Boots lying in the corn field after Tom drove through. I'd never seen him so jittery as when he had to tell his mother what happened.

In a place where you have lots of cats you have a leader, the alpha male. In all my life I've never known a more amazing animal than the leader of the pack on that dairy farm. His name was Toughy. A truly large tabby with noticeable muscles more suitable on a bull dog than a barn cat. He was friendly to me, but ruled the other cats, and some of the cows, like he was the king.

One day we heard a great commotion up on a hill behind the barn. When we went to look, I saw six wild dogs in a mad frenzy attacking something in their midst. We couldn't see what it was, but as fast as one dog rushed in, two others would yelp and come flying out. Fur flew, blood ran, the dogs got cut to shreds. It looked like a real battle. While I watched them fight, Tom got pretty agitated, said something about "those damn dogs" and ran into the farmhouse to get a rifle. By the time he returned, half the dogs had whimpered their way out of the fight. The rest were still giving it a go, so Tom fired a couple of shots at them and they all took off. When we arrived at the spot where they had been fighting, we found a slight depression in the ground about two feet across and six inches deep. Crouched in this defensible position was Toughy. He came out a little over excited and a bit scratched up, but generally in good health. *Next time,* I thought, *those dogs better bring the whole pack if they're gonna take on our cat.*

The rest of my first week continued as the first day had started. Milk the cows twice a day, clean the gutters, get beat on by Tom when I least expect it, and work my tail off. I had some trouble breathing those first days and Penny did give me one shot, but after that we all forgot about it. My congestion disappeared before the second week. In our opinion, the farm had so many things to which I had allergies, they gave it up and quit bothering me.

One morning, after we finished milking, Tom told me we had to plant corn. I'd have to help him, so off we went to the future cornfield. As he hooked up a big planting machine behind the tractor, Tom explained how things worked. It had a row of wooden hoppers with tubes running out the bottom into spikes stuck down in the dirt. Below the hoppers lay an eight-inch running board and behind that a big chain blanket that dragged along the ground. Tom filled the hoppers with seed corn, showed me where to stand on the running board, got on the tractor and took off. I hung on in fear for my life. "Watch you don't fall off, that chain can really tear you up. Just walk back and forth so you can make sure the corn keeps flowing down the tubes." How Tom thought I should do that and not fall off as he tore over the bumpy ground was a question of great concern for me. I held on with one hand and pushed seed with the other. After a while I got my sea legs so pushing corn got easier. Besides, it was better than shoveling out gutters.

In addition to trains, Tom liked cigars. Anytime I saw him, he'd likely have a big, cheap, stinky, stogie sticking out of his mouth. I knew they were cheap because I looked at the box they came in. Fifty cigars for $10.00. Only the best for our Tom. While planting another field, with me surfing the corn planter as usual, Tom sat puffing away in the driver's seat of the tractor. He noticed I was looking comfortable with my job and must have thought I needed something to occupy my mind, because he yelled "HEY, DO YOU SMOKE?" I had limited experience with cedar bark cigars, and once tried a few puffs from a cigarette, so I yelled back "SURE".

"WELL, HERE, SMOKE THIS ONE," he yelled as he pulled the lit cigar out of his mouth and threw it at me. I, being a bit of a dim bulb, caught it. After burning my palm I got it turned around, stuck it in my mouth and took a pull. It made me cough, but I must admit it was way better than cedar bark. Tom thought it was a great laugh, and I smoked the thing down to a nub without getting sick.

After mastering the fine art of corn planting, I got to learn the joy of harvesting hay. There are two categories of hay harvest. One is for immediate use, so the hay is just piled loose in a hay wagon. The other is baled hay that has to be stored till the cows get hungry during winter. I experienced both, many times, but baling was way more work. First you have to rake it, then you have to bale it, then you have to stack it in a wagon. After all that, you take it to a barn and store it. The whole operation has to move quickly in case it rains. Hay does not like rain. On the Canne farm, we got things started by dragging a baler with a powerful throwing attachment behind our tractor. Behind the tractor, we pulled two hay wagons. One person drove the tractor around a field of cut and raked hay. The hay was packed into seventy pound bales, thrown over one wagon that's twenty feet long, into the second wagon where some poor sucker catches them and stacks them. Guess who got to drive and guess who got to catch? Look at the picture below and imagine a second wagon behind the first. Do you have any idea how hard it is to catch a seventy pound brick being shot over fifty feet? Plus, they come at you every seven seconds. On the first few rows, you can't so much catch the bales as block them aside, being careful they don't break apart. That would be bad.

Catching hay bales. Photo by blimp pilot, Al Judd.

Apart from the physical abuse it can inflict upon one's body, hay will make you crazy. It gets into everything you wear and it itches. I spent half my free time picking pieces out of my shirt and socks. Once the wagons were full, we delivered them to the barn. There we had to load the bales onto a hay elevator to lift them into the upper rafters, otherwise known as a hay mow. The bales stayed out of sight in the hay mow (rhymes with cow) until pulled down for winter feed.

After a few weeks on the job I started to act like a somewhat useful hand around the farm. I'd learned to milk a cow by hand and could hit a cat in the mouth with a stream of warm milk, making me very popular with the cats. Tom told me when my friends asked what I'd been doing I should "tell them you pulled tits all summer." Twice a day I'd lift a dozen or more heavy milk cans chest high to drop them gently into a top loading cooler. I stacked hay, shoveled gutters and moved cows, almost like I knew what I was doing. Tom continued to clobber me on a regular basis, but not like child abuse or real bullying. He never got mean, or hurt me. Our horseplay seemed more like wrestling with an older brother. I finally asked him why he bashed me every day and he told me "To toughen you up, of course. Your folks think you need it."

My parents told him to beat me up? Well crap. After that I did my best to fight back, so getting pounded was more fun. Even though I was growing stronger, I never got the best of Tom. The man was built like a rock. Not a fair fight. Still, he seemed to enjoy my renewed spirit pretty well. In between chores and thrashings, Tom taught me things about working a farm. He showed me how to drive a tractor, fix things with bailing wire, and even how to straighten old nails when we wanted to reuse them. I guess we didn't have money for new nails. That realization made me consider how they could afford to pay me? I wondered if mine was a "mercy" job? You know, give young Rog a job so he can play at working. *Man, that would really rot my socks. How's a guy supposed to toughen up or even grow up if he's being set up?*

A hay wagon used for daily feeding is just a hay crib on wheels. It has a wooden deck with V shaped 2x4s along its length to hold up the hay. Ours were old, so the wood was as hard as iron. One sunny morning, Tom and I filled the wagon with fresh hay and delivered it to our bovine ladies. Once Tom found a good spot to leave the wagon, I jumped off to unhook it from the truck. As I jumped, Tom thought it would be a good laugh to take off without me, wagon and all. I, having become a fit, limber fellow, jumped back up on the wagon and turned my face forward to laugh at him. Fearing I was trapped between the truck and wagon, Tom slammed on the brakes. Two independent actions happening at exactly the same time. My face met an upright hard enough to crack the 2x4, and I passed out. Lucky for me I was on a hay wagon so I fell backward into a nice bed of hay where I lay until Tom came running back. I've heard Welshmen are hard headed so I guess I should be thankful for my ancestry. Given a few minutes to remember who I was, I seemed none the worse for my experience, and we went on with the day.

After lunch we directed our efforts to a lovely afternoon of stacking hay in the barn. Tom had taken pity on me, considering my morning mishap, and instead of standing in the hot rafters stacking bales, I got to load them on the elevator. I'd put a bale on at ground level and it got lifted way up high to a small door where my partners, Tom and a State School worker we had hired, picked it off the belt and stacked it. That's how it works, assuming all goes well. As you might expect, it did not. We were on our second wagon of bales when Penny came along and took over the job of loading. I was puttering around raking loose hay from below the hay mow door. One bale must have been off center. When it got to the top, it caught the edge of the door, Tom missed catching it and down it came. Seventy pounds, twenty feet, right on my head. I was out for the second time in a day.

Hay sent to the hay mow. By Theresa Westaby, Rootstock Coop.

When I came to, Penny decided I needed to sit quietly for a while, so I pulled up a bale, and sat watching as everyone else worked. I've also heard bad things come in threes. Tom's dad, Vince, chose that moment to show up. Vince was a tough old guy with rotted teeth from chewing leaf tobacco for fifty years. I think he once made a living as a fur trapper. I knew little about that, but I'd seen all the animal traps he kept in the back of his garage. Looking at me he yelled, "Tom, what the hell's he sitting on his ass for? Get him up and working." He was kind of a grumpy old guy and stomped off before anyone had time to explain my bad day. I didn't figure he'd care much anyway, so I got up and went back to work. I'd learned a lesson. Even if you're bashed up a bit, nobody ever yells at you for working too much.

Not every day turned out as bad as that one. All of them lasted too long, and I got so tired, I developed the habit of sleeping any time I got the chance. I hadn't worried about my cot since the first night I arrived. If we had to drive somewhere, I'd fall asleep. If Tom took me back to the house for any reason, I'd fall asleep on the living room floor. In the morning, I'd sleep until Penny woke me up. When Penny worked nights, getting up didn't always happen at the crack of dawn. Lots of days, getting up didn't happen at all. If Penny called to check on us, the phone rang in the house and in the barn. We were in big trouble if nobody answered with barn noises in the background. Usually, the phone rang and rang until Tom woke up to answer it. She always called back later to be sure we were up. When that didn't work either, Penny had to leave the hospital to come home and get us out of bed... that was scary. After the second time, I could be dressed and down to the kitchen between the time I heard her car tear into the driveway and she came in the door. On those days, I left Tom to his own defense.

Fortunately, life on the farm amounted to more than work and sleep. We goofed off as well. Penny and Tom each had horses. I rode double with one or the other throughout their few hundred acres of fields and pastures. I also learned to drive the old farm truck. My driving was passable as long as I didn't have to change gears. I never did get the hang of that, and Tom didn't try to teach me. I think he figured if I couldn't get out of first gear I couldn't go too fast. He'd just get us going in a pasture, jump out and leave me to drive. You can do that when the throttle is on the steering column. Tom set it to the speed he wanted and left it. The old truck could go real slow without stalling out. Tom would get it going, tie off the steering wheel and walk along beside, throwing hay out of the bed with nobody driving. If I was driving and wanted to stop, I'd press the brake pedal until it stopped moving, then turn off the key.

The family across the street from our barn had kids close to my age. In the evening, if we got chores done early, I'd go to their house and hang out with Robyn, Dillon, Dale and their baby sister Dixie. As the summer wore on, our activities grew beyond kid stuff. One night they "borrowed" some beer from their dad and the four of us, not the baby, drank it. On another night, I shared cigars I'd pilfered from

Tom's box with Dillon and Dale. We talked about girls when Robyn wasn't around. She was the oldest, a year older than me, and the boys were younger. They all seemed to know a whole lot more about adult subjects, like sex, than I did. Both boys tried to educate me by asking if I knew what this word or that saying meant. I rarely had a clue. When I pretended I did, I'd just make a mess of it. Robyn took a more direct approach to my education.

Her family got milk straight from the pail like we did. Every few days, one of the kids would come over to pick it up. One evening, when I happened to be there by myself, Robyn showed up. It was raining a little, so she was wearing a long raincoat when she came into the milk house. As she handed me her pitcher, the smell of fresh flowers hit me. *Wow. That doesn't smell like the barn. Robyn smells good,* I thought, turning to the refrigerator. After filling her jug, I turned back towards her. *Holly crap!*

Robyn had taken off her raincoat and faced me wearing nothing but a nightgown. Not the kind of nightgown your grandma wears. This was short, pink and frilly. I could see right through it! I could see everything! Robyn just stood there smiling, letting me look. My eyes bugged out, my mouth fell open, and my heart pounded like I'd soon pass out. Then she opened her arms wide and said "Well?"

I made intelligent noises like "oh", "aug", "wa" and kept looking.

After a few moments, she said "Don't you want to do

anything?"

To which I managed to choke out "Do? What?" Robyn seemed a bit put off by that.

"Boys are so stupid." she said, then picked up her coat and left in a huff. She never even took her milk.

Not all my experiences as the object of another's affection were as pleasant as my encounter with Robyn. When Tom had an extra job, requiring little intellect, he'd occasionally hire workers from the State School. The Newark State School for Mentally Defectives housed men and women with advanced to severe mental disabilities. I visited it once with Tom. Several dismal, red brick buildings greeted us as we drove through the gates. Steel bars covered the windows of their upper floors. Tom warned me. "You have to be careful. Don't let them get too close and leave everything from your pockets hidden in the car." Inside the building we'd entered, several men looked up from benches along a hallway. Strange sounds assaulted my ears while the smell attacked my nose. *Geez, this place smells worse than our barn. Like disinfectant mixed with puke and pee.* The men surrounded Tom and me giving hugs and patting us on the back like long-lost brothers. Everything about that institution gave me the willies. *These guys are sure friendly.* I thought. *Some of them are a little too friendly. Get me outta here.* The stories Tom told me later about one patient, a shovel handle, and our cows made my mind cringe.

During the visit, Tom hired a guy named Raymond for

a day's labor. I'd met Raymond a few times before, so his small size didn't fool me into thinking he wouldn't do much work. Once you got Raymond to understand what you wanted him to do, he was a dynamo. He'd get the idea in his head and just keep at it till you convinced him to stop. After delivering Raymond to the farm, Tom left him and me to clean out the barn. "I gotta go into town," he said. "Don't worry, I'll be back by 1:00 to pick you up."

With Raymond's single-minded efforts, we finished our clean-up early. Tom, of course, didn't arrive at 1:00, leaving us nothing better to do than sit outside the barn waiting in the shade. It got to be 1:30, no Tom, 2:00 o'clock, no Tom. As usual, with no chores to do, I started nodding off. Watching me sleep must have put an idea in our Ray's head. I woke up quick when he came over and sat down next to me. Right next to me. So close he was touching me. This made me a little nervous, but Raymond was a friendly guy, so I didn't run away, I said "Hi Ray" in a happy voice.

Raymond said "Hi" back, while moving his hand to my leg.

OU-OH! I jumped up and moved through weeds to the hood of an old car, abandoned in the barnyard. *Maybe he'll like the shade more than he likes me.* Raymond stood up, came to the car and again sat beside me. At fourteen, I didn't know the word lust. He smiled and his eyes looked like he had a fever. Sometimes it took a direct command for Ray to let go of an idea, so I yelled, "RAYMOND, YOU STAY HERE, OK?" then left him to stand under a tree by the road. Apparently he wasn't ready to let go of his idea. He quickly followed me to the tree.

Raymond seemed to be getting more urgent in his approach. A tingling sensation crept up my neck and scalp like the time I'd watched a creepy horror movie. My eyes darted around looking for rescue. Scared into desperation, I took the only direction of escape left. I climbed the tree. Ray refused to be stopped by a simple thing like a tree and climbed up after me. When I got so high I thought the limb might break, I figured I only had one option left to save myself. I broke off the biggest dead branch I could find and poked Raymond in the head with it. The first one didn't stop him, but it slowed him down, so I rattled it all over his head and shoulders. That seemed to take the desire right out of him, and he let go of his idea. Raymond climbed down the tree and went off to pout on his own. He actually seemed put out that I was being so unfriendly.

I stayed up the tree, swaying in a light breeze, until Tom arrived a half hour later. He didn't quite grasp the depth of my agitation with him. From his point of view, I'd had a good lesson about real life and survived in good health. What more could I ask for?

One of the best rewards from the farm was that having gotten over my allergies, I could have a pet of my own. When I returned home at the end of the summer, I took one of the farm cats with me. He was a kitten named Little Dipper, son of Big Dipper, whom Penny said got his name for being such a big dip shit. The Dipper family's only claim to fame was that they all had six toes on their front paws, presumably because their family tree didn't fork so much.

A few years later, after Little Dipper had grown, we got a Samoyed puppy named Vola. Dipper decided to be Vola's mother, Vola seemed to like the idea, and a family was born.

Dipper and Vola

Dipper taught Vola to clean himself like a cat by licking his paws and play like a cat by batting at toys with his paws. When Dipper was outside and wanted to come in, somehow he communicated his request to Vola, and the dog would come barking until Mom went to open the door. When Dipper got so old he could no longer take good care of himself, Vola took time to lick him clean. After Dipper died, Vola would often run to the door and bark, only to be disappointed that no cat was there to be let in.

The Proverb says, "Foolishness is bound in the heart of a child." When I went off to the farm, I did not understand what I was getting into. I worked over a hundred hours a week for $25.00. That works out to about 25 cents an hour. On the plus side, I did more growing up in three months than many boys do in three years. I found out many years later that the whole thing really was a setup instigated by my parents to build my maturity. All the aunts, uncles, and cousins were taking bets on how long I'd last. I outdid their expectations. After my week off, I went back and continued to have my eyes opened to a more realistic view of the world.

Today, I wouldn't trade the education I received that summer for any degree you can name. Over Christmas break the next winter, I returned to the farm after getting a call from Penny. With Tom laid out by the flu and Penny very pregnant with their first child, they had no one to work the farm. Could I come during my break and help? Of course. I owed them far more than that. Still, I was never tempted to become a farmer. The people, animals and experiences of that summer have stayed with me for a lifetime. When my mind wanders back to the early days, I always find great joy in remembering our time together on the farm.

5

Summer 1968

Dear Taidy,

The most amazing sight happened up on Shark Lake last weekend. Dad and I had been out fishing for a few hours Saturday morning and caught lots of bass in a bay just past the island where we always camp. Dad says the fish like hiding there because of all the lily pads. When we ran out of live frogs, I fished with a worm harness. You know, that thing with spinners and three hooks in a row that holds a fat dew worm. When I caught two big ones at the same time, Dad couldn't believe it. He teased me about putting them on there when he wasn't looking. I told him I was just a more skilled fisherman than he was, so he said he'd try to concentrate a bit more. What a laugh!

About noon we quit for lunch and came back to our island. The weather was great, not many clouds, not much wind, high seventies, perfect. After lunch we were just sort of goofing off on the island and both of us happened to be on the east side where the rocks rise so steep a mountain goat couldn't climb them. Suddenly we heard a really loud roar from out in the lake. It was like a jet buzzing us or something. Both our heads snapped 'round to look. I didn't see a plane, but I did see a giant wall of water going straight up into the air. No kidding! It had to be as big around as our island and way taller than the trees. And it was moving. Moving toward us! It was

79

like a miniature tornado, sucking water right out of the lake. Neither one of us spoke, nor moved, nor nothing. We just stared at this thing. Then, after about thirty seconds, it dropped all the water, and the racket stopped.

At least the racket the water made stopped. We were yelling like crazy. Then I saw a big circle of waves moving fast over the lake toward us. As it got closer, Dad yelled at me to grab onto a tree and hold on. I did, just as it hit. The wind passing by our island was blowing like I'd stuck my head out the car window on the highway. Not quite enough to lift me off my feet, but stronger than a sunny afternoon in Ontario has ever seen before. After passing us by, it hit the cliffs on the mainland and just broke apart. It was gone. Dad guessed it must have been a waterspout caused by a lake breeze and heat off the cliffs or something. Go figure.

Sport

"Hastings Rod and Gun club didn't pan out." Dad informed me with a twinkle in his eye. "They went belly up so I've been looking for a new place. Some men at work told me about a spot called Shark Lake. They say it's loaded with bass. How about we try it?" At twelve years old, of course I wanted to go. Given a choice between fishing with Dad or seeing the Beatles when they played Maple Leaf Gardens, I'd still have gone with Dad.

His theory on catching fish seemed to involve going where most people don't. An idea often demonstrated during trout fishing trips to the Adirondack Mountains. When he learned about Kawartha Lakes Provincial Park and Shark Lake, we started a habit of canoeing, camping and fishing that lasted until I graduated college. Those trips are the canvas upon which many of my best memories were painted.

Like much of northern Ontario, the Kawartha Lakes region is a beautiful, unspoiled land, largely free of roads and lacking in people due to its remote nature. Nothing but forests, lakes and granite within the confines of a park. One hundred and forty-five square miles of preserved wilderness that is as wild today as it was when I was young.

The chain of five lakes Dad and I paddled began with Coon Lake and ended at Shark. In those days the portage landings were not well marked on maps or shore so, for a time, Dad missed seeing a designated path going beyond the third lake. We'd found a good campsite and plenty of fish, but Dad seemed dissatisfied. He wanted to find a path forward. As a veteran of many a compass trek through the Adirondacks, he considered the lack of portage markers to be no great obstacle at all.

With logs for chairs, we laid our topo map on a big granite rock while looking for a route to the next lake. Dad led the discussion. "It seems like we can make our way from the north end over there somewhere and go around this big hill where it stays pretty flat. I'll bet it's fairly short, only about half a mile." Then he stood with his compass in hand and pointed. "We have to go that way." I nodded my head like a veteran who'd actually done this before and agreed with his assessment.

Going "that way" was not so easy. Hauling a tent, packs and a canoe over a portage is work. Doing so through granite ridges, thick woods and a large swamp is painful. Our short trek became a titanic struggle lasting two hours.

Howard Geiger, "Dad", at Shark Lake.

After that, finding the portage from the fourth lake to Shark presented no problems. On the return trip, locating the misplaced portage back to the third was not an issue either. I'm grateful we never had to make the compass trek again. Dad found the path we'd missed in a little bay next to our original campsite.

Isn't that the way things usually work? When the path we should take is just around the corner, we often miss it. We expect life to be hard and assume our way forward must start "over there someplace." Once we get where we're going, hindsight lets us pick out the trail we should have taken from the beginning.

Dad in island campsite.

Our map of Shark Lake showed a campsite near a stream flowing in from the north. There we found a pleasant, if somewhat buggy, place to spend a few days. A long stretch of sandy beach backed by scattered stands of maple and birch, with gray cliffs of rock behind. It wasn't bad, but Dad looked across the lake as we stood on shore and said "Let's check that little island." Maybe he figured there would be less bugs on an island, maybe protection from wolves and bears, maybe it was direction from divine providence.

Back into the canoe we climbed and across the lake we went. The island was perfect. Just the right size with a small rock beach to land the canoe. It had a nice campsite with a good fireplace and even a little table with a shelf above made from branches nailed between two trees. We'd found what was to become our wilderness home.

Although a unique sight, the waterspout I saw on a sunny afternoon in July was not the only interesting event to cross our path during trips to Shark Lake. Another appeared as Dad and I paddled up to the trail head of a portage. We immediately noticed the landing was occupied. Not by other adventurers such as ourselves, but by a large brown bear. I'd seen bears up close in cages along the highway. I never expected to see one face to face, on a trail where I intended to hike. The experience proved intimidating.

Being intelligent woodsmen types, we decided it would be best to stay well out in deep water. Bears are good swimmers, but we were pretty sure we could paddle faster if we got a head start. From the safe refuge of the lake, we watched for a while in fascination. Mr. Bear didn't seem to be too concerned with us and in fact didn't seem to be too concerned with anything. He, or she... I never got close enough to decide, was a big fellow, and if he wanted to hang out at the portage, that was fine with me. I could wait. Dad, however, wanted to go fishing and got tired of waiting. "Ok Sport, let's make some noise and see if we can scare him off." Both of us yelled and banged our paddles on the gunnels of the canoe and in the water. After a few minutes of concentrated commotion, the bear stopped whatever he was doing and looked at us. With an irritated "harumph", he took off into the woods.

During the sixteen years I'd been his son, I'd never known my father to be a foolish man. Firm perhaps, but not aggressive. He was soft spoken, even when he was giving me the heck, and his decisions were based on knowledge and experience. Common sense and a level head guided all his actions. On that day he made an exception. As soon as the bear took off, Dad shouted "COME ON. HURRY. LET'S GO." and we paddled full speed for shore. The bear had only passed from sight a handful of seconds when we landed. I didn't think landing was real bright, but Dad said "Wait here." and off he goes into the woods after the bear.

"Dad… DAD… **DAD!**"

Well darn, I thought, *now what do I do? I'm here and where's Mr. Bear? Where's Dad? Why would he take off to meet up face to face with an old bear anyway? What if he gets eaten? Hell, what if I get eaten?* Dad didn't do things like this! I stood alone in the forest with a growing sense of panic. My heart pounded like a flat tire on a bumpy road. First, I took a couple of steps to follow after him. Next, I changed my mind and turned back toward the canoe, then changed my mind again and turned around to look off into the trees. *Is that something moving?* Fear of the bear crawled down my spine and started my legs going in every direction at once. A little healthy fear can be a good thing. It tends to keep me from making stupid choices. Panic prevented me from doing anything at all. I was jumping from one idea to the next so fast my brain got tired. When I stopped for a breath or two, it started working again. *Should I get a stick or rock for a weapon? No, that will just piss him off. I've got my knife. As if that's gonna help.*

I still couldn't decide what to do, so I did nothing. Not so my dear old Dad. He wanted to follow the bear and even if it wasn't the best decision he ever made, he made it, and he did it. I wanted to be just like him; smart, brave and always sure of myself. My usual source of composure had just run off into the woods. Without his presence, I failed to emulate his poise. *What's that noise? Something's coming. Oh geez... Oh, it's Dad.*

"The bear gave me the slip," he said. "Let's go." I looked at Dad like he'd lost his mind. Here I stood, frozen with fear, while he acted as if it was nothing. Did he ever feel fear or doubt? I'm sure he must have, but rarely did he let anyone know about it. Instead of bringing my confusion to his attention, I again stood there and did nothing.

He'll never understand what I'm worried about. I thought. *Drop it and go fishing.*

Did you ever notice that some experiences seem to repeat themselves? That's how it went for me when I ran into another bear in the wild. The second time, I was in a considerably more compromised position. It was not at Shark Lake but several years later, in the summer of 1980, while on a fly-in fishing trip to Two Peaks Lake. Dad, my brother-in-law Fred Cousineau, best buddy Steve Finlayson and I had just arrived at a remote cabin in far northern Ontario. I had a bad case of the green apple quick steps and needed to find relief. The outhouse behind our cabin was three walls of rough cut logs with a roof but no door. Behind the outhouse, a trash dump. As you might have guessed, the dump was occupied. Not by other fishermen, but by a large black bear. I guess my experience with the previous bear had given me some confidence, and it is a true measure of my gastric distress that I had no trouble deciding what to do. Bear or no bear, I was headed for the outhouse, so I had to face him. As I sat there I yelled "Steve, you watch the bear. If he starts coming for me, throw something at him."

"No way," Steve replied "you smell so gross he won't go near you. He'll come after me." Steve had always been a true friend, so I well understood that there was no shame in his being timid about coming any closer to the bear than necessary. He agreed to watch from a distance and give me a shout if it started toward me. As I sat there contemplating friendship and my fate in the near future, I called to him again. "Hey Steve, do you know the difference between a friend and a true friend?"

"No," he replied, "what's the difference?"

"A friend will help you move." I yelled, "A true friend will help you move a body. If the bear gets me, move mine to a nicer spot than the dump."

Thankfully the bear was more interested in the contents of the trash heap than the outhouse. He just kept snuffling around the garbage as I finished my business. During my second opportunity to face a bear, I had no choice but to overcome my fear. I again didn't get eaten, and all was well except later the boys had a good laugh at my expense. We saw his tracks again several times, so had to keep a watch for the bear during the rest of our trip. Dad named the bear Gladly, said he was cross-eyed and that he must be a Baptist. "Gladly the Cross I'd Bear." Not one of his better jokes.

I never saw another bear near Shark Lake, nor did I often see any other people. We did occasionally see evidence of their passing. An improvement to a campsite, or a bit of garbage left along the trail, told us other people used the lakes for hunting and fishing as we did. Dad had a rule that we should always leave a campsite cleaner than we found it. He seldom slacked off on that rule, so we would pick up the garbage left by others if it was practical to do so. Perhaps it was the habit of looking for litter that made me more observant than others. Probably it was just dumb luck. On one trip I found more than trash along our trail. I found a little bit of treasure.

In 1970, I took my first excursion to Shark Lake without Dad. Steve Finlayson, Jeff Simon, who attended school with Steve, and I went off on our own for a couple days as men of the woods. We spent a lot of time together as teenagers. This was a chance for three guys to prove themselves on an adventure all their own. When joining this sort of expedition, there are unwritten rules that should be observed. Rules like my father had about cleaning the campsite. Steve had been camping a few times with my family, plus he'd had other outdoor experiences with his own family, so he knew what was expected when one spends time camping. Everyone pitches in, you don't have all the comforts of home so get over it, and above all else, no whining. Jeff, however, was not what you might call a woodsy fellow. At mealtimes it didn't even occur to him to take part in cooking or cleaning up because he didn't know how. "How do you wash a frying pan without a sink?" he asked.

"In the lake. Use lake sand to scrub off the tough stuff and a rag with a bit of hand soap to finish it off."

"I'm not going down by the lake. Too many bugs." Jeff's hands waved about his ears as he tried to drive off black flies. We had bug spray so the mosquitoes and other things didn't bite too bad, but you have to learn to sort of ignore them flying around your face. Jeff had trouble mastering that bit of mind over mosquito Zen. Throughout the trip, he'd drop garbage without picking it up and complain about the hard ground when we tried to sleep. Our non-existent bathroom facilities totally surpassed his suburban experience. Steve seemed to take all this in stride, but I have to admit Jeff bothered my sense of what was proper behavior. I should have been more understanding.

Steve and I came from good homes. Jeff's home life was often difficult. He had no opportunities to learn anything from his dad. Our trip was the first time he'd slept a night in the bush and without someone to teach him, how could he be expected to know the rules? Teenage boys rarely give each other's values serious consideration, so I didn't think Jeff would listen if I explained how he should behave. In truth, I didn't try. I just shook my head and felt superior. Still, we had fun, no one got hurt, and far too soon we had to go home.

The hot summer sun warmed my back while I pushed our loaded canoe from shore early Sunday morning. A long paddle, with a long portage at its end, left us hot and sweaty as we worked our way through the lakes. Jeff's hair stuck to the side of his face in greasy black strings. His denim shirt clung to his chest and belly. "It's too hot," he complained when we approached our next landing. "The mosquitoes are biting right through my shirt. God, I'm thirsty. Wish we had a beer, eh?"

"Drink some lake water." I told him while bringing our canoe alongside a makeshift dock. The trail head often had an old broken down rowboat pulled up on the rocks. That day it was there. While I suggested Jeff should drink water, and we bumped past the rowboat to land, I noticed a flash of gold. A true treasure sitting in the shade under a cracked wooden seat. A gift from God on a hot day. The merciless guy hiding within my mind declared "You know, I'm kinda thirsty too. I guess I will have a beer."

"Yeah, right. You gonna go to the beer store?"

"Sure, in your imagination." Their jeers served only to enhance my joy. I reached under the seat, pulled out a full, unopened can of Molson Golden Ale, popped the top and took a long drink. The warm beer tasted great. Screams of anguish from my companions were priceless.

Although we remained close for a few years, Jeff never went camping with us again. I lost track of him after I left Canada to work overseas in oil exploration, then found him again after an intense effort in 1987. Steve and I remain good friends to this day. We still get together as often as possible to fish, talk, and share each other's lives.

Over the years, Dad and I fished everywhere on Shark Lake and only found two places where the bass seemed plentiful. That always puzzled me because there were lots of bays and rocks that looked like good fishing holes, but every time we tried them we came up empty. One place was where the stream came into the lake at the campsite marked on our map. We usually caught fish there, but they were seldom big. The other was a lily-pad-filled bay just behind our island. That spot always held lots of huge smallmouth and largemouth bass. As long as our bait held out, we caught great big fish.

On one of our last trips to Shark Lake, I asked him "Dad, we're good fishermen, why'd we quit trying other spots on this lake?"

"You know Sport," he replied looking at me thoughtfully, "there's not much point spending time where fish don't bite, just to be stubborn." I suppose he was right. It's better to accept things as they are and go with it. Dad wasn't long winded in his explanations and rarely shared any philosophy with me. He taught by example rather than lecture. When he did share, I tried to listen. As I started thinking about what he'd said, an old proverb came to mind. Something Dad often mentioned when we played cards, "Well son, you can't beat the pencil," meaning you can't beat the guy keeping score. In life you can't beat the pencil either. God, fate or lady luck, whoever you believe is in charge, will let things happen over which we have no control. Quietly accepting those things seemed like a good rule to live by.

6

October 1968

Dear Taidy,

WwaaaAAAAHHHHHaaaaaarrrr... how do you write the sound a stock car makes going around the track? It's loud, fast, exciting and these fans have turned Langhorne into a hotbed of anarchy and carousing. Penny tells me we're somewhere south of the Pocono Mountains, near Philadelphia but you couldn't prove it by me. All I've seen is the speedway, fan parking lots and flesh the women in Agincourt keep well covered.

Last month, Tom called and asked me if I'd be interested in going with him and Penny to the race. He and I went last year. Sure I wanted to go, but had to work out how to get to his place without being able to drive. I won't get my license 'til the end of the month. Besides, I needed permission from my folks. No worry there. It had already been arranged, and the asking was only a formality. My parents sure are out of it. They think going off with Penny and Tom will keep me out of trouble. Heck, they're the ones leading me astray. Well, Tom is at least. Penny pretty much makes certain I don't get injured, arrested or otherwise damaged. I guess what my parents don't know won't hurt them and all the better for me.

Dad drove me to the farm, and Tom got someone to take care of the cows for a few days. After talking for a while, we piled all our stuff in the trunk of his car and the three of us hit the road. Now you gotta understand that this was a low budget trip. We didn't really have any place to stay and we didn't really have any food or a whole lotta money. And oh yeah... did I mention we had to stop and pick up Penny's friend Diane? Lucky for us, Tom's big 'ol Chevy Malibu is a beast of a car with plenty of room for four. Good sleeping in the back seat if you're sixteen and not too picky. A twenty mile detour got us to Diane's house where Tom pulled into the drive and honked.

My first sight of this woman was as she bounced down her front walk with suitcase in hand, and I do mean bounced. Well the top half bounced for sure. They threw her bag in the trunk, and she bopped into the backseat with me. Looking at me like the witch looked at Hansel, she said "Hi, I'm Diane, you must be Roger." I gaped with my mouth open and the others laughed like I was the only one not in on the joke. Obviously, I didn't know much about girls and nothing about women. Diane was a type of lady I'd never run into before. She wore tight jeans, a loose fitting white shirt with too many buttons undone and a lacy blue bra. I hadn't actually seen many bras before and certainly not one so well filled! Except for bathing suits, I'd only ever seen one girl who showed me anything at all. And Diane was old too... had to be like, twenty-three. The woman spooked me, but I couldn't take my eyes off her. Kind of like a car wreck on the freeway. I was fascinated by something that scared me.

It takes quite a while to drive from upstate New York to eastern Pennsylvania, and after a few hours of talking and listening to country music on the radio, I guess Diane got bored. With nothing better to do, she turned her attention to me. "Gee, Rog, with those long legs of yours you must be getting a little cramped."

"I don't have long legs," I thought, but replied, "It's OK, I'm alright."

"You sure? You can stretch out if you want. Put your feet up here in my lap."

I noticed the hungry smile was back and also noticed Penny adjusting the mirror so she could see what was happening in the back seat.

"No, no. I don't want to bother you any."

"Oh, it's no bother honey, I'll even rub your feet." She replied, smiling as she leaned over, pulled one of my feet into her lap and started untying my shoe. One foot over there and the other over here got a bit uncomfortable. I gave in to the inevitable and put the other foot in her lap. She removed that shoe as well. My experience with foot rubs being kind of limited, I didn't really know what to expect, but it felt good and Diane seemed to be enjoying it.

Soon she was enjoying it more than I considered might be normal and started leaning into her work. In fact the leaning quickly became the focus of her exercise, and I found my feet in full contact with her large American breasts. I know I'm slow, but I figured out real quick that this was no accident. She was really getting into her work when she pulled her shirt out of her jeans and stuck my feet underneath. Even though I liked it, I'd become oddly confused and nervous. I made a feeble try to remove my feet, which she quickly prevented and kept a-rubbin. My only hope sat in the front seat. While thinking "Oh boy, this is heading for a problem," I stared at Penny in the mirror, my eyes filled with panic. She took pity on me. "Knock it off, Diane." Tom exited the highway at the next gas station.

Wow Taidy. What was I supposed to do? Run or have fun? She acted kind of indecent, but jeez, chances with women don't come along every day. They come along, like never. Still… she's too scary.

Two more hours of driving brought us to the speedway and a spot in outfield parking. Outfield parking is basically a big cow pasture a long walk from the track. Rows of cars park side by side, tents are pitched and people camp during the race weekend. There were facilities in the form of port-a-potties, but that's about all. Tom pitched our small tent behind the car to save our spot, and we headed off to a grocery store for a few supplies. With no pots or pans in our meager stock of gear and no way to heat food anyway, our choices were somewhat limited. I guess we managed because I didn't starve.

Diane seemed a lot less enthusiastic during this part of our trip. Penny must have gotten on to her about molesting her little cousin. I'm sure she didn't want Diane to take her game any further. That was the last I saw of Diane for the rest of the day. Next to us in the field, three guys in a camper arrived and parked for the night. They were more her speed. Let's all be thankful for missed opportunities.

"Ahhh" sighed Tom, blowing out a puff of cigar smoke and taking another drink of Genesee's best. "It don't get no better than this." He was sitting on the hood of his car, his back resting on the window and looked like the king of his world. I was fighting indigestion from the can of cold spaghetti I'd just finished and Penny looked at him like he needed a lobotomy. I guess when you milk cows every day of your life, relaxing in the sun seems pretty

good. "Let's walk up to the track and see what's going on." He continued, "That's where the rich folks camp. I'll bet they're hav'n some good parties up there."

"NO, TOM," replied Penny in her best you-better-listen voice. "We can't just leave Diane and take off. She'll be on her own."

"Ha! She's with the guys in the camper and I doubt they want to be disturbed right now. Look."

We both turned to gaze at the camper parked beside us, and it was rocking. I mean literally rocking side to side. When we moved closer, Penny and I could hear muffled sounds coming from inside. She suddenly decided a walk would be a great idea. "Come ON, Tom. Let's go." And off we went toward the track.

Up near the raceway, campsites changed in appearance. Instead of cars and tents there were trucks, Winnebagos, converted busses and travel trailers. The smell of fresh meat cooking on dozens of grills reminded me again how I wished my guides had been a little more organized and actually brought food.

We heard the beat of the Beach Boys or something coming from a radio in a nearby trailer and Penny grabbed Tom's hand to dance. He dances like a three legged bear so the moment soon passed, and we moved on. I bet there were several others around who would have taken her up on her offer because the atmosphere had gotten pretty festive. Lots of people seemed to have the same idea as us, and many had brought alcohol to liven the mood. I think some of the women must have gone to the same fashion school as our friend Diane. There were plenty of things visible to make a boy happy.

I managed to pull my eyes away from those things when I

heard a loud cheer from directly in front of the gate going into the speedway. It was locked for the night, but a large crowd had gathered for an impromptu sporting event. Shopping cart races! The nearest grocery store was about a mile down the road. I don't know where the carts came from, but several people had apparently organized the area for a race. I saw people in carts, a pit area and cheering sections. They even had lanes marked out in the parking lot.

A starter held his makeshift flag high and yelled "On your marks. Get set. GO," while jumping into the air and whipping the flag to the ground. It was heads up, one-on-one drag racing with one person pushing the cart and a girl riding inside trying not to spill her beer. When they got to the end of the lane, a second guy with a checkered flag would bring it down with a flourish and point it at his declared winner. As they finished each heat, everyone drank lots of beer and the fans cheered or jeered, depending on how they liked the result. Bets got settled, and they did it all again with another pair.

As it got darker, more fans showed up, more carts showed up, the crowd got louder and the races got more sophisticated. First, they added numbers to the carts. Then, they started modifying them so they would go faster. When it became too dark to see, a Good Samaritan brought in some large floodlights on a pole and lit up the whole area. Someone provided a bullhorn to help keep heats running on schedule. Things progressed well, though somewhat drunkenly, into the night. Then the cops arrived.

I've got to say that this bunch of drunken shopping cart racers were not the most cooperative group I've ever witnessed. When told it was time to "shut her down" as the nice deputy put it, they yelled and booed and made no move to comply at all. I distinctly remember several comments to the effect of "up yours", "make us" and "get lost asshole" coming from the crowd. Tom, our leader (when Penny let him) and the most experienced with these situations said, "Oh shit, time to go!" We soon made our way back to the car and our welcome beds.

Penny and Tom got the tent, and I got the back seat where I locked myself in, having recently realized the unpredictable nature of drunks, and drunks being so prevalent at this event. There I settled into the sleep of exhaustion and the effects of my one beer.

Tap, tap, tap... knock, knock, knock... pound, pound, pound! "Roger, wake up. I gotta get in the trunk. It's cold out here, I gotta get my clothes."

"Huh, what?" I pulled myself up on the seat and looked out the window. It was pitch black out but light from a small flashlight let me see Diane's face. I opened the door. "What are you doing? What time is it?"

"It's three, and I need to get in the trunk. I don't have anything to wear."

With sleep still fogging my brain, I looked at her in the dim light and AAAAUH! She had on some guy's t-shirt but that was it. No pants, nor nothing! "Son of a biscuit." I thought, "This lady is what Mom always warned me about." I fumbled with the keys Tom had left hidden under his seat and tried not to look as I opened the trunk. "Where are you going to sleep?" I asked, praying it would not be the car.

As she pulled clothes out of her suitcase and put them on she explained "I'll go back to the camper. Those guys are so drunk they'll sleep 'til noon."

"Are you sure that's safe?" I asked.

"Don't worry about me," she laughed. "It's them you have to worry about."

That's the last I ever saw Diane, but I understand she survived the trip. Maybe I'm supposed to regret not taking advantage of my opportunity but I don't. I'm all for hitting the open road to adventure, but there are some roads that even I know are a dead end.

A few hours later, with light streaming in the windows and heat making things uncomfortable, I awoke to someone pulling on my leg. "WAKE UP LAZY BUTT. IT'S TIME FOR BREAKFAST." Tom yelled as he pulled me half out of the back seat. I managed to catch myself before I hit the ground and stumbled to my feet. Penny handed me a carton of milk and a bag of cellophane-wrapped honey buns fresh from the Jiffy Mart down the street.

"Yum," I thought, "health food".

Tom encouraged me to make haste in his always thoughtful way, "Hurry up and get that in your belly so we can get to the stands. They've already started firing up the cars. They'll be running soon. We're leave'n in two minutes, so move it."

A gobbled breakfast, a long walk and more indigestion got me to our seats just past the finish line, high up on the first turn. In no time, the cars started to move out onto the track and make their practice runs to get things set up the way they ought to be. The engine noise was loud and I could smell the fumes from burning fuel *and rubber. I loved it. After a couple of hours of watching cars coming and going, the public address announcer spoke up to let us know that pre-race practice would be over in ten minutes. A short time-out, then the parade led by a band of Mummers. They were the fanciest looking bunch of feathered highsteppers I've ever seen. Once the ceremonies finished, marshals directed cars onto the track and got 'em moving.*

All lined up, a lap to get up to speed, then the green flag to start the race. WwaaaAAAAHHHHHaaaaaarrrr, the mass of cars running past at full throttle was so loud I could feel it pounding on my chest. Two abreast, three abreast, passing, falling back, spinning out. On it went for the rest of the afternoon. When it was over, Dutch Hoag took the checkered flag.

We made our way out to the car, packed up our gear and headed out. Nothing much was said about Diane, and I thought it best not to ask. I guess I slept most of the way back to New York, 'cause I really don't remember anything about the ride.

Rog

The farm proved to be too old to prosper in the modern world. Penny and Tom moved away to settle north of Syracuse where I could still visit them occasionally during holidays when I had enough time to get away. Those trips often seemed unremarkable. Filled with the comfort of a family sharing good fellowship, they provided a source of contentment in my life. On other occasions, like when I traveled to Langhorne with them as a teenager, they were the catalyst for serious misadventure.

I should point out here that I never considered myself a drug-addled hippie. Still, as a child of the sixties, I had certainly partaken in mind-altering inhalants a few times. Add to that the cultural norms of friends who often rode in my car, it is only natural that some small bits of contraband might have been lost there. Normally, this would not be a problem. Even the ever vigilant Mr. and Mrs. Geiger were not diligent enough to find such small samples of evidence. It could, however, prove to be an issue if you had to cross the border to visit your cousins in New York.

On Christmas day, 1971, I decided to pack up my steel blue Valiant and go for a drive. The car had been my wheels for five years, and before that my mother's, but I was fairly certain it would make it to Penny and Tom's home in Central Square, New York. I arranged things with Penny, got my plans worked out with my folks, and was ready to go. A teenage kid, from an upscale suburb of Toronto, taking off at a whim. I hopped in the car, turned up the music and cherished my freedom. All I had to do was head east a couple hundred miles, turn right, cross the St. Lawrence River and drive south for an hour. The only possible hassle was the border, but they never stopped anyone. I'd even walked across while hitchhiking.

I arrived at the border shortly after noon on a sunny winter day. The good thing about traveling on Christmas is you're pretty much alone. The bad thing about traveling on Christmas is you're pretty much alone. No traffic means bored customs inspectors, and considering I looked kind of like your basic hippie, mine decided this was an excellent chance to practice his detailed car search skills. That man put on his evidence gloves and ran his hand through every nook, cranny and crevice of my reliable automobile. At one point, as he was running his hand along the underside of my seat back, he stopped. Slowly he pinched something between his thumb and index finger, got out of my car while turning toward me with a big old border guard grin on his face. Standing in front of me in the inspection area he said "Son, hold out your hand." I did, and he dropped a tiny, round, greenish brown marijuana seed in my hand. "Son, do you know what that is?"

I looked at the seed in my palm with dismay. *Well crap, I don't even smoke this stuff anymore.*

It was true, I didn't. During my first semester at college, I had decided pot was not for me. I just didn't like it so I quit smoking it. Regrettably, some habits can really take hold of some people. In this case, those people decided they ought to take hold of me. A few of my dorm mates grabbed me one night, tied me to a chair, then took turns blowing pot smoke in my face. They tried to get me high against my will. Unfortunately for them, I was a scuba diver and could hold my breath for well over a minute. I held my breath while they were blowing and took another breath when they quit. My tormentors wasted so much pot on me in half an hour, they finally decided I was serious and gave up. Once released from my bonds, I seem to have been released from any urge to return to pot smoking as well. The emotional commitment I made to beat them left little room for backsliding.

Rog with Steve and Shona Finlayson. Picture by Kate Finlayson.

My customs inspector stood in front of me expecting an answer. I thought, *this officer is way too serious. It just wouldn't be fair for me to get busted for a seed now!* I looked the officer right in the eye and said "Yes, I know what that is," and tossed the seed back over my shoulder into the grass behind me.

The inspector smiled while saying, "Merry Christmas son. You can go."

My life's road has run like that. A few bumps, some unexpected turns. Maybe I'd get lost for a while then pass over a hill and find the highway again. My mission was to avoid situations that took me to the end of the road before I found my way home.

During Christmas break of 1973, I convinced my best buddy, Steve Finlayson, that making a run to the great state of New York would be just the ticket to relieve our cabin fever. Even though they were both working, Penny and Tom graciously pretended they would be glad to have us. A road trip was in the works in no time. Our decision to travel to the snow belt in winter turned out to be the first of several poor decisions on that trip. Not only was the driving treacherous, there really wasn't much to do once we got there. After an initial day of boredom and being left to our own devices, Steve and I ended up in a North Syracuse establishment where young ladies demonstrated their dancing skills without the hindrance of clothing. We started our entertainment early and stayed late, with Steve and I matching each other drink for drink. He drank CC and Coke while I enjoyed shots of tequila. At one point late in the evening, I recall going to the bar and asking the barman, "Another shot of tequila please?"

To which he replied, "I can't give it to you."

"Well, why not?" I asked.

"You drank it all."

"Well how much was there when I started?"

"Twenty-three shots more than there is now."

"Oh, I guess that's enough then." Whereupon I retrieved my great good friend Mr. Finlayson and departed for home or Tom's house or wherever it was we were staying. Steve didn't resist my idea that it was time to leave, but neither one of us could walk too well, so we had to help each other. Once we found the exit and entered the great outdoors, we discovered a winter storm had covered our part of the world in ice and snow. "You know Steverino, I'm not sure it's wise for us to drive, but I don't suppose I can walk on this ice, can you?"

"I'm quite sure I can't," he replied. "Just wouldn't be safe to try."

"Well, I guess the best thing is to drive, don't ya think? I wouldn't want to do anything unsafe." We departed the parking lot slowly. I was driving when I had no business walking. The snow and ice were so thick on the windshield I had to wait several minutes while the defroster cleared enough of a spot for me to see a little of where I wanted to go. We made it about a mile toward the highway when Steve mumbled "I don't feel so good. You better pull over." I did, and Steve got out to lean against a tree in some citizen's front yard. I continued sitting in my car, along the side of the road in upstate New York, minding my own business. Shortly, I sensed a shadow fall across the window on my left and being an inquisitive sort, I rubbed the fog away so I could read the sign that had suddenly appeared just outside. *Onondaga County Sheriff's Department? Hey, that's not a sign, it's a car. IT'S A COP CAR.* A revelation like that could have sent me into a panic. I, however, managed to keep my head, rolled down my window, took a couple of deep breaths and addressed the deputy as he got out of his car. "Good evening officer."

"Hello, is everything all right here?"

"Well, my friend here has had a little too much to drink but I'm OK. We'll be back on our way north in a minute or two."

"Ok, it's a rough night out there tonight, you guys be careful."

"Thank you." I replied as he left us without further comment.

Who knows if he saw my Canadian plates and figured we'd be out of his county soon anyway, or just didn't want to deal with us out in the cold. The question is irrelevant. He was as big a fool for letting me go as I was for driving intoxicated. I've heard that God takes care of fools and drunks, so maybe He took care of us that night. It was a miracle we made it back to Tom's house without hurting ourselves or anyone else. Our road could easily have come to a dead end.

During the summer of 1974, Penny, Tom and I hooked up for our last road trip together. I've always liked races, but never became good at working on cars or driving them fast. I'm more of a natural born spectator, whose talents progressed in more questionable directions. The three of us decided to attend a big event at Mosport Raceway, east of Toronto. A weekend of continuous races at a site that allows camping all around a long road track. Penny and Tom came to our house in Toronto where we loaded all our gear in my little Renault and drove east.

"Ok, the gate's about a mile away and we've still got that little problem to take care of before we get there." We only had two tickets because we never had much money in those days. Without enough to purchase a third ticket we decided sneaking into a race couldn't be much harder than getting into a drive-in. All we had to do was hide someone. Experience gained working at a drive-in told me they always look in the trunk so we had Tom lay on floor of the back seat and covered him with camping gear. He lay there under a tent, sleeping bags, Coleman stove, lantern, bags of food and a few blankets thrown in for coverage. We had to leave the suitcases in the trunk for appearances. I expect Tom was a little squished, but we told him to take one for the team and be quiet, then took off for the entrance. At the gate the usher accepted my tickets, took a quick look inside and asked "Can I check your trunk sir?"

"Certainly," I replied, "let me open it for you." I could hear Tom snort and groan a little under all the junk as I opened my door, but I ignored him. After checking the trunk the fellow said "Thank you sir" and passed us through. Once in, Tom complained constantly until we stopped to dig him out of his camouflage, a process made all the more difficult with endless laughter from the two doing the digging. Back on the road, we soon found a good camping spot at the bottom of a long hill right on turn eight. *Perfect*, I thought, *not exactly like camping for peace and quiet, but that's not what we're here for.* As a public service disclaimer, I'd like to point out I no longer condone deception as a means to an end when trying to enter an event without benefit of a ticket. It's stealing, it's wrong and I would not do so today. At the time, however, my moral compass was a little out of calibration, so whatever worked seemed just fine.

Motorcycle coming into turn eight at night, Mosport.

As evening turned to night, we were sitting near our camp, as close to trackside as the marshals would allow. Motorcycles came tearing down the hill and hit our turn with the rider's knee inches off pavement. One poor guy was going too fast, missed the turn and wiped out right in front of us. He and his bike flew off the track and slid through the grass, coming straight for us. "We better move!" yelled Tom as we all scrambled out of our seats, but we needn't have worried. Safety nets caught him and the motorcycle before they got to us and before he got to the trees. We moved anyway.

Even with lots more racing the next day, we had plenty of time to wander through the stands and other parts of the track. I had made arrangements to meet a high school friend named Don at the pits about noon. Don said he had a pit pass and I had two, but Don also had a friend with him. How were five people, all wanting to get a close look at the cars, going to get into the pits with three tickets? "Why don't Tom and I hang around out here and you guys can go have fun," Penny suggested. It appeared Tom wasn't so keen on that plan. Our recent success with sneaking Tom into the park got me thinking. "Wait a sec, I've got an idea," I said. "Don, give me your ticket." I took my two tickets, splayed them apart about a quarter of an inch and folded them in half at a slight angle. If I held my hand over the bottom part, the tops clearly looked like four tickets. Then, sliding Don's ticket behind the four halves, it looked exactly like the top of five tickets.

I knew this alone wouldn't be enough, and any illusionist will tell you the key to trickery is distraction, so I figured I'd need a little distraction to get away with this. Everyone in the group was carrying something: a blanket, camera, binoculars, even a small tote bag. I stuck the tickets in my shirt pocket so the five tops were easily visible. "Now give me all your stuff." Gear filled my arms and hands so it was impossible to reach into my pocket for tickets. "Let's go to the gate." Our little parade marched right up to the ticket taker where, pointing to the tickets with my nose, I said "Five, myself and the four behind me." I stuck out my chest so he could get a good view in my pocket and paused long enough for him to count five tickets. We moved again before he wondered why I was carrying so much and the others were carrying nothing. I got a polite Canadian "Very good. Thank you Sir." as we passed him by.

By this time in my life, I had become a rather competent photographer, at least in my own mind. I'd had my work displayed in photo shows at college and even gotten one image published in a small Florida environmental magazine. How I got that image is a good story of its own.

A bunch of us, all long-haired, hippy-looking college kids in a photography class were walking the beach taking nature pictures. We came upon an older gentleman doing some surf fishing but tried to give him his space so as not to disturb his efforts. I guess we didn't give him enough space because as we passed by, he pulled a pistol out of his tackle box, cocked it and stared at us. Without saying a word, everyone quickly moved along. Well, almost everyone. A dead fish on the beach caught my eye, and I stopped to take a close-up, with our fisherman as my background. I know fishermen, so I figured I wouldn't get shot for taking a picture of a fish carcass. He never suspected his indiscretion would get his image into a magazine and now a book.

Gun toting fisherman, Jensen Beach, Florida.

A photographer finding himself at a major sporting

event will keep his eyes open for the best vantage point from which to take pictures. I was no exception. Not just anyplace would do for an artist of my commitment, it had to be inspired. As we exited the pit area, I saw it. The starter's tower. *Oh yeah, that's the place for me. Perfect.* Before the marquee race on Sunday, I had to find a way into that tower. They do not, of course, let every schmuck with a camera into the starter's box overlooking the start/finish line, and they don't sell tickets for the privilege either. Only race officials and the press are allowed in that gate and up those steps.

I needed a plan. I'd seen a few press photographers in the pits and noticed they all had large red press passes visible on their vests or cameras. *Well, I've been successful twice so far this weekend. If I'm bold enough, I bet I can make it three.* First, I hunted around until I saw some red paper of about the right shade laying in the garbage. Using my pocket knife I cut it to about the right shape and size, found string and tied it to my camera. I watched the gate for several minutes until a particularly young guard took over, put on my best "I belong here" attitude and walked through the gate.

"SIR. SIR. DO YOU HAVE A PASS?" called the young fellow.

"Yes," I replied as I half turned, tugged on my red paper and kept going. I spent about two hours in that tower and got great pictures.

The rest of the weekend we watched races and had loads of fun sharing campfires with other fans that thankfully never got as rowdy as those in Langhorne. That was a relief because drunken crowds tended to scare me. I'd like to conclude Canadians are too polite to become an unruly mob. It probably had more to do with the relative seclusion of Mosport, which offered no easy access to alcohol.

In some ways, the end of the race was the end of an era in my life. Penny and Tom headed home the next morning. Soon after, I drove back to Florida for my last year of college, then on to work in the North Sea. Life is a chapter book, and the chapters of our times together were over before I realized they'd ended. After working overseas for a few years I moved on to Texas. Penny and Tom had separated and gone different directions in their lives.

I visited Penny a few times until life got in the way, then lost touch with them both. Several years ago I was working through a self-help book that asked me to identify the three men who had the most profound influence on my early life. One, obviously, was my father. Another was a professor I had in college named Nikos Orphanoudakis. The third man who greatly influenced my young life was Tom Canne. Where Tom's influence waned, Penny's flourished. One way or another, much of what I now understand about manning up, people, and life, hatched during days spent with Penny and Tom.

7

November 1968

Dear Taidy,

"The mail has been delivered. I repeat, the mail has been delivered." Good code eh? We worked it out so I'd be able to let everyone know when our ransom had been paid, and I was sure no one was staking out the drop. As soon as I made the call, our hostage was released, I claimed the loot, and that was it. We got away with a perfect kidnapping.

It wasn't all that hard, really. Kidnapping the school mascot is loads easier than grabbing a real person, especially when your mascot is just a stuffed animal. Ours is a big raggedy lion, symbol of the mighty Agincourt Lancers. I'm not sure why the other guys decided it was important to take the lion hostage, but a couple of weeks ago the three of them came up with the idea and needed my help. Since my sister is a cheerleader, on the student council, and into school spirit like a toddler eating ice-cream, I figured it for a pretty good idea. Heck, the only thing she'd ever done wrong in her whole life was to help Rick and me steal a bus stop pole. This was my chance to goof on Amy with a good prank. Opportunities like that don't come often.

My part of the operation called for me to be a lookout, which I thought should be fairly safe. The rest of the plan was simple. Lancer the lion is the perfect size to fit in a baritone case. Jim has a case because he plays baritone in the band. Dave stole Lancer from its display late one day after school, just as Jim was walking by with his empty instrument case. Quick as you please our victim was in the case and out of the building. As soon as he was driven away to an undisclosed location, Doug taped a ransom note to the door of the school newspaper office. Our demand for Lancer's release... one bag of penny candy like we get from the smoke shop down on the corner. The guys wanted to include me because I live across the street from a mail distribution box where the ransom was to be delivered. From my second-floor window I can see up and down our street, plus have a good view of the side streets close to our house.

The payoff worked perfect. Right on time, a car pulled to the box, a girl stepped out and placed a small brown paper bag on top. After fifteen minutes of watching for cars, I made my call. The best part of the whole affair was my sister's ideas on who did it. Her favorite theory was that it was the newspaper staff because they wanted to have something good to write about. We never got caught, and no one ever even suspected we were to blame. Kind of a shame really. My standing in school society could have used the boost.

Rog

My life back in Agincourt during the late sixties seemed to occupy a different continuum from times spent with Penny and Tom. Demotion back to childhood, after returning from a summer away on their farm, surprised me. I'd matured on the farm. When I got home, the same restrictions that were in force when I left still applied. I thought I'd grown up, why didn't my parents acknowledge it? Pranks like kidnapping the school mascot were an exception. They might have let up a little had it occurred to me to talk with them about it, but we weren't a family that went in for a lot of discussions. Actions were more the norm. When boredom led to a series of bad ideas on my part, Dad took action. "Time for you to get off the couch and out of the rec room, Sport. How about finding yourself a job?"

Jobs for kids in the winter are scarce. My halfhearted efforts produced nothing until the spring of 1968 when I read in the paper that Scarborough Drive-In was hiring ushers. They accepted fifteen year olds, and with experience as a paperboy and farm hand, I got an immediate job offer. I started working the evening of my interview at the minimum wage for adults. $1.00 an hour. That's four times what I'd earned on the farm.

"Here's your flashlight kid. Stand in the drive lanes with the other ushers and make sure cars take their turn getting to the windows. The senior over there will fill you in on the details."

Exciting work for the first hour. Once I got the hang of directing traffic, and my feet got sore from standing on tarmac, the luster quickly wore thin. We couldn't even see the movie.

A fledgling attempt at organized labor rescued me during my third week. Mr. Rob, our manager, saw my mother drop me off and popped his head out an open window. "GEIGER. NEED TO SEE YOU." Inside, I found him sitting at his paper-littered desk, glaring at a ledger book. He didn't waste time with pleasant chit-chat. "Geiger, a pack of lads just quit. I know you've only been here three weeks, but you've been here longer than most of the boys I've got left so you're senior usher. Pay's $1.15 an hour and you don't work the lines. Teach the new boys what's to be done and work the lot."

Working the lot meant I got to come in early and walk around testing for broken speakers or inspecting for wires running down poles in the back row. People would sneak in during off hours and connect wires to speakers behind the drive-in. When I found them, I cut them. Once dusk set in and cars showed up, I'd wander around helping with problems and looking for people drinking alcohol. Concession stand employees passed me free food while I watched all the movies without having to pay, even the restricted ones I was too young to view as a customer.

Well look at that. Empties lying under the car. It's not easy hunting down booze in a drive-in. The last row was a good place to start. Steamy windows and no one in the front seat confirmed my suspicion of a back seat bash. When I tapped on their window, nothing happened at first, then slowly it lowered. Light from my flashlight exposed an unbuttoned shirt doing little to hide healthy breasts. The young woman to whom they belonged didn't seem to mind at all. The guy upon whose lap she sat was going red in the face. "I'm sorry, sir, you're not allowed to have alcohol here. You can either give it to me for disposal or leave the theater." The man's eyes narrowed as his mouth worked on a snappy comeback. I lifted my walkie-talkie, ready to call for backup.

"Oh, give the kid your beer, Gord. We don't need to go yet, do we?"

Gord, who still hadn't come up with a reply to the first question, looked at each of us, then handed me half a six-pack. The nice lady smiled, rolled up her window, and they went back to whatever it was they were doing. People in the back row caught little of the movie. I'd just turned sixteen, so the government didn't let me buy beer. Theirs went to my car for disposal at a more convenient time and place.

On October 26th, 1968, my life took another turn for the better. "Congratulations son, you passed. Just take this copy inside to the clerk and she'll issue you a temporary license." The first Saturday past my sixteenth birthday saw me emancipated from the bonds of immobility. I had a license to drive. I was free. True, I had to borrow my mother's Valiant if I wanted to go anywhere, but at least I could drive myself. A whole new world of opportunity had opened, and I intended to take advantage of it.

"Our teachers said no high school kids are allowed to come to the dance," Steve informed me. "Leave your car here. If we walk, how they gonna know?" Outside, light snow fell in our faces as we headed up the hill towards his school. Zion Heights Middle School was the epicenter of juvenile male desire. At their dances, we did our best to attract a hint of interest from heedless girls. My best rarely progressed beyond a single dance.

"If you get cold, I've got the anti-freeze," I said to Steve. I'd purchased a half mickey of vodka from an acquaintance at my high school, then filled the bottle with Coke. By mixing, I hoped we'd be able to drink it without gagging. If it was too nasty for us, how would we get a girl to try? "With any luck, who knows what will happen?"

There seems to be a law of northern culture that says outside cold needs inside heat. Thermostats got set on eighty to compensate. I thought if seventy-two is good for July, it ought to be good for February. It would clearly have been better for our plans. I'd entered Zion Heights with the bottle hidden inside my coat and everything was fine until the place started to get hot. Who wears a winter coat inside anyway? Besides, we'd tried a few sips and the warm concoction tasted awful. "Dang, no girl's gonna drink this stuff. I can't drink this stuff."

"Dump it," Steve suggested.

"No, let's hide it. We'll put it in some snow and get it later." As I made my way toward an exit, good sense almost triumphed over temptation. I decided I should toss the bottle in a garbage can. Then someone tripped, we collided, I spun around and as I was catching myself, I heard a faint pop, like a Christmas bulb breaking in my pocket. Liquid soaked down my leg as its stench filled the air. *OH SHIT... THE BOTTLE BROKE!*

"FINLAYSON, WE GOTTA GO!" Pandemonium broke out around me.

"God, what's that stink?"

"Is that booze?"

"Hey, somebody spilled a bottle of whiskey!"

"Who's got alcohol?!"

Girls stared, administrators converged, guys howled with delight. I lowered my head and hurried out of the gym. Alone in a bright tiled hallway, the first refuge I laid eyes on was the boy's restroom. *Maybe I can hide there and clean the smell off.* Running through the door and into a stall, I dumped pieces of broken glass into the bowl and flushed. The wet part of my coat followed. Two quick flushes, then I wrung it out as much as I could. That seemed to help somewhat, and I was about to repeat the process when the administrator threw the main bathroom door open. "Son, if you're in here you'd best show yourself now."

I stood on the toilet seat and watched his shadow bend down to look for feet. He must have been in a hurry. Not seeing any feet, he left. After several ragged breaths, I followed. At the door, I popped my head out and seeing him way down the hall, I took off in the other direction for an exit.

"HEY YOU! STOP RIGHT THERE!" I kept going as fast as my fat butt would carry me and reached the door as a new group of kids came in. One of them looked familiar. I *know that kid from Camp Comak.*

"VANSTRAWBERRY! How ya doin man?"

"Roger?"

Just when you think you'll make your escape, wham, a chance encounter stretches the limits of personal safety. *Should I stop and greet a friend I haven't seen in a couple of years or beat it before that old fart makes it down the hall?*

"Ya, but I gotta go. Really," I said while smacking his hand as I ran by. "That man's trying to catch me. Bye." Off I went, out the door and down the sidewalk. Around the corner from his school, I found Steve waiting. We made our way back to his parent's house like fugitives, hiding in the bushes or behind a parked car every time we saw headlights on the road. In his kitchen sometime later, we proclaimed my escape complete.

During my early years, I occasionally put myself in situations where something could go wrong. Small things, capable of triggering consequences beyond all proportion. Was the incident at Zion Heights Middle School the continuation of a trend started with a pipe bomb? A poor decision, leading to near disaster, followed by exhilarating escape? Probably so. A better choice, one following the rules, would have been far wiser, but then I would not have experienced the thrill of a successful getaway. Risk versus reward? That was a question I faced often throughout my young life.

8

June, 1969

Dear Taidy,

At school they say "Happiness is a warm puppy" but what do they know? Happiness is a new job away from home. I'm out of the drive-in, heading north and hoping it'll be sorta like Camp Comak, except I'll get paid. Crothers Twin Lakes Marina, way up in Orillia. Do ya suppose they have a canoe at this place?

I think that summer going off to the farm spoiled me. I sure don't miss all the work, so being home was a big relief and all, but staying in Agincourt last summer was kind of boring. Last time I left home I had the best time of my life once I got over the hard parts.

The most excitement I've had since then was visiting Penny and Tom a few times, and fishing trips with Dad. While I'm home I never do much other than hang out with Steve and Jeff, drink tea and smoke. I'm not griping, but I've noticed my friends and I don't do a whole lot. Where's the future in that?

Nope, I've got this worked out. If you want to have any fun, you need to pull yourself up off your butt and leave the comforts of home. I wonder if the other guys ever think about this stuff? I say, get yourself out the door and onto something new. Everything will be there, just like you left it, when you come back.

Rog

Making our way up from the dock on a dark rickety stairway, Dick Crothers led me to what would be my home for the next three months. The smell of mildew, creeping up from the water below, seemed to season the place with the flavor of age. Through a short hallway at the top of the stairs I got my first view of a rundown attic apartment. It two tiny bedrooms, a ripped vinyl couch and tatty old chair in a small sitting area. A kitchen with fading appliances. The stained floral wallpaper and tired furniture took me back to Penny's farmhouse. At least here I don't have to sleep in the hall. "Take your pick of rooms," Dick said, "or take them both. You're the only one who's gonna live here."

The room on the left had barely enough clearance to let me slip past the bed while dipping under a sloped ceiling. I stuck my head out a small screenless window to watch water flow past the docks below. *Cool. I can open the window for air if the bugs aren't too bad.* It wasn't much like home but seemed clean enough. Kind of nice, really. I stuffed my duffle bag under the bed and returned to Dick's tour.

"The fridge and stove work ok, but try to clean up after yourself. Our roaches can get aggressive if you feed them. That's the bathroom on the right just down the hall there. You'll need to empty it every couple of days."

From the hall I peered into the only door available and found a tiny closet. Inside, a camping style "bucket a day" commode sat on bare floorboards. To use it, I'd have to pull the bag before it got full, carry it down the stairs and dispose of it… somewhere. *Great, my second job away from home and I'm back to moving manure. That's gonna get ripe when this place heats up.* Then a small shadow shot past my head.

"JEEZ, WHAT WAS THAT?" As I ducked in alarm, I heard Dick chuckling behind me.

"You're not afraid of bats are you?" he laughed. "They're your roomies. They live in there. Get yourself settled in and come down to the office. We've got work for you." Once Dick returned down the stairs, I sat at the kitchen table and gave my new home a good look. *Damn, an apartment all to myself. This could be paradise!*

Welcome to Crothers Twin Lakes Marina. I spent the summers of 1969 and 1970 working and living on the shore of Atherley Narrows between Lake Simcoe and Lake Couchiching. Ninety miles north of my home in Toronto, the crossroads of Atherly sat a mile east of Orillia. Bill Crothers, a Canadian Olympic medalist, was an absentee owner but his younger brother, Dick, ran the marina. Their third brother, Dave, had once been my sister's boyfriend. When the marina needed cheap labor, I got my chance.

Gopher work at a marina requires little advanced training. How knowledgeable do you have to be to pump gas, mow the lawn, clean restrooms and empty septic tanks on expensive yachts? Although simple, the job was never easy. Moderately demanding labor filled most of my daylight hours. At dusk, all the chores of independent living patiently awaited my attention. Still, I rarely wanted to complain. I was my own man, made a steady income and lived on the water, all without oversight from my parents. What sixteen year old could ask for better than that?

As part of the Trent Severn Waterway, Atherley Narrows sat on the best recreational boat route through southern Ontario. The marina saw plenty of traffic of all types. Luxury yachts, sightseers, fishermen and riffraff all graced our docks. Some were rich, like the fellow in his polo shirt and a captain's hat who'd come gliding up in a classic Chris Craft runabout. Looking like a squire come-to-town, he'd flip a few rope bumpers between his polished mahogany and the weathered mystery wood of our dock. He acted like he was afraid of anyone touching the pristine beauty of his baby.

Some like Jim and George Church, twins from my public school back in Agincourt, had little. Those two hobos came cruising through one morning on a pontoon raft, boasting nothing but an old outboard and a tent for shelter. They said hello, filled up with gas, then continued on their journey north.

Another memorable visitor almost didn't stop at all. Our dock was deserted when I saw a boat coming full speed straight at me. I waved my arms in the air to ward off the young man driving. "SLOW DOWN! YOU'LL CRASH THE DOCK!"

"NO! NO! I CAN'T. I CAN'T STOP!" The guy kept coming full blast until he swerved and crashed sideways into our dock. In one motion, he killed the engine, jumped out and secured the stern of his vessel with a stout line. As his boat filled with water and sank, I saw it had split right down the middle. Soon, only his engine remained above water. Between quick breaths he tried to explain, "I kept her afloat by going full out. Not sure why she didn't break in half. Water sprayed up like I was skiing!" With help from two fishermen, we managed to save his outboard.

Of all the traffic through Twin Lakes, I enjoyed the fishermen most. The marina sold fishing tackle, so many of the weekend fishermen thought we had knowledge as well. These sportsmen assumed I'd be up to date on the latest fishing report, which lures worked where, and how to fish them. As we talked over an early morning coffee, I learned to make up tales about this lure or that, to see how much I might get them to buy. "Yes sir, Mr. Stewart, I heard they were catchin 'em shallow on a Flatfish Frog off Grape Island yesterday. We've only got a few left. Been sellin 'em like crazy." Once I figured out that most fishing gear is made to catch fishermen, not fish, it became a sport all its own.

Unlike the farm where work was twenty-four/seven, the marina provided occasional free evenings, plus a day off every week. Not that I had anywhere to go. I couldn't even make it into Orillia without a long walk or hitchhiking. I only had a small red rowboat, courtesy of my dad. Our engine repair man let me borrow a souped-up ten-horse Mercury outboard which fit my boat well. The combination proved anything can be converted to racing in the mind of a teenager. My little boat would positively scream when opened up. I used it to do a little fishing, sightseeing, or slow cruising around to get away. That's how I met Gerald, a local boy who'd stop in at the pumps occasionally for gas. When we'd see each other out on the lake, we'd wave. After meeting a few times, we started racing and chasing each other's boats for fun. Through Gerald, I met a few other locals and, with the cottage kids I knew from Toronto, gathered a handful of acquaintances. No lasting friendships, but others my age to save me from being alone all the time.

"Hey Gerald, I'm off Friday afternoon. You wanna pick up Alain and boat over to Orillia? You can show me around your big city."

"Ok. Not much to see though. I'll ask if he wants to come and meet you here about 4:00."

A couple days later the three of us took in all Orillia had for excitement in short order. "I told you it didn't have much to offer," Gerald said. "Let's go back to the park." Alain had wandered off somewhere along a sea wall, so Gerald and I headed off to where we'd beached the red boat at Couchiching Park. With little else to do, we climbed the broad gray steps of the Champlain Monument and sat to wait on Alain's return.

I looked up at the large gray statue. "Samuel de Champlain, larger than life. A giant voyageur with his ten-foot Indian friends. Oh, and they threw in a priest for good luck. Not bad company for the evening eh? Whaddya suppose old Champlain would think about walking on the moon?" I asked. "A few hundred years ago he was exploring Canada, now they're way up there looking around. Go figure."

"Yeah, I watched it on TV. How'd they get live TV back here?"

Lying flat on the cool granite I looked up at passing clouds, "Don't know. Sure is a long trip. I know one thing, I love this time of year when it stays light so late, especially up here where you live. We could stay another hour and still be back before dark."

"Yeah. Not much to do here though, eh? You guys in Toronto are lucky with Yonge Street and all. Up here it's either sports or drugs. See that bunch behind me, over there in the playground? All a bunch of speed freaks."

I sat up to watch a dozen scarecrows sitting on the jungle gym and swings doing nothing, pretty much like us. It's never a good idea to stare at druggies, but I noticed this group was looking in our direction as they left their swings to huddle up. With few other people around the park, my uh-oh senses began to stir. "Gerald, take a gander at the junkies. Ya think they're up to something?" As we looked at them, they looked at us, went back to talking, then turned again in our direction. When they broke up to spread out, while slowly heading our way, my uh-oh's went on high alert.

"That looks bad," Gerald said, "get ready to run." As we stood, the pack quickened into a trot.

"HEAD FOR THE BOAT!"

We had about thirty yards on them when we reached the beach, pushed off up to our knees and jumped in. "ROW!"

Gerald got the oars moving as I dropped the prop below the surface while desperately yanking our starter cord. "DUCK!" Gerald yelled as a rock hit our bow. Soon more rocks were whizzing by our heads to splash into water around us. Pull… nothing. Pull… nothing. "MOTOR PLEASE!" Gerald cried. Now in a panic I gave the throttle a twist to pour on the gas while giving the cord another yank. BRROOUMMM, the engine fired up and we were off. A sharp turn put her nose toward deep water and took our butts out of range. Back at the beach, we saw a bunch of frustrated junkies giving us the finger and shouting.

"YA GOTTA GO BACK," Gerald yelled.

"WHAT? WHAT THE HELL FOR?"

"ALAIN. THEY'LL GET ALAIN."

"Well, crap." I turned around, and we headed for the seawall where we'd last seen him walking. I guess drug addicts aren't excited by a lot of exercise. Ours wandered back to their playground and lost interest. With no lights on board the boat, we gave up our search to return to the marina as dusk settled over the lake. "Ya know," I said to Gerald, "Orillia really doesn't have much to offer. I don't expect I'll be going to town again real soon."

Roger at Crothers Twin Lakes Marina, circa 1970.

Is there a child of the early fifties who didn't come of age during the summer of sixty-nine? The Americans landed on the moon, English and French were recognized as equal Canadian languages, and the Woodstock Music and Arts Fair came to life in upstate New York. My world was changing all around me while I tried to keep up. For most of two summers I had a great time working and playing in the recreational heart of southern Ontario. Fast boats to drive, pushing my boundaries, learning new skills. Most of my experiences were wonderful. The times that left scars on my spirit were not.

A few days after our run-in with speed freaks, I again saw Alain and learned he wasn't even aware of our adventure in Couchiching Park. He'd met up with a girl he knew and departed long before Gerald and I found trouble. Gerald came from a nice family with little experience in the way of adventures. They encouraged him to spend time with more wholesome companions. After that, I spent more leisure hours in the company of older marina guys. An apartment right above their workplace made a convenient haven of retreat for Dick and another employee named Tommy. The two men kept my home well stocked in beer. As we sat around the table listening to Dick's stories of life as a Sudbury cop, or Tommy's bragging of his conquests, I'd gratefully accept any drinks sent my way. Dave, the friendly ex-boyfriend who'd recruited me, had better things to do, so spent little time with his brother. Sadly, he only remained at the marina for a short while after I arrived.

Although Dick clearly dedicated himself to running the business, his evening hours were directed to more boisterous pursuits. The ambitions of his sidekick seemed to be limited to drinking and sex. I'm not sure how to describe Tommy's official position with Twin Lakes. Sort of a salesman trying to be assistant manager. He was friendly in his own crude style, but rough enough to make "my way or the highway" a viable philosophy as he bullied himself through life as an Orillia townie. He'd buy beer for me if I asked, then claim a few as his finder's fee.

Another employee, Reg Gaudaur, was a bright spot in my relationships at Crothers'. Reg was our sixty-something-year-old boat repair man. Friendly, steady and willing to talk or teach is how I remember him. No recounting of Twin Lakes Marina would be complete without mentioning his name. When things got too crazy, I could spend a few hours working with Reg to remind myself some people still had pride in their work and the life they led. He set a quiet example of respect as he dealt with others, and I shall always think of him as a friend. The rest of the team… not so much.

I love apple pie. Sweet, fruity, crusty goodness just begging to be washed down with cold milk. Mine, baked by my mom, was waiting for me as soon as our marina store closed for the night. So where was Mr. Crothers to perform that task? I had no idea. With no boss in sight, I locked up on my own then ran up the stairs to my apartment with lust for pie in my heart. Apparently, Dick had lust of a different sort in his heart. He and a woman were vigorously occupied in the extra bedroom. I know this to be so because they left the door wide open. Visible sex was an experience for which I was woefully unprepared, but who wants to be known as someone who can't handle a shock? On the contrary, I felt being steady in a crisis was an important part of the manly persona, so continuing on with my original mission seemed my best course. Without giving them a second glance, I went to the fridge to retrieve my pie, sat at the kitchen table, stuck in my fork and ate.

Lost as they were in their own appetites, the amorous couple never slowed down to notice me at all. Things continued like that for a while, me eating pie at the table as they squeaked away in the bed. By the time I finished, my mind had morphed to a place where all this seemed sort of normal. Still, sitting around without the obvious consumption of pie as an excuse became a bit too weird. The fact that I had nowhere else to go prompted me to try to reclaim possession of my home. Besides, Dick had a payback coming for throwing a kitten I'd rescued out the second-story window and into the lake. "HEY DICK. DO YOU THINK YOU COULD STOP USING MY BED FOR A TRAMPOLINE?"

Two heads popped up from the sheets, looked at me and giggled. "Done in a bit," Dick whispered as he got up and closed the door.

Although I was no longer the naive boy who'd left home two summers before, sixteen years in Agincourt had not groomed me for the misconduct I faced around the marina. I was seeing people every day who lived by standards with which I had no experience. Even the customers baffled me. One customer made a point to let me know he thought I was pleasant enough to talk to, but basically a piece of crap because I was an American. "All Americans are worthless, kid. You might try to amount to something, but you'll fail. You can't help it because that's the way you were born." This from a Canadian, the most polite group of humans on earth. Maybe it was our reputation for bigotry that turned him off. I don't suppose he would have been too happy had he known how friendly his lovely Canadian daughter and I had become.

I don't claim to be an innocent bystander in the matter of misconduct. My first choice was seldom to shy away from participation. In my mind, if funds and opportunity allowed, why not try it? Not in an "anything goes" sort of way that often leads to disaster, but rather a more cautious, eyes-open approach to the road to ruin. Where were my boundaries? No one was around to set them for me. My parents had laid the foundation, but here I had to find limits for myself.

With the sun sinking under Atherly Bridge I put my mop away and locked up the restrooms for the night. Tommy and some friend of his named Tork were pulling through the lot in Tommy's old Galaxie as I made my way back to the dock. "Hey Rog, we're going to the Shangri La for Chinese. Wanna go?"

My first thought was money. I never had much while I was working because most of my pay packet went straight to a savings account until I'd gathered enough to buy a motorcycle. Once, I was so broke I worked three days without food. I was too proud to ask for help and unable to take funds out of the bank due to a holiday weekend. This day I had cash and quickly agreed. "Sure, let's go."

You would think the short drive into Orillia could be accomplished without incident or distraction. With Tommy at the wheel, you'd be wrong. We'd almost come close enough to smell the chow mein when he saw a woman walking along the highway and pulled over to roll slowly beside her. "Hello sweet Danielle. Where's the best girl I know going tonight?"

"Crazy, you wanna come?"

"No but we're off to eat. Want to go with us?"

Tommy had stopped as Danielle took a quick look inside. "Yeah sure. Why not?"

"In the back, Tork," was Tommy's only reply.

As soon as we resumed moving down the highway, Tommy whipped the wheel around, sending us back in the opposite direction. "Got to take care of something first." We passed the marina, but didn't stop. We passed the Atherley Arms Hotel, but didn't stop. A few miles and several turns later we were way out in the country when Tommy took a hard left onto a farm road surrounded by corn.

I thought, *oh crap, this can't be good.*

"Um, Tommy, where are we going?" Danielle asked.

"You'll find out. You'll all find out in a minute." Around the next corner, he pulled into a small hidden clearing and cut the engine. "You lads sit up front. We'll need the back seat."

Oh jeez, get me outta here. Could I make a run for it? Hell, it was getting late, and I didn't even know where we were. Make a stand? The naive fantasy of a kid. Besides, Danielle didn't seem to mind all that much, once she got past noticeable resentment at having to be carnal in the backseat of a Galaxy while two spectators watched. Survival being high on my priority list, I did as instructed. Tommy told Danielle to get busy or walk.

In the front seat, my mind seemed to stumble off to lala land. It drifted back to occasions when I'd lain awake thinking of home. On those nights I enjoyed going down to sit on the dock alone. No boats, no cars, no people. Just sweet smells of nature accompanied by the songs of crickets and frogs. If the call of a loon gave voice to my loneliness, all the better to echo my mood. Could my immediate crisis be overcome by focusing on something less disturbing than the profanity performed behind me? I tried to distance myself from the experience by dreaming back to better times. Perhaps if I'd been able to shut off my mind completely, I could have held on to a few shreds of the innocence. I tried. I failed. I managed to cope. My childhood left forever, and I never thought to say goodbye. *Good God, this is too gross.*

Their act completed, we skipped the restaurant and returned to the marina with the happy couple laughing it up like they were at some great party. At least now they'd leave me alone, right? What a fool. Tommy moved the party back to my apartment, insisting I come along. In the bedroom I normally occupied, my companions each took a turn with Danielle. Could it get any worse? Well of course it could. After wearing themselves out and apparently not fulfilled with the deprivation they had already inflicted upon this woman, they looked to me. "Hey, I bet young Rog'd like a go, eh? Right. Now's your chance son."

"No, thanks. Not interested."

"Sure you are, boy. In you go."

With few alternatives, I let myself be guided through the door. She lay there, naked on the bed, smiling like I was about to be her next victim. Maybe so. Maybe I was about to be drawn into a web from which I would not soon escape. The immediate consequences of refusal played through my mind. They wouldn't be good. As I looked down at Danielle, one thought overwhelmed the rest. *In my family we don't do this!* To hell with consequences. "Not a chance." I muttered turning for the door. "You're not my type."

The price paid in mockery for my decision was high for a week or two, yet not so dear as had I succumbed. Nor was this the last of these situations I faced during my time living between the lakes. The daughter of one of my fisherman customers went missing for two weeks. She was hiding out with the cook from a fancy resort on Lake Couchiching and spent some of her time in my apartment servicing Tommy and his buddies. As with the first offer of "get in line" sex, when I again had to make a decision I again declined. An old proverb teaches. "Train up a child in the way he should go: and when he is old, he will not depart from it." I admit I have departed from ways I should have gone many times, but not those times.

During the summer of 1970, things at the marina changed. When I returned for a second season at Crothers', I was surprised to learn Tommy had gone, apparently leaving the area. Dick settled down with the woman who occasionally occupied my spare bedroom while I moved to my father's travel trailer parked in the marina's back lot. All good news for a young man who, now a year older, was ready to take on life and return to work wearing the worldly attitude of a veteran.

Unfortunately, my ideas of worldly behavior quietly slipped into rationalized larceny. Heck, Dick wasn't exactly an angel, why shouldn't I keep a little back? I convinced myself that pocketing a few bucks when I got the chance was merely a tip for hard work. I deserved it, didn't I? Slack off working and still get paid? Sure. It's OK so long as you don't get caught, right? On a hot afternoon in August, Dick called me into his office. "Here's the last of your pay. Pick up your stuff and go home." I'd been fired. Dick never told me exactly why. If it wasn't for stealing from him, it should have been. On my way out, I wandered through a boathouse to say goodbye to Reg. After putting a note on my trailer door, thanking my few friends for their company, I walked to the highway and stuck out a thumb.

My journey back to Toronto that night provided plenty of time to consider the extent to which I'd fallen. Clearly my father's boundaries were firmer than my own, and I had character issues in need of repair. Howard Geiger's boy fired and sent packing. We didn't do that in our family either. I dodged my parents for two days before I got up the nerve go home. True to form, Dad refrained from asking for details about my termination from Crothers' Marina. Life offered better options than dwelling on mistakes.

9

July, 1971

Dear Taidy,

"Riders on the storm... Into this house were born. Into this world were thrown... Riders on the storm." Jim Morrison died last week. I saw it in the paper this morning as we got ready to go. Think about it, man. Last fall Janis Joplin OD'd, the Beatles broke up just a few months ago and now this. I liked the Doors. My whole world is falling apart.

My day's not gone so good either. I made it for trout fishing with Dad, so that's cool, but I got no sleep at all last night. That's a bummer. Ontario changed the drinking age this spring. Seeing as one of us can drink legally for a change, Steve and I went to the Algonquin Tavern. Lots of Willowdale lads there. I suspect one of them slipped something into my beer. Steve and I closed the Big A, then returned to his place where we talked through the night. I only split when I realized Dad would be up before I got home if I didn't.

Half way through changing into my fishing clothes, Dad rapped his knuckles on the bedroom door to deliver a five AM wake-up. "It's OK, Dad. I'm already up." I tried my best to sound cheery and good to go.

"Yeah? You were up at 4:30 too. Where were you?"

"Oh. You knew about that? Well, I stayed at Steve's and

came home real early so I'd be ready."

He gave me a hard look for a second. "Uh huh. You're driving today. I hope you got plenty of sleep." My father is a master of creative torment when he figures I've done something I shouldn't.

Single day trips are tiring at the best of times. On this one, I had to drive three hours before we got to the stream, and trout fishing ain't a walk in the park. By 3:30 I was draggin'. When I started making noises about packing it in, Dad was all smiles. "Let's fish till we get our limit and try to be on the road by about 5:00. Oh, and I'm kind of tired. My heart doctor said I should take it easy. You get to drive. Maybe I'll take over after we stop to eat."

Dad and I usually stopped at A&W on our way back to Agincourt. Today, as I drove through Burke's Falls, he told me to pull into a sit-down restaurant. Inside, he looked at me over a large menu. "I think I'll have a beer with dinner." Dad never drinks beer! "You want one too? Oh wait, it might make you sleepy and you've got a long drive before we get home."

Thanks for the lesson, Dad.

Rog

To say Dad was particular about his equipment would be an understatement. He bought gear made to last, kept good care of it, fixed it when something broke and stored everything in its designated, proper place. His camping and fishing things were more than tools; they were his friends. Woe be unto any kid who lost one except for my sister Amy. She dropped his rod over the side of the canoe once and got a pass. He treated her special. Two of his favorite items were his fishing knife and coffee pot. They'd been with him on every trip to every lake and stream since long before I came along.

Thankfully, I was not involved in the actual disaster, only an attempted rescue, so the first part of this story is second hand. As Vice President of an international chemical company, Dad occasionally enjoyed sharing his Canadian wilderness with visitors from other countries. On one of these visits in the late summer of 1970, he took Mr. John Collins from England to Shark Lake. Mr. Collins was not strong in his canoeing skill and, in fact, had not been in a canoe prior to this trip. I'd been scheduled to work that weekend at Canadian Tire, so Dad decided his skills were more than sufficient for both of them. Poor judgement by Mr. Geiger. They made it to Shark Lake well enough, but as they paddled out a long inlet, heading for the main lake, the wind got up about the same time as John's confidence. A few gusty whitecaps met a few gusty strokes from the bow and over they went. The canoe capsized.

The two men held fast to the submerged canoe as their gear floated off in thirty feet of cold dark water. When John's swimming skills proved as limited as his canoeing, Dad figured it would be bad for Canadian / English detente to let him drown. He helped John to shore, leaving his faithful tools sinking to the bottom. My father never discussed that decision, but just like facing the bear, I'm sure he made it in a moment and didn't look back. Swamped canoes don't sink, nor do paddles, which allowed him to rescue those essentials as well. Ever the experienced woodsman, Dad carried emergency matches, encased in paraffin, in a buttoned pocket. He soon started a fire over which they warmed up and dried out. Once rested from their mishap, he and John made their way back to Dad's car before dark. It was, after all, a quick trip with nothing to carry but themselves and a canoe.

Like many old school gentlemen of his generation, Dad talked little about his feelings. He grew up one of seven children in a home with an abusive father. His parents provided no guidance in his life, so Howard Geiger had to provide his own. According to his brother, Chuck, "Our father had a mean disposition and bad temper and 1 was always afraid of him, especially when he was drunk. I could come and go when and where I pleased. I didn't have to ask permission to go places or do things. When I stayed out late at night, or didn't show up at meal time, no one was concerned about where I was or what I was doing. Howard was the Superman of the family. He and I slept together. Often, before we went to sleep, he would tell me stories of things he had read." My father was a special man.

I think I would have enjoyed knowing more about Dad's past as I grew older. What did it take for him to succeed on self-discipline alone? I had little knowledge of his childhood, but his aversion to serious discussion seldom bothered me much at the time. He was my idol and my hero. It never occurred to me to wonder about the deeper questions of his life. As to the loss of his gear, I find it difficult to imagine he ever dwelt upon his feelings as we might today. Still, I could tell he was upset by losing so many of his trusted tools. Things that had been with him on dozens of happy trips throughout his youth.

I, a product of a different generation, do ponder what might have been lurking around the shadows of his mind as he watched part of his life sink to the bottom of the lake. At fifty years old, he'd already had two heart attacks, and now another slice of his youth was slipping away. He made a decision to get it back. To do so he planned a rescue mission for the next weekend. That's where I came in. I'd earned a scuba diver's certification in the winter of 1968. With my air tank and wetsuit, this would be a piece of cake. Right? All he asked out loud was for me to lend a hand in recovering his camping gear. Within that request hid the reality of a father asking his young son to help him do something he couldn't do for himself. Was he asking me to do something he couldn't even express to himself? A new experience for both of us.

To get things started we had to consider the first rule of diving - always dive with a buddy. I didn't have one. *OK, the old hard hat divers didn't have a buddy either.*

"Let's tie a rope to your tank and use pull signals," Dad

suggested.

If I got into trouble, I could signal Dad and he would haul me up. *Oh yeah, great plan.* Then there's the extra weight and bulk. A steel dive tank, full of air, with harness etc. weighs about forty-five pounds. A quarter inch wetsuit weighs about ten and both take up a lot of space, plus there are regulator, mask, fins and dive weights. Together, that's considerable extra baggage. You don't need extra baggage when you go on a trip to recapture someone's youth. We left all the non-essentials behind.

The last days of summer can get cold in northern Ontario. On one September trip we paddled through snow flurries while making our way home. Although the dive gear slowed us, we made it to Shark Lake before dark, then spent a cool night in a makeshift camp close to where the canoe went under. Dad had lined up two intersecting landmarks that gave us a rough idea of where it had happened. The next morning, overcast skies blocked warmth from the sun as wind shook down leaves boasting fall color. I wriggled into my wetsuit top, then began loading gear into our canoe. As I was about to climb in myself, Dad said "It's not a good idea for you to ride in the boat. I'll have to drag you."

"What?"

"If you jump out of the canoe with that stuff on, you'll probably sink us again, and I can't see any possible way you'll get back in again without dumping us. I'll tow you out and back."

147

"Good thinking. Hold on a minute while I wade out. When you go by, I'll hitch a ride."

After lining up his landmarks, Dad said "Ok, we flipped about here. See if you can find it, Sport." We tied on the tender rope and down I went. Like the first time I'd met a bear, I was separated from Dad and on my own, but this time he was waiting as I took off searching. Our roles had reversed completely. Despite the danger, I knew what I wanted to do. Once the decision was made, I acted on that decision. No fear, just determination to see it through. Dad's job, sitting in the boat watching my bubbles while waiting for a pull on our rope, must have been far more nerve wracking. I had a quest to fulfill. He had to worry about sending me into the depths to retrieve his past.

When diving these Ontario lakes, there's good news and bad news. The good news is the water is fairly clear so visibility is not bad. The bad news is the thermocline. A thermocline is a sharp drop in temperature at various depths as one descends into a body of water. Here there was a change every six to ten feet. The water was less than seventy degrees at the surface. By the time I got to the bottom the temperature had probably dropped to fifty. I was fine from the waist up, but bare legs in fifty degree water don't work very long. Wearing old sneakers instead of fins, I walked along the bottom like that hard hat diver who goes it alone. Didn't they lose a lot of those guys? I could see well enough, and didn't stir things up too badly, so I worked a search pattern with no grid to guide me. I guess I made it about ten minutes before I lost feeling in my legs. At fifteen minutes, the cold got so intense I had to start making my way to the surface.

Um, this could be a problem. I'd never really tried to surface with almost full gear, no fins, and no use of my legs. It's not easy. Ah, but I was once a boy scout, so I was prepared. Three sharp pulls on the rope meant "pull me up, slow but steady." I gave three tugs and Dad started pulling. When I got to the surface, I gave him the bad news that so far I had found nothing and explained my problem with the cold. He wanted me to give it up right then, but I insisted on giving it another go. "Listen Rog, I don't want you getting yourself hurt doing this. Let's quit while we're ahead."

"No way. We came all this way. Carried all this stuff. I'm not givin it up after fifteen minutes. Besides, it's your old knife and coffee pot." I'd made a decision to face the bear and give it my all no matter what. After giving my legs time to recover in warmer surface water, I went down again. Within ten minutes I'd reached the end of the radius of my tether and the end of my endurance. Dad again pulled me to the surface, and I let him know I could no longer continue. "Oh well," he said, "at least we tried Rog, let's go home."

We learned that day that things lost in deep water shift around a lot and it's hard to find them again. It's kind of like when trying to recapture the past. You might find that time has shifted things out of place and you're having trouble finding what you're looking for. The attempt can be cold and often painful. On this rescue mission, we tried our best but failed to find Dad's gear so he got new gear. It was also the event where my status matured from being Sport to being Rog. Sure, he still called me Sport sometimes, even in his last days while under Hospice care, but I was no longer his little boy. I was his son, yet a man. Did he see this as passing the reins from one generation to the next? I doubt it. Nor did I see it as some life changing transition. If anything, it was something I sorely needed at that point in my life. Evidence of a depth of character that had been obvious in its absence. We'd both confronted new questions mixed up with a new dimension in our relationship. In answer, we simply accepted the change and went on with life.

10

September 1971

Dear Taidy,

Have you ever heard the saying "No good deed goes unpunished?" Well, I'm living proof. I tried to help a lady out and look what happened. Yesterday was already supposed to be my last day to work at Canadian Tire. The schedule said I was off at 4:00. I got fired before noon. A real bummer 'cause I worked there for over a year. It seems they don't appreciate warehouse grunts who defend sales girls from idiot department managers. The guy was being a jerk. All I did was make sure he knew it. A bunch of the other ladies came by to see me off, so I guess they were into what I did, even if the store manager wasn't.

Hey, stuff happens, life goes on, and my life is going on to Florida. Saturday we leave to drive to my parents' house in Key Largo. We'll be there for a couple of weeks, then head back north to drop me off at college in Cocoa Beach. At first I had an idea to work the Alaska pipeline instead, but Amy says college will be the most fun I'll ever have. I figured it would be worth a try. Besides, the campus is right across the street from the beach and it's warm all winter! That's so great. When all the guys up here are freezing their buns off, I'll be lying 'round getting a tan. What a laugh, man. My folks are thrilled their boy is actually going to college, and I'm just glad to be skipping out on winter. Oh and get this, I'm studying oceanography. I'll be going out on a boat to check out coral reefs and fish like Cousteau does on TV.

Sun, the ocean, scuba diving and bikini girls. Ain't life a hoot?

Rog

During my final twenty years of organized employment, hiring student workers was something I did every spring. I tried to find the brightest, hard-working kids from the group entering their senior year in high school. Occasionally, I'd get one who had already worked a paying job, but I didn't find many. Most had never been employed. At the same age, I was in my fifth job. Does that say more about our society today or my own twisted path? I suppose it reflects on both.

With the shame of my demise at Twin Lakes soon forgotten by all, it was not long before I again found myself working a new job. Canadian Tire, a sells-everything megastore, hired me as a stock clerk to unload trucks, build store displays and learn other skills of limited value. I learned to assemble bicycles. I learned to stock shelves. I even learned to roll a tire so it would turn a corner at a place of my choosing. Enticed by the dubious incentive of working my way up to department manager, supervisors encouraged me to follow the rules, stay diligent and study all aspects of store operation. In the midst of all this learning, I also discovered you can ride down a roller transfer line.

Imagine a thirty foot conveyor of large ball bearings going from one level of the stockroom to another. That's a roller transfer line. They were designed with a shallow slope angle, which was fortunate, as anything steeper might have been dangerous for novice participants. Riding the line is somewhat like tobogganing until you hit the metal bar at the end. Great fun if you don't crash or get caught. During a particularly slow evening shift we'd gotten bored, when a bright young fellow came up with a suggestion. "You know," this person said, "if we make something to sit on, I bet we could slide down this thing. It'd be kinda like a ride at the midway. No ticket required."

Doug asked, "Well what do you expect me to slide on?"

I replied, "I dunno, flatten that shipping box and give it a go."

"I ain't doing it. Get Larry to try."

We all looked in his direction. "Yeah, OK." Larry said. It shouldn't be too bad, eh?"

Larry did little to stay fit, so he took a minute to clamber up the steel framed side of the transfer line and sit on a piece of cardboard. Nothing happened. "Lie out flat on your back. That'll distribute your weight," I suggested. As Larry adjusted his position, he started to move. Slowly at first, then picking up speed until his feet ran into a green stopper at the end of the line.

"I could never get moving," Larry complained. "The cardboard's too soft. Find a piece of wood or something."

"Here, try this." I handed him the wooden lid from a reusable shipping coffin.

Larry's second run was far more successful. The sound of whirling ball bearings accompanied his descent even after he barely avoided flying off the end of the line. That was fun, so we tried two guys on a eight foot plywood shelf. They lived! Next it was three and before good sense reared its ugly head, we'd prepared ourselves for the ultimate Olympic four-man-run. On the night shift, who's to know? Four guys, sitting on a piece of wood, counting down to liftoff.

"WHAT THE HELL ARE YOU FOOLS PLAYING AT?" The sport department manager glared at us from a doorway. For a few seconds we looked at each other, our eyes bugging out as we contemplated unemployment. I figured *What the heck, swing for the fence.*

"What's 'a matter. You want a turn?"

He stared hard at me as his scowl slowly morphed into a smile. "Yeah, one of you boys needs to move."

I didn't learn much at Canadian Tire, but one lesson changed my life's path for several years. Working as a stock clerk until I made department manager promised no future. I didn't want to be a dairy farmer or pump gas at a marina either, so the necessity of higher education became obvious.

With high school occupying low status on my priority list, getting accepted into an accredited college seemed a lofty goal. My academic success could be summed up by the physics teacher's comment as we wrapped things up for Christmas break 1970. "Roger, as far as physics is concerned, you're dead." I dropped his course and another of similar progress the same day. That left only three classes. My prospects of being considered for a Canadian university were dead as well. Both my parents, two grandparents and my sister had attended college. I would not get a pass from our family tradition without consequence. After some discussion, we decided an American school would have to be my salvation.

Thinking on the problem one evening I wondered just how I had gotten to this state in the first place? I'd heard my mother mention a few times that tests indicated I had notable intelligence, but every report card I ever got commented "Roger does not live up to his potential".

Hell I thought, *potential would be a damn sight easier if I could read worth a flip.* I'd also been told I was reading before I entered kindergarten. Teachers didn't understand things like dyslexia in the fifties, so before long they broke me of the reading habit by insisting I do it their way, not mine. *I don't even like to read. What am I going to do in college? Those people have to read everything. Maybe I should get better at it.*

Procrastination would have gotten the best of me but for my father's daily routine of reading the paper. He had left the family section open on the kitchen table one morning and there, on a page opposite the funnies, I read "York University to offer speed reading course. Classes to be held two nights a week."

Hum, speed reading. That would be cool. I wonder if my parents will pay for it? They did, and I learned well because it was a skill I wanted.

That decision, made of my own accord, was a turning point in my life. I'd faced up to a need, found a practical solution and successfully enacted that solution. Clearly a new way of doing things. By the time I left for college at the end of the summer I'd started reading books just for fun.

"Hey Dad, you look like Mr. Allnut in that old Bogart movie. Hold up the fish and I'll take your picture." Two weeks prior to being dropped off in Cocoa Beach, my parents and I made our first trip to the Florida Keys. One day, as Dad and I stood on the sea wall of his Key Largo cottage, I noticed how his skin had turned a healthy brown. Gone was the pale pallor of heart disease. All problems from work laid aside. He looked like the cares of his life had been washed away by saltwater and sun. *What a wonderful thing it must be to have a home on the water*, I thought. *Like a personal fountain of youth.*

Howard Geiger in the Florida Keys. Circa 1971

Soon his reprieve ended, and we found ourselves unloading the station wagon in front of a small, two story office building turned college. Even with the palm trees, it can't have been very impressive to the two who were providing funds for my tuition. If they had misgivings, they also had the good grace not to mention them. A hot Florida sun beat down on the three of us standing in the parking lot of

Hydrospace Technical Institute. All my possessions lay at my feet in a duffle bag and new green foot locker.

Roger at HTI, circa 1971.

"Well, you're on your own now son. Write when you can and stay out of trouble." Mom gave me a hug, and they were off, heading north on the coastal highway, to follow the beach for the first few miles of their trek home. Goodbyes could be a bit short in my family.

Now let's be clear here. Any college that would accept my academic record was not an institution with stellar academic standards. The college and I both showed remarkable growth during the four years we were together.

The single building campus I so eagerly attended as a freshman moved a hundred miles south and evolved into Florida Institute of Technology's School of Marine and Environmental Technology. Occupying one hundred and fifty acres of tropical splendor, the campus at which I spent my last three years improved our living and learning standards considerably.

The HTI campus, one building with classrooms and cafeteria on the ground floor and dorm rooms on the second, offered little in the way of luxury, but who cared? It was right across the road from Canaveral Pier, the small-board, surfing capital of the east coast. That made it paradise. We called it Hydrospaced Technical Institute because "spaced" was a condition in which many students passed their time. Upon finding my dorm room I discovered an area smaller than a one-car garage, arranged to house four young men. A communal bathroom with an open "locker room" shower was available several doors down the hall. I thought it was more than acceptable. *Cool, I've got a real toilet and a shower on the same floor as my bed.*

"Hi. I'm Donn. All this stuff," he said, pointing to a load of stereo equipment, surfing gear and food, "belongs to Frank. Our other roommate, some guy named Mike, didn't get here yet. You make it to the pier yet?"

"Nope, but I bet I'll be there pretty quick." With that introduction, Donn Eyman and I were off to begin a daily routine of poor food, limited study and lots of beach time.

The next morning found the two of us, forty other guys and two girls loaded on an old Bluebird school bus heading for the main FIT campus. Registration had to be handled by the serious bureaucrats.

"Name?"

"Roger Geiger."

"Major?"

"Oceanographic Technology."

"Home town?"

"Toronto, Canada."

"Date of birth?"

"August 21st, 1950."

"1950? Everyone else says '52 or '53. I wasn't born yesterday son. I'm not showing you as twenty-one on your ID unless you can prove it. Let me see your driver's license."

"Don't have one. I don't have a car."

"Ok, let me see your draft card."

"I don't have one of those either. I'm from Canada."

"Well do you have any ID? Anything to prove you're really twenty-one?"

"I have a Canadian social security card, but it doesn't have my birthday on it."

After looking at the long line behind me, the nice lady gave up trying. "OK, you win. Next."

Far out. I just aged two years. Now I can buy beer in Florida. That'll make me popular in the dorm.

My new friend Donn and I made a good team. He had a 1964 Volkswagen bug, robin's egg blue, that he'd driven all the way from North Dakota to attend HTI. I had lots of good ideas as to where his wheels should take us. "Hey Donn, my cousin Jack runs a Penny Saver newspaper down the road a bit. It's right beside the topless shoeshine place. You drive us down there and he'll pay us to stuff papers for the afternoon."

"Really Hodji? Sounds like too much work for low pay. Are we that hard up?"

"Come on, we're broke. How bad could it be?"

I'm not sure how I earned a silly nickname like Hodji. I got tagged with the name by one of the guys in our dorm based on the old Jonny Quest cartoon. The main character's sidekick, Hadji Singh, was a cool orphan kid from Calcutta and his name stuck like glue.

Students of the seventies were at least a generation away from having cell phones, nor did we have phones in our dorm rooms. Our telecommunication relied on a pay phone in the stairwell of each floor. When it rang, whoever happened to be closest answered, then went looking for the intended party. During my senior year, Mom called the dorm and asked to speak to me. Even though I'd known everyone for years, those standing around the phone didn't know who she was talking about. One of my old friends, Dave Clarke, still uses my nickname when we talk. The title "Hadji" is also said to be a respectful term for Muslims who have made the pilgrimage to

Mecca in Saudi Arabia. A title that proved to be prophetic in coming years.

A few weeks later I found another opportunity for work. "Donn, I got us a cool job. A place called Roberts' Farm over on Merritt Island is looking for pickers. All you have to do is drive us over there a few days a week. We get paid by the orange."

"Orange pickers? That sounds worse than papers."

"Come on, at least give it a try." You can talk a broke student into just about anything to make money, so we were soon headed north out of Cocoa Beach into orange grove country. As newcomers, we didn't understand why the old guy who owned the place seemed surprised to see us. "You boys are here to pick? Have you ever picked before?"

"Well no, Mr. Roberts, but we can learn. Besides, if we don't work hard, you don't have to pay us much."

"Yeah… well go over to the flatbed and pick a bag, then we'll get you a ladder. We'll see."

Orange picking was probably the hardest, most painful job I ever had. By late afternoon our aching arms were scraped up like we'd been fighting cats and our legs wobbled from climbing ladders. We'd also learned the source of Mr. Roberts' surprise when we answered his ad. Donn and I were the only white pickers on the farm. All the others were Negro families who picked as a team. Even the kids worked, picking their oranges off the ground and putting them in the collection crates. These kids had no shoes. They worked barefoot without ever stopping to horse around, talk, or complain. Above them, men and women with sunken faces and ragged clothes worked on ladders from dawn to dusk to make a few dollars. This was a part of society I'd never known.

When I was in third grade, our teacher led a discussion on poverty. As a naive kid from the suburbs, I thought the poor people she mentioned were the men who worked on garbage trucks or "workies", the Italian immigrants who worked construction. I had no notion of what real poverty looked like. Neither did I have any notion of other races. Everyone in Agincourt was white. As a picker, I worked side by side with truly poor people of color. Everything I'd seen on TV (race riots, protests, killings) indicated I might need to be afraid of these people. In the grove, fear seemed a ridiculous notion that simply did not fit. The family pickers initially ignored us. When they saw how useless we were at picking, some left their own work to come by and show us how to be more productive. Up on a ladder, we were all just people trying to earn our pay.

By the end of our day, Mr. Roberts had come by a few times to check on us. He helped us with our picking and let us pad our count a little so we'd at least go home with a few bucks in our pocket. "You boy's worked hard today. Come back tomorrow, it'll get better." We came back the next day and more. Every time we showed up, Mr. Roberts seemed more interested in our progress. He gave us a tour around the farm, introduced us to other family members and fed us oranges from his private grove. Those were the best oranges I've ever eaten.

Unfortunately, try as we might, we failed to improve our picking enough to make the effort worthwhile. At the end of our fourth day I was about spent. "We ain't making squat, man. I don't know if we should come back."

"I've had it too," replied Donn. "This ain't worth it."

"Yeah but listen. You see how much the old guy likes us. If we keep at it another week, Mr. Roberts will have us out of the trees and driving a tractor. It'll be a good job. I just don't think I'll make it."

Donn's reply sealed the decision, "I know I can't."

"Ok, you've got the wheels, it's your call." We never returned to the groves.

Life at HTI settled down to a routine of more fun than study. My feet became so hard from walking barefoot I could put cigarettes out on their bare soles. Even the dreaded sand spurs had a hard time penetrating my tough hide. I saw several Apollo launches, took trips inland to fish the St. Johns River and generally had a grand old time. Classes were not high on my agenda. Still, I attended regularly, learned something in most of them and ultimately did well when measured against the not too rigorous standard. Fortunately, that low standard did not apply to math.

In the fall of 1971, real math and I met for the first time in the class of a young professor from Greece. Nikos

Orphanoudakis held high expectations and taught in a style I had never encountered. With Nikos, we didn't learn math; we discovered math. His eyes gripping us from under a mop of black hair, Nikos would flash a grin while asking, "Learn a formula? Come on, what is that? Do you understand why it is done this way? First you must see how the rules were created." Then we would explore a path of realization that lead to knowledge. With Nikos as my teacher, I experienced success in the classroom I had seldom known. I developed a taste for learning and enjoyed new discoveries greatly. Prior to this revelation, my only enthusiastic encounters with education had been learning to make gunpowder and speed reading. The boy who needed a tutor to complete high school math ended up working for his college math department, teaching remedial algebra and tutoring other students in advanced calculus. After graduation I rarely used higher-order math again. That may seem disappointing, but it was not. Never did the math itself represent a true legacy of what I learned from Nikos. His real lessons were far more important. He taught me how to think and he showed me the extent to which an individual can grow. Those are lessons worth remembering.

11

March 1975

Dear Taidy,

Oh wow, you are not going to believe what we saw at sea yesterday. Really weird! As the sun sank over Florida, Donn Eyman, Dave Clarke and I sat up on top of the wheelhouse enjoying the ride and shooting the breeze about nothing. Off to the north, we saw this bright light glowing on the horizon. We watched it get bigger, then bigger and BIGGER. It was coming from under the water! A few seconds more and WOOSH, a missile broke the surface and shot off into the sky! It must have been off a sub from the base up at Port Canaveral. Man, it was sooo cool.

We're on the Aquarius doing a research cruise out to the Bahama Banks. The Aquarius is one of the boats from our fleet of oceanographic vessels. Some fleet. We've got three boats. At seventy-seven feet, the Aquarius is small but not too bad. With a ship's crew of two, a few bunks below decks and a small wet lab, she's just right for students to play oceanographer for a couple of days. Our leader, Capt. Pierre Dallemagne, is FIT's resident oceanographer. His claim to fame is that he knew Cousteau back in the old days in France. I guess he doesn't think much of Jacques 'cause every time we mention him as an oceanographer, Dallemagne says "Cousteau, 'e is jus de film makher." He also says if we have a piece of equipment that doesn't work, "Jus' toss er over de rail. Den they muss replace her, no?" Not sure I trust everything Pierre tells us.

Yesterday afternoon, the ship's captain said severe weather was coming in from the Atlantic. We had to motor back inside the Gulf Stream and get closer to shore to ride it out. Have you ever noticed how different some people are with problems like bad weather? When most of the students beat it below decks to take shelter, Donnie, Clarkie and I went to talk to the captain. Clarkie asked him if we could go up on his roof to watch the storm come in.

Captain Fred said sure, if we didn't mind a rough ride, and then, as Donnie climbed the ladder, shouted for us to come down if we saw lightning. After dusk, the seas got so wild we had to grab a railing to keep from rolling off. Waves sent spray over the wheelhouse and soaked us as the boat splashed its way toward land. It was the best ride ever! We were having a blast while the poor lubbers who'd retreated below got sick as dogs.

The ride lasted well into the night, eventually ending when we got close to the coast. Still up top, we caught some sleep until the sun peeked over the horizon back where the storm first found us. It was time for breakfast! Who's gonna eat nasty boxed meals from the cafeteria when you've got subs from Joe Shakra's deli? Below decks in the sleeping quarters, Donn pulled our cooler from under a bunk. We sat at a small table surrounded by sea-sick students and made a great show of peeling foil wrappers from our food. A sausage supreme for me, Clarkie had the meatball and a roast beef supreme for Donn. The smell of provolone, red sauce and fat drifted throughout the little bunk room as Clarke offered a bite to any who

might be hungry. As we laughed, several oceanographers in training
ran topside to feed the fish.

Hodji

Spiced with minor adventures and a little mayhem, my
year at Hydrospace Technical Institute passed as quickly as a
daydream. The following summer, while I worked in my
father's factory back in Toronto, the college moved south from
Cocoa Beach to Jensen Beach. HTI ceased to exist, with only a
few students mourning its passing. Nestled along the shore of
the Indian River, FIT's new home for oceanographers boasted
a real campus surrounded by emperor palms, tropical plants
and waterways teeming with life.

I never intended to spend four years living on campus,
but having a room to myself on the top floor helped convince
me to stay. The view, facing east over the river, was fantastic.
From my windows I could see most of the lush habitat of our
school as well as that of our neighbor, Frances Langford's
Outrigger Resort. Out past the river, only a narrow barrier
island obscured a distant view of the Atlantic ocean. I loved
living so close to water.

In a rare display of wisdom, college administrators
soon added two degree programs, environmental science and

health science, with the express goal of attracting more female students. This excellent and successful idea added about a hundred women to our meager population and led to the creation of a dedicated girls' wing in the residence hall. Good fortune blessed me with a dorm room directly adjacent to that wing. In real estate, location is everything. Mine provided many opportunities to build rewarding relationships with my neighbors.

The building in which we lived also inspired a unique opportunity for mischief. In an architectural adaptation I never understood, the planners had attached a wide ledge to the face of our structure on upper floor levels. The ledge offered no access by door, nor a railing of any kind, so could not be considered a balcony. It looked like a suspended sidewalk, going nowhere. A determined young fellow could, by worming his way backwards out a narrow window, reach the sidewalk if he put his mind to it. With the third floor being so far above the ground, few tried. For my feminine neighbors, our ledge provided an ideal spot in the sun where they set wet shoes out to dry.

An opportunity like that is irresistible bait for a troublemaker. Tying the laces of those shoes into knots, without getting caught, might be an interesting challenge. On a night with just enough moonlight to let me see, I slipped out the window, easing myself onto the ledge. *Cool, it didn't even wobble.* When I thought about standing, my legs trembled with determined reluctance, so I crawled along on hands and knees, trying to avoiding looking over the edge. Four rooms down, I found three pairs of shoes and got to work. The reaction of the ladies the following morning was better than I'd dared hope. They were in a wound-up tizzy about who had tied the shoes. I struck again a few days later, waited a week, then hit them again. At all hours, the Shoe Monster would strike when they least expected. The mystery of his identity grew.

Twice the women laid traps for me, placing shoes on the ledge while hiding to see who came along. The first time, luck saved me when I overheard a conversation. By the next, I'd given up on the game, fearing accusations of voyeurism. As I moved on to other pursuits, a lovely young lady named Lauren let me know she'd figured me out. "All the girls say the Shoe Monster's been quiet for a good while. Ya think he'll ever come round again?"

"Now how would I know anything about that? That monster doesn't seem attracted to my shoes."

"Oh yeah, you know. If he does come back, no way he'll get mine. They stay on my feet or in my room."

"And you think that will stop him? I hear he's kind of shifty."

"Of course it will. We always keep the door locked. It's not going to happen, guaranteed."

Smiling I said, "Guaranteed, eh? So what'll you pay if he manages it?"

"Whatever he wants, 'cause it's - not - possible."

BAM-BAM-BAM-BAM "HODJI, GET UP! THE DORM'S ON FIRE!" My eyes popped open with a faint whiff of smoke filling my nose. Throwing on pants and work boots, I was out the door in seconds.

"Where is it?"

"Second floor. Under the girl's wing."

Thin wisps of smoke were already drifting through the hall. I looked around, trying to recall the fire training I'd had back in Cocoa Beach. A few HTI students had volunteered with the Cocoa Beach fire department and participated in several hours of training and practice. We gave it up when the paid staff decided washing the fire trucks was an important part of our service.

"Smoke will be filling the stairwell pretty quick," I replied. "We'll need to help get people out."

As the commotion of shouting and the fire alarm woke others, a friend named Dan and I ran through the girls' side of our building. Several were already standing at the top of a stairwell in their pajamas, afraid to descend through smoky shadows lit only by emergency lights.

"Just stay together, hold your breath and get to the bottom as fast as you can. The air will be better there. GO!"

Dan and I then moved down the hall, checking every room for stragglers. Half way along, the door to a room right over the fire was still locked. I pounded on the door yelling, "ANYBODY IN THERE?" Getting no answer, I stepped back, then gave the door a massive kick with the heel of my boot. It flew open, splintering the frame, and leaving bits of wood lying on the floor. The room was empty, so we moved on to the next.

As we finished checking the last room, I asked Dan to follow everyone down one stairwell, saying I'd go down the other. "I'll be down in a minute. I've got to check one more place." Don't be confused, for this was no heroic act. I'd decided to get sneaky. Back at Lauren's room, I entered her unlocked door. There, under her bed, sat a neat row of shoes. I picked one pair, tied the laces in knots and placed them on her desk. With pen and paper borrowed from a drawer, I wrote a note and stuffed it in a shoe. "That guarantee?"

Hodji, circa 1974

School administrators opened the cafeteria next to our dorm as a temporary shelter, while fire crews doused the flames and cleared smoke with large fans. I knew I wouldn't get any grief for busting open a door. The man in maintenance who fixed that kind of damage was my boss. Later that day he had me helping him with repairs. I later learned the fire was caused by an unattended hot plate, too close to the curtains. I also learned guarantees from cute girls are not worth much.

The final scheduled adventure for students soon to graduate was their senior cruise. This two-day trip on the Atlantic offered us a small taste of life at sea. Did we really want to take on a career in which our home for weeks on end might be a ship? I'm sure I did. I had a great time. Donn, Clarkie and I faced the storm like my father once faced a bear. Rather than retreating below deck to endure discomfort until it passed, we challenged our situation intending to overcome it. Though still a bumpy ride for me and those who rode with me, facing our bear provided greater comfort.

Viewed through the perspective of time, my years at FIT passed quickly, leaving a trail of stories in their wake. Trips to the Florida Keys with Donn; scuba diving through reef and cave; the day Clarkie and I set a record by driving a hairpin corner at fifty-five miles an hour. I earned poker triumphs I'd love to repeat, joined parties I'll never live down, and knew women I'll never forget. Many friendships from those days are still alive forty years later. These times are a joy to recall, yet by graduation I was ready for the next chapter. I wanted to celebrate my degree by going to work.

How does a fresh graduate go about finding a job? In 1975, the Web was twenty years away, nor did we have access to computers. We didn't even have calculators. The method I chose was the shotgun approach. I got a book listing oceanographic organizations from the library and wrote three hundred and sixty letters of interest. While on my way to buy stamps for these letters, I read a poster advertising representatives from Texas Instruments would soon be on campus for student interviews. These worthy gentlemen turned out to be with a subsidiary of TI whose business was seismic exploration for oil. Geophysical Service Inc. operated vessels all over the world and were looking for people who could handle the rigors of work at sea. I submitted a resume immediately.

Clarkie and another classmate received job offers during their interview. Donn, who was heading to grad school in Colorado, didn't bother to apply, and I waited in limbo with a "we'll get back to you."

"Hey Clarkie, where we goin to celebrate? You're off to see the world. That deserves a beer." Donn and I took Clarkie to Chumley's, the best seafood place in our area. At a fern shrouded bar, we slurped clam chowder and talked of futures exaggerated by vivid imagination.

"Here's another round for y'all," the bartender said, "from the gentlemen at the end of the bar." Looking up I saw the two GSI recruiters lifting their glasses in a toast. Not wanting to close a door when opportunity knocks, the three of us had a quick chat to plan strategy before making our way to their stools. "Thanks. How bout I get this round?" I offered. As we'd hoped, one round led to another and several more while we explored their experiences at sea and inflated the adventures of our lives in college. I don't suppose we won the contest of tall tales, but we had a grand time and by the end of the evening they had invited me to Dallas for another interview. A good plan, well executed. I could hardly wait to call Dad. Here is my side of that call:

"Hey Dad, guess what? I'm flying to Dallas for an interview."

"Yah, a big exploration company. They have ships all over the world."

"I know. It's great, eh?"

"A suit? Why do I need a suit?"

"OK, ok. They'll expect it. How about just a sport coat?"

"Yes, I promise. I'll buy a coat tomorrow. Um, do you think you could pay for it?"

The second call to Dad:

"Hey Dad, thanks for letting me use your credit card."

"Yah, I got a sport coat and dress pants like you said."

"What color? Well the pants are blue."

"The jacket? Oh, ah, well the jacket. It's white."

"Yes, WHITE. Hey James Bond looks good in a white jacket. I thought I looked pretty cool."

"Dad? Dad? Guess he hung up."

Despite my choice of jackets, the interviews in Dallas went well. I was offered a job as Quality Control Engineer on a marine seismic vessel. The wonderful people at GSI intended to send me all over the globe, plus pay an unimaginable salary of eight-hundred and ninety dollars a month. Things worked out just as Dad said they would. I'd gone to college, found a job and was now officially a success. I tossed all those letters of interest in the trash.

12

July 20, 1975

Dear Taidy,

Can you believe I'm in England? Tomorrow I leave for Aberdeen, then on to Lerwick, way up north in Scotland, to meet my ship. A month ago I left my home in Toronto to take on the big world, or at least some of it. I figured they'd send me to Tahiti or Singapore or some other exotic place. I got the North Sea. What a bummer. Kind of reminds me of that summer working the farm. If I can stick it out, I know I'll have proved what I'm made of. My friends back home think I'm the luckiest guy ever. I am for sure, but it's gonna be a drag sometimes. So what? I've been through worse. God, I'm scared!

My first few days here have been a blur. All new and exciting and as good as I could hope. Funny looking row houses, all built of gray blocks, cart vendors selling veggies along the "high street," little pubs where locals meet every evening. It's all so different. Last Saturday I traveled into London to see all the sights. After a bus tour I just started walking, then kept at it all day, covering all the landmarks, castles and monuments I could find. Walking is a bit dangerous if you don't pay attention because over here they drive on the wrong side of the road. I kept looking to the left, but cars come from the right. After seeing all of London I could manage in a day, I took a train back here to Croydon and then straight off to bed at the Alpine. That's the hotel where all GSI folks stay.

Yesterday I toured around Surrey and saw a cricket match. Now there's a boring game for ya. Pretty civilized though. Players stand around drinking beer between innings. Marion, a cute waitress from the Alpine, and I had a real picnic with cheese, wine, a blanket and everything. Just like the movies except I gotta leave for Aberdeen in the morning and I didn't even attempt to get "friendly." I was trying to be all on my best manners 'cause a man I met on the plane said English girls weren't like ours at home. He said they don't like guys "who don't behave properly." Well la de dah. You don't suppose he was jerkin' my chain do ya? I kinda got the idea Marion was a little disappointed. I don't guess I'll see her again anyway.

Well, that's where I'm at today. It's off to bed for me 'cause I gotta get up and out'a here early tomorrow. In the pub tonight, I met two GSI guys who just got in from Egypt. Man did they look beat. Found out it was the party manager and quality control engineer from a boat that hit a mine in the Suez, but they're not allowed to talk about it. Seeing them face to face brings everything close to home. You know, more real somehow. Kind of makes me wonder about my future.

Rog

When a young man leaves home for work at sea, he should really expect to encounter a few unusual situations. In 1975, a week after graduating college, I left home to become a doodlebugger with Geophysical Services Inc., headquartered in Dallas, Texas. According to Urban Dictionary, a doodlebugger is a "term for field seismic personnel. Doodlebuggers search out oil the world around by exciting the ground with explosives. They work in the most extreme climates, brave the most dangerous countries, and are renowned for their ability to drink massive amounts of alcohol without dying. Doodlebuggers often work in camps in the middle of nowhere and are easily identified by their pot bellies and lack of shaving. They tell the BEST stories." To the lads back in Toronto, I was a minor celebrity because I'd finished school, found a job and would get to see the world. During my last interview before I joined GSI, a manager mentioned that they "lost" three or four guys every year to accidents. "Well, what kind of accidents?" I asked.

"Foolish accidents," he said "Try not to be foolish, it can kill you."

I signed up anyway.

International travel with GSI proved to be a challenge not suited to the faint of heart. They didn't feel the need to provide detailed travel instructions, typically assuming you knew where you were meant to go and if not, you had the wherewithal to figure it out. A week after arriving in Dallas, I got pulled out of training by a supervisor who told me to pack and head to the airport. "You're going to Croydon. Here's your ticket. Plane leaves in three hours so you better move it. When you go through customs, don't tell them you're working in England. You're working in the North Sea. That's different."

My ticket said Heathrow Airport, London, so I figured Croydon must be around there somewhere. Then I found an address for the office listed in a company information binder I'd received my first day. What more did I need? Just get on the plane, get off the plane on another continent, go through customs without letting them know I would be working in England, find an office who-knows-where outside London and hope they had a place for me to stay. Simple, right? Not simple, but the next day I presented my exhausted self at GSI's Croydon office and soon got squared away with a room at the Alpine Hotel. For years, the Alpine had served as home away from home for GSI men passing through England. I imagine that's why they employed lots of pretty young ladies. Expecting to continue on to Scotland in the morning, I fell into bed early. Pretty English girls would have to wait.

"Plan's changed," the area manager said. "The Arctic Seal is still at sea. You'll have to hold tight a couple days." A couple days stretched into a couple weeks of little work and lots of sightseeing. I got to spend plenty of time touring London, sampling English pubs and meeting lovely British women. When I finally got the call to head north, I was sorry to leave, yet eager to get on with the job I had come to do.

True to form, my superiors again gave me little direction. "Here's your tickets to Lerwick. It's a fishing village in the Shetland Islands." No information on who to see, where the ship might be, or how I should find it. Just go.

I didn't realize this, but the Shetland Islands are way the heck up north, past the line where trees no longer grow. Up there, the guys I worked with had a saying. "There's a naked girl behind every tree." No trees, only gray rocks of a color similar to the cold gray skies of the North Sea dot their barren landscape. When I got off the plane at a tiny airport, I found nary a town nor harbor in site. Outside the terminal, a lone bus waited alongside the narrow lane. When several passengers from my plane got on the bus, I pointed and asked "Lerwick?" A few heads nodded in reply, so I got on as well. Right or wrong, I figured a pleasant bus tour beat standing on the sidewalk in the drizzle. Our bus followed a road that hugged coastal cliffs and beaches as we rolled past emerald green fields full of sheep. Everywhere, boulders pushed up from hills bald of trees, as if trying to offer birds an alternative roost. Engrossed in this magical landscape, I watched in wonder until a sign proclaiming "Lerwick" passed by my window. The rain had stopped, and I looked ahead to a little village nestled below high hills surrounding a small bay. I could see ships at rest in the harbor. *Ships! Better get off the bus.*

Who doesn't love a guy who comes to the North Sea wearing a wool turtle neck and cap? With a duffel bag over my shoulder, I looked every bit a man of the sea. Before me, gulls cried for food as they circled fishing boats making their way home to port. The aroma of their catch lay thick on salty air. *Now how the hell am I supposed to find my boat?*

"Excuse me, sir? Do you know where the Arctic Seal might be?"

"Gang doon th' quay thaur pest th' hoose 'en up tae those taa maists."

Right. I had no clue what the man might have said, so moving on seemed a better idea than standing there like an Old Spice commercial. I wandered along the docks as if I knew what I was doing. Several rows of boats later, I came upon a small white ship with the name Arctic Seal painted in blue on her bow and a fellow in overalls working on deck. "HELLO," I yelled "I THINK I'M SUPPOSED TO JOIN YOUR SHIP."

"Oh, aye," he replied, "you'd be the new lad. You'd best get yourself aboard then."

Those first few weeks on the *Arctic Seal* were a study in contrasts. Twelve hour shifts where efforts to analyze data would often be sidetracked by the urgent demands of physical toil. Hearty meals of simple fare intermingled with dishes of dubious origin that only a highlander could relish. When off shift, restless sleep on a lower bunk in a cramped cabin shared by eight men. We had Englishmen, a few Scots, a couple of Americans and me. Weeks of work, where the most enjoyable event of my day was taking a shower, were occasionally interrupted by brief views of striking scenery, rarely surpassed in all my travels.

The Arctic Seal, circa 1975

After leaving Lerwick, we headed north past Muckle Flugga, the most northerly point of land in the British Isles. Along the way, we passed close by several of the rock islands that combine to make the Shetland chain. Cliffs, topped with brilliant grass, rose hundreds of feet out of the water providing homes to thousands of exotic sea birds like the fat billed puffin. This was grandeur in bigger chunks than I could imagine or adequately describe.

But the North Sea is rough. Some days, I'd have to shove life jackets under the outer edge of my mattress when I wanted to sleep. Their bulk kept me from being tossed out of my bunk onto the deck when the ship rolled hard to one side. Meal time proved to be another adventure. How does one

183

hold a plate and glass steady while leaving a hand free to eat? You have to be quick. Working in rough seas for long periods left me aching. I'd stagger through passageways and workspaces like the ball in a pinball game, smashing a shoulder on a bulkhead or a hip into the corner of a desk. Throughout the day my muscles stayed flexed, constantly straining to keep me vertical or secured to any stationary object. The biggest surprises came when descending a stairway. If our ship happened to drop down a steep trough, the next step would fall away under my foot. I'd be left hanging stiff armed on side rails, as my body tried to fall. After enduring several days of strong weather I felt bruised, like a boxer surviving a fifteen round bout. Thank God I never suffered sea sickness.

Seismic work consists of recording the echoes from sound pulses we'd send deep beneath the seafloor. The returns are picked up by a three kilometer line of hydrophones pulled behind the ship. Towed cables are a great system when the seas were calm, but a potential disaster when the waves got up. In rough weather, one of my jobs was to guide that hydrophone cable onto a giant spool bolted to our stern deck. You can't simply pull the cable in like slack line onto a fishing reel. That would break it. The ship has to back down the line. When the waves got big, they'd come crashing over the stern as we'd try to get the cable on board. Sometimes, the waves were so large I would look up twenty feet one moment to see its crest and down twenty the next to see its trough. When waves broke over the stern, all I could do was grab the cable with both arms and hold on for dear life. No railing; no safety net; no harness; just the deck over cold, open water. We had a long standing motto for that type of thing. When a tough job needed to be done, we'd shake our heads, say "Do or die for GSI" and get to work.

Rumors suggested anyone pulled out to sea with a receding wave would die of hypothermia before the ship could turn around. On a rough morning in August, I tempted that rumor. Halfway through a midnight to noon shift, our party manager came into the instrument room. "Waves are rising boys. Better get to the back deck and start bringing in cable." As we backed into freshening seas, the four foot swell grew to ten and waves washed over the deck where we worked. Bone numbing water swirled over our knees, then rose to our thighs. When a wall of water came rushing over my waist, it proved stronger than my hold on the cable, then sent my submerged body tumbling under the reel. Cold took my breath away as I found myself wedged between the spool and its frame. I fought to grab hold, never having time for fear. On its way back to sea, the wave again tried to break my grip while desperation helped me hold strong. The wave receded without me. As fast as I'd gone down, I regained my feet, my body shaking with relief as I climbed back to relative safety on deck. I'd survived. To validate my position as a doodlebugger in good standing, I went right back to work. Still, that kind of experience will lead a young man to consider his priorities in life.

Jeff Goodman and unknown on the back deck. By Jeff Cunkelman.

Safety harnesses, shown in the image above, were stowed somewhere on board but I never saw anyone use one. Perhaps that's why we had foolish accidents. A few years later, habits changed when safety became more popular. My friend, Jeff Cunkelman, might have been more impressed with the company's campaign for safety had his ship not gone down in the North Atlantic a year after he captured this photograph. His mates, who didn't jump for life boats fast enough, didn't survive. Fortunately, Jeff did. Do or die for GSI.

Despite brief periods of heart stopping danger, three months in the North Sea dragged tediously from one day to the next. Beyond the routine of work, we had only a few mundane activities to pass the time. Eat, work, read a book, eat, sleep, get up, work some more. Like a man serving time, my mood darkened with every passing day. When a fire in our engine room reduced the ship to one propeller and minimal power, my reaction expressed relief rather than worry. A good disaster provided a fine break from our daily schedule and a chance to spend a few days in port.

A man at sea can change when he goes too long without touching land. At around three weeks, some became mentally unstable. Our stressed out crew, a few near death experiences, dark clouds and waves, it's no wonder we spent most of our port time in pubs.

During one extended voyage, our first mate decided to consume all the contraband booze he'd smuggled on board. The ship was infested with cockroaches, so he determined it was his duty as an officer to fix the problem. His solution was to seize the ship's .22 rifle, and "Shoot the little buggers. Every damn one of em." His first shot lodged in a companionway wall. The second took an errant route out to sea, just before he passed out on the back deck. After securing the rifle and the mate, the Arctic Seal made a quick return to port where police hauled him off in handcuffs, never to be seen again.

If I've learned anything over the years, it's that everything evolves given time. Be it the smell of gutters filled with cow-slop or the crush of a four-man dorm room, we can generally get comfortable with difficult circumstances. Circumstances we can't overcome can probably be outlasted. The North Sea was no exception. By mid-September, rough seas persuaded our bosses to move on to other latitudes. The *Arctic Seal* was reassigned to work its way down the west coast of Africa. Staying on board to make the transit, I got to experience an accelerated change of seasons. The wet, cold, depressing climate of the north passed through spring and into summer over the course of two weeks. As we headed south, the seas warmed, and so did my disposition.

Africa, and our main port of call, Dakar, proved to be an awakening for me. An education in the harsh realities of the world and the poverty in which most of its inhabitants live. There I again realized how blessed I'd been as a child, and the advantages I held as an adult. Just as hard work and poor accommodations had been maturing my expectations of comfort, Africa matured my appreciation.

Still, sunny days sustained a generally good mood until my tour on the *Arctic Seal* came to an end in the middle of November. One evening, as we tied up at dockside in the port of Douala, a forlorn young man called up to those of us working on deck. "I'm the new QC. They told me to join your boat." My replacement had arrived at last. That joyful news meant I'd be leaving for home in the morning.

Sitting on a homebound plane the next day felt strange. Like returning to North America would make life too easy. The experiences of five months at sea had conspired to shift my world view. I recognized how privileged my early life had been. I'd evolved, become more confident. How could I continue to grow back in the land of plenty? Would my parents notice a change? How would they react? A moot point really. They'd moved to Brazil. It was Christmas before I got to see them again.

What is it about long hair, a shaggy beard and a ticket from Africa that makes customs inspectors assume you'd have drugs? They'd gone through every pocket, sock and container in my bag before officially declaring me free to re-enter Canada. *Fifty days off with money in my wallet.* I hadn't had that much time without obligation in ten years. I could do whatever I wanted. While standing in the terminal of Toronto International, I only wanted to go home. The closest I had to that was my sister's house in Guelph, an hour east of the airport. *Cool. I've always liked surprising my sister. This will be a good one. Better call ahead just in case.* Her failure to answer deterred me not at all, and soon I was on the shuttle heading for my temporary home.

My sister's front steps were not an unpleasant place to sit on a sunny November afternoon. I'd arrived to find the house locked tight, but figured a wait wouldn't hurt me any, as long as it didn't snow. I think their neighbor got a little nervous seeing a scruffy looking fellow sitting with his duffle bag on Amy & Fred Cousineau's walk. "Excuse me, but can I help you?" she asked from a safe distance.

"I sure hope so. I wanted to visit Amy and Fred but they seem to be out shopping or something."

A puzzled look crept over her face as she moved a few steps closer. "Um, are they expecting you?"

"Well, no. I've been gone quite a while and had no way to let them know I'd be home."

Then her eyes lit up, followed by an excited smile. "OH! OH! Are you Roger? Amy told us about her brother who's overseas."

"Yes, I am. I left Africa yesterday and was hoping to stay here for a while."

"Oh my. I'm afraid Amy and Fred aren't just out shopping. They've gone up north for a few days. But don't you worry, they've given us a key. I'm just going in to get it, and I'll let you in." The surprise that two days later met my sister at her front door outdid anything I could have planned.

Throughout November and December, I visited every close friend and relative from Ontario to Florida. Amy and Fred, Steve Finlayson, Penny, Taid, Nikos back at college, and even my parents when they returned from Brazil for Christmas. All those lucky people got to experience the exciting world traveler's return. I hope our reunions provided as much pleasure for those I visited as they did for me. Probably not.

January found me back to work along the Gulf coast of Louisiana, onboard the *MV Navasota*. Compared to the

Shetland Islands or Africa, the scenery was dull. At least the locals spoke English (after a fashion), served great food, and partied like "Laissez les bons temps rouler!" (Let the good times roll) was the eleventh commandment. Beyond that, port towns along the gulf seemed much the same as the rest of the world. During my time on the southern shores, I encountered a gun-wielding Cajun in a lunch grill, almost took a beating for dancing with a black girl, and learned oysters with beer makes a fine breakfast. Had our work contract and my stay on the Gulf Coast not suddenly ended shortly after I arrived, I fear Louisiana may have done me in.

In the spring of 1976, with oil prices dropping, worldwide exploration slowed to where GSI had nothing immediate for me to do. Although this may not have been the best circumstance for future employment, an unexpected month of leave was welcome indeed. It seemed to me that a trip to see my parents in Brazil would be in order. Not wanting to find myself sitting on the steps trying to speak Portuguese to the neighbors, I first had to make a call.

"Dad? It's Rog."

"Yeah, your son."

"I know it's only been a few weeks. Listen, I'm on leave again so I thought I'd come for a visit."

"No, I'm back in Dallas now. I've got a ticket to Sao Paulo."

"Well, tomorrow. I leave first thing in the morning."

"Yes Dad, Brazil is a long way. Don't worry, I'll see ya

tomorrow. OH, isn't Carnaval about to get going down there?"

Brazil at any time would have been wonderful. Brazil during Carnaval was fantastico. Every city, town and village celebrated the coming of Lent. It was samba, grilled meat and shots of pinga every night for a week. The remaining three weeks I spent sightseeing. Some with my parents and some with a beautiful young teacher from Santos. A month was not enough.

As soon as I returned to our Dallas office, I learned from the human resources manager that work for GSI's marine division had all but dried up. "Sorry, Geiger, we don't have any open quality control spots and probably won't have any for several months. How about transferring to land operations in Saudi Arabia?" Only one question came to mind. *Where the heck is Saudi Arabia?* The nearest map provided an answer. Was this a joke? I had a degree in Oceanography and the only position available would send me to a Middle Eastern desert. With no other options, I reluctantly accepted.

Although different from what I'd experienced at sea, life in the Saudi kingdom proved to be no less difficult. After several months of enduring oppressive heat, oppressive people and oppressive authority, I'd earned enough time off to spend a few weeks on an island in the South Aegean Sea. This place had everything. Ancient history, beautiful seascapes, great food, all surrounded by hotels packed full with available women. The Isle of Rhodes offered all the distractions a young man could desire. The Papillon Restaurant offered second floor rooms for a reasonable price.

Mornings at the Papillon came with no pre-dawn cries of *Allahu akbar* calling the faithful to prayer over loudspeakers from the nearest mosque. Instead, I listened to birds singing in a flower-lined courtyard below my window. Their songs, along with aromas of pastry and lamb drifting up from kitchens below, conspired to rouse me out of my bed every morning. Outside, a short walk led to the yacht harbor. I often sat along shore sipping strong coffee while watching the "beautiful" people advertise their wealth on million-dollar vessels. Then I liked to stroll through the Agora, a marketplace where high stone walls enclosed an ancient city full of shops and cafes. Inside, I'd enjoy a breakfast of sweet bread and tart yogurt while listening to old men gossip across their sidewalk tables.

The island provided an endless supply of interesting sights and experiences, surrounded by cold, crystalline waters from the northern Mediterranean. Days spent exploring coastal grottoes by motor bike were highlighted by fine meals of fresh seafood, followed by wine sipped under the shade of an olive tree. After dark, my pursuits shifted to tourist discos and dancing the night away to the beat of Abba with lively young ladies on vacation.

A week into my stay, I met up with some other GSI

men, including an American named Brian. Compared to most Doodlebuggers, Brian's conduct was easygoing and sober. He'd spent considerable time on Rhodes and established friendships with some of the local residents. Of particular interest was his friendship with a group of unattached nurses. These lively ladies, originally from Britain and Sweden, worked in the city hospital and had expressed to Brian an interest in worthy young fellows like ourselves as dinner partners.

His lady friends had experienced difficult local relationships, so they avoided Greek men in favor of foreigners. Clare, a lusty girl from England, had curly brown hair with bangs covering much of her forehead. Clare's eyes sparkled through the curls whenever she talked. In contrast, her Swedish friend, Ulrica, resembled a petite blonde angel. Ulrica was the quieter of the two. Brian, Clare, Ulrica and I soon joined two other couples for a Saturday evening at a late-night taverna.

Located high in the hills outside of town, the whitewashed walls of a modest cafe greeted us as we exited our taxis. We entered through a cobblestone courtyard surrounded by lush gardens. Inside, waiters served a delicious meal as local singers performed rousing folk songs. A taverna really needs to be experienced to be understood. After dinner, everyone drank wine and danced a Zorba style line dance until long past my bedtime. "Come, my friends," called the leader of a small band. "Join the line and dance the Syrtos. As you dance, we will play." In a strange reenactment of ancient Greek tradition, plates were broken throughout the evening. Performers, customers and waiters all smashed plates on the floor whenever the mood struck us. Our hilltop taverna offered entertainment fit to cleanse a dusty soul. The ladies had fun, our conversation turned intimate and time lost its hold on our lives. At 4:00 am, the party had to move on. Even a Taverna has to close sometime.

Outside, light leaked from old lamps above us as we waited for rides that would carry us down to the harbor. "Can you smell that?" I asked Ulrica, while pointing to vine covered walls. "Smells sweet, like the honeysuckle we had in Florida. It smells sweet like..."

"Oh bugger," groaned Brian's date. Clare's angry eyes cut toward a group of Greek fellows who'd wandered into our courtyard.

Hello, I thought, *where did these bright boys come from? They weren't in the pub.* Sure enough, Clare took another look at one of them, sighed and said something to him in Greek. Turning to Brian, she said "I know this berk. He used to chat me up a bit. We went to dinner a couple of times before I told him to bugger off." Berk is British for dork, which the guy proved himself to be when he yelled at Clare in Greek, then switched to broken English.

"You do damn turistas now? We no good for English beech?"

I looked to Brian for a reaction, but he appeared frozen

in shock. When Clare said something unflattering back in Greek, our visitor took it poorly, came over and gave her a hard shove that sent her stumbling backwards. With my companions still stunned, I stepped in front of her while loudly informing the fellow "YOU'RE NOT DOING THAT AGAIN BUCKO!" That's when he punched me in the nose.

I'm not much of a fighter. In fact, I'd never had a fight in my adult life until that punch. I had, however, prepared myself prior to going overseas by reading a book entitled *Effective Unarmed Combat*, written by a tough old veteran of the Chicago Police force. In this moment of reaction, all I could remember was that I should be as sudden and violent as possible, and that a ridge hand to the throat worked well. My right hand shot out, striking his adam's apple. My left hand came around to join the fun and together they got a good hold of his throat. Then I bashed his head against an ivy covered wall while yelling at his friends to "GET THIS GODDAMN, SON OF A BITCH OUT OF MY SIGHT NOW! WE DON'T" (another *bash*) "PUSH GIRLS WHERE" (*bash*) "I COME FROM AND" (*bash*) "WE'RE NOT GOING TO" (*bash*) "STAND FOR IT HERE". Before I got further into this scolding, his friends had pulled the guy out of my grasp and dragged him off, apologizing richly as they left. I guess they didn't push girls in Rhodes either.

Shock morphed into astonishment amongst my friends. As I stood there shaking, they all looked at me like Leonidas the Spartan had come to life in their midst. I doubt any of them were more surprised than me. How did I react so quickly, so effectively? I'd heard these guys usually carry knives. How did I survive? Did I enjoy this? My adrenaline-charged limbs twitched like jumping beans while I contemplated the new being who had borrowed my body. Silence overshadowed the trip as we road down to town. When Ulrica and I arrived back at the Papillon, I put aside my questions for another day.

During my visit to Rhodes, I was a year and a half into a three-year journey of discovery. Mostly, I'd been discovering the world. During an early Sunday morning on an island in the Mediterranean, I was discovering myself. Here are two lessons I took from the experience. First, I never got around to being afraid. Even when some guy plants your nose all over your cheek, it doesn't hurt so much. At least not until later. That fact has something to do with our fight-or-flight response. When we go with fight, our bodies release stress hormones like adrenaline and norepinephrine to help us do a thorough job of it. All those chemicals combine to make a great pain killer. Even though I've successfully avoided any more fights during my life, I've never been as worried about the possibility as I might have been before that first one.

The second lesson was considerably more rewarding. I learned that in a triumphant defense of a woman's honor, sometimes the winner gets a lively reward. I really enjoyed being the winner.

My adventurous trip to Rhodes established a prototype

for travel I would follow for the next two years. Skiing the Italian Alps; beach front in Thailand; Bavaria during Oktoberfest. Why would a guy go home when the world had so much to offer? Each was better than the other as I pursued a quest for wayward gratification. In payment, my work demanded long hours, rough quarters and loneliness. At all times, my home, friends and family were thousands of miles away and I missed them dearly. Stress, danger, ragged living. These were the dues for a career choice easily made.

13

Summer of '77

Dear Taidy,

In college we used to sing a song by Goose Creek Symphony. In it, there's a line that goes "...it was fun, but I'm on the run. If they catch up to me, there's a price I must pay." Those words have been running through my head as I sit here writing. Outside our safe house, the sun has just passed its peak. I hope I survive to see it set again. When the military showed up this morning looking to haul a few foreigners off to prison, three of us climbed the wall. We don't even know if they've noticed we're missing yet. I expect we'll be OK for a few hours, at least long enough to plan our next move. To my way of thinking, getting out of the country is the only option, but difficult seeing as the Saudi's have our passports. I can't speak for Mark and Tim, but I'm more scared than I've ever been in my life.

Did you hear about the Saudi princess who got executed for running away with a commoner to get married? It happened not so long ago in Riyadh. They shot her and cut his head off just because they disobeyed. The staff house owner thinks we tried to poison his family. How do ya suppose they'll execute us?

Tim's uncle agrees we're in some serious trouble, but he doesn't yet know how much, so he's trying to find out without letting on anything to arouse suspicion. He figures he can get away

199

with hiding us one night before we have to move on. Tim and Mark are getting some rest. They're better men than me if they can sleep. As I sit here, I've been thinking a lot about Doug. Why'd he stay behind? Is he brave or foolish? With the exception of our most recent history, I've never known him to act foolishly. He must be doing what he feels is right. Is it? He's got to be as scared as I am. Is he more brave? This country isn't exactly known for its fair minded justice. What if some of the others end up being blamed for what I did? Can I let them pay the price? That's sure not doing my part for the boys. It would be hard to live with. Can I live with it? No.

So I guess that's my decision. Go back and see what's happening. I can't sit here without finding out if someone else has to take the rap for me. I've got to know. This disaster is like a big, angry bear. I've got to face my bear, even if it kills me.

Lord this place is nuts. Sand storms, giant bugs, insane drivers, morality police, and nothing to do. I think if I live to get out of the Kingdom it will be the happiest day of my life.

Rog

A roach the size of a hen's egg crawled up the wall beside my work table. With a smack of my hand, I squished it flat, then returned to opening the box of data sent in from one of our field crews. Across the room, an older man who'd been in Saudi forever, called out a warning. "Geiger, check that box for critters before you open it!"

Oh yeah. May have some bugs hiding in my box. I gave the box a little shake, then pressed it to my ear to listen. *Nothing… still nothing… a little scratching, something moving?* "Hey, I think there's something in here."

"Excellent! Be careful you don't get any hitchhikers when you take the tapes out. We'll see what you've got when it's empty."

A man who worked in the desert told me camel spiders often chewed holes in the flesh of laborers while they slept in their tents. The giant black scorpions would crawl right out of your worst nightmare. When GSI's field engineers got bored, they'd hide spiders and scorpions inside boxes of data tape destined for the processing office back in Dhahran. Those of us in the office didn't mind as much as you might expect. Two nasty insects could be provoked into a fight. A fight on which bets would be laid during a few minutes of deadly entertainment. I found a spider in the box and we'd captured a scorpion from an earlier shipment. "Two bucks says the spider takes it," the old guy called, knowing inexperienced men usually bet on a scorpion. With their big deadly stinger, those black monsters looked mean, but they moved slow. Camel spiders run circles around them. In Kingdom, we took fun as we found it.

Life in Saudi Arabia was difficult for an infidel Yankee. Four years of Florida sunshine in no way prepared me for its extreme weather. In Dhahran, temperatures regularly topped 120 degrees, with ninety percent humidity from the Arabian Gulf. Sandstorms blew in off the desert to line the corners inside my widow with grit. I once visited a field crew down south in the Rub al Khali. They had recorded temperatures over 150 degrees. The name for their province means Empty Quarter. Kind of fitting for a place where only the dunes seemed alive.

Dune buggies and our supply plane in the Rub al Khali.

After coming to grips with the heat, my next challenge was driving on streets where the rules of the road were best described as suicidal. Traffic lanes had little meaning, increasing from two up through whatever the available space would allow, and back at a whim. Right of way went to the largest, fastest and whoever was in good standing with Allah.

When driving through the desert on a raised two lane highway, I had to be wary of oncoming rock haulers. These huge Mercedes dump trucks, full of boulders, barreled down the road side by side at 70 miles an hour. If an oncoming vehicle got in the way, they didn't stop. Inshallah brother, God's will. As a Saudi man once said while trying to enlighten me, "If the leaf falls from the tree, it dies."

Heat, crazy traffic, strange beliefs and the wickedest insects I'd ever care to see. Even a camel spider had trouble with some of the critters over there. The worst I ran into appeared during a party put on by the guys from Halliburton Oil Services. With fifty of us gathered in their company clubhouse, several sliding doors had been opened to take advantage of a cool evening breeze. Our hosts provided plenty of homebrewed beer and booze to ensure their guests enjoyed the festivities. As we stood around sharing jokes and jibes, an uninvited guest came scrambling in through one of the open doors. This newcomer was the biggest, fastest, scariest, multi-legged creature that ever lived. A giant centipede, twelve inches long, with great big pincers ready to skewer any slow legs. Who would believe fifty rough, tough, oil and gas men could turn into a bunch of screaming little babies so fast? The centipede was tearing from one end of the floor to the other while men took off in any direction available. Stand on a chair, sit on the bar, knock your best friend down, but don't let that thing get you! The beast must have gotten winded because after a few minutes it moved to the now empty center of the room and stopped. It looked around the place like a schoolyard bully choosing his next victim. From my perch, well out of the way on top of a couch, I heard a muttering grumble from the behind the bar. Out stomped Les Evans, wearing a faded Hawaiian shirt, his stubby shorts, and a pair of flip flops. This tough old Aussie carried his stout body on short legs and didn't much care what we thought about him. The clap, clap, clap of his flip flops echoed as he crossed the floor alone. "Bloody bunch of Pommy pansies." Les ended things with a squishy splat. His foot stomped the critter to paste. Cheers filled the room as we toasted a brave man.

The rest of the single GSI men and I lived in a twenty room staff house, inside a walled garden, with two Pakistani cooks, three house stewards and a gate guard. I kind of liked the cooks and the stewards for being friendly and willing to joke with us. The old gate guard never smiled at anything. He just stood around scowling, with his fat gut hanging over a six inch belt that held up his long skirt, and the big shabria dagger he always carried.

I suppose all being in the same circumstance kept us going. Misery likes company. As with my mates on board ship, the lads in our staff house stuck together. All of us worked six days a week in Dhahran, the headquarters and corporate village of Aramco Oil. When not working, we had to make our own fun, often involving large quantities of homemade booze. We even had our own pub in the staff house. It had been cobbled together in a spare room by adding a small bar and a couple of tables. Trinkets retrieved from exotic destinations decorated the walls. Alcohol has been forbidden in Saudi since the time of Muhammad, so if the mattawa, their religious police, caught us with any, they'd send the offender off to one of their prison compounds. If they caught you stealing, they cut off your hand. Adultery? They'd stone you for that. These people were serious. Still, almost everyone made some kind of hooch. With so much of it going on, if they had busted us all, Saudi would have run out of oil with no expatriates working to find it for them.

My particular specialty, affectionately called Looney Juice, seemed to make people a little crazy. I'm not sure why fermented apple juice, with a little sugar in the bottle to give it a sparkle like Champagne, made folks lose their minds. The first time I brewed it, I used a tablespoon of sugar in each bottle instead of a teaspoon. A few of the bottles, which were aging nicely in a closet in my room, exploded one morning. The blasts gave my roommate, Paul, flashbacks to his Aussie army days. He thought we were under attack, yelled "MORTAR", and hit the floor, trying to roll under his bed. Paul, a large fellow who had at one time played professional rugby, didn't fit so well in his bedroom foxhole. His next words, unkind and unsuitable for this record, are best forgotten. We rescued most of the bottles but had to empty them for a second fermentation and re-bottle with less sugar.

That second trip made for a rather strong brew. Maybe that's why it affected people so much.

Paul didn't make his own brew. He had to purchase a locally made moonshine called Siddiqui, which is Arabic for "little friend". Not long after the exploding bottles incident, he was transporting some of his purchase, sampling a little along the way, when he crashed his car into a parked police van. That's not tolerated in Saudi and Paul got two years in a local prison camp. Unlike western jails, Saudi prisons made survival an every-man-for-himself affair. They didn't even give him a bed to sleep on. Only a bit of ground alongside one of the gray, sand-worn walls that kept him locked in. "Find a spot and lay out your blanket," is the only instruction they gave inmates. Other than the rice and chicken provided once a day from a communal pot, there was no support for prisoners.

With limited supervision, conflict occasionally became physical. Paul towered over most of the Pakistanis, Indonesians and other third world men imprisoned with him. He had little trouble staying safe, but incarceration seemed to take a toll on his health and mind. Several mornings a week on the way to work, we stopped at the prison to leave food for him. We never got to talk to Paul. Our closest contact was an occasional glimpse and a shouted word when we dropped by or reports from our managers about his condition. He was essentially on his own. Luckily, after about a year, King Fahd pardoned him during Ramadan, and the company flew him home.

Another friend, Tim Kent, and I spent a whole night on the roof of our house drinking and talking in celebration of his release. We were having a fine discussion on how one should treat our house stewards when I learned Tim had grown up a rich kid with servants and other advantages of wealth. "Servants are just people like everyone else and you have to treat them with respect like you would anyone. You can't provoke people just because they work for you, even if they live with you."

"Tim," I asked, "if your family's so rich, why are you suffering here in Saudi like the rest of us? You should be doing something great back home."

Tim on the roof at dawn.

"Aw, when I was in high school dad's business went south on him. We lost everything, the money, the big house, the servants, all of it. That's Ok though, it was really a pain sometimes. I had to be taught how to live like that and then I had to learn how to live without it." He took life's ups and downs in stride, so wasn't too bothered about having to ship off to Saudi like the rest of us. If fact, he seemed to enjoy making his own way.

"Well here's to Paul," I said, raising my mug in toast. "May his return home be happy."

I spent most of my time in an office, so when I got out in the field for a week or two, I considered it a treat. I have to admit the Saudi desert could be impressive if not exactly beautiful. Every time I stopped to look, its rugged landscape painted in shades of brown and gray seemed to stretch on forever. It could also be dangerous. I'd heard the nomadic people, the Bedouins, who still lived in tents out in the heat, believed everything on earth belongs to them. If we happened to have something, it was only because they allowed it. If they wanted it back, they took it.

One of the field crews I worked on told a story of a Bedouin tribesman who came into camp asking for a water pump for his truck. They had one but their party manager told him we needed it and refused to part with it. The Bedouin returned to his truck and came back with an AK-47 to *explain* to our manager why he must not hold on to what was not his to keep. He made a good point, so the pump was handed over with no further debate. The authorities would do nothing because the rights of Arabs always trumped those of expatriate workers.

I do not wish to imply that these men were without honor, for that was not so. The headman of another field crew I was fortunate to visit proved it for me. Our seismic surveys worked like a big echo sounding operation. Large thumper trucks sent vibrations deep into the earth and arrays of geophones picked up the returned signals, which were recorded on tape for processing in a computer center. Every field crew had a base camp from which they departed to wherever the current data collection line happened to be that day. The line often ran far from base camp, and in the desert everything in every direction tended to look alike. Some of us had to pay close attention to detail if we wanted to stay on course.

One morning I got a little off track. Even with no defined roads and few identifiable landmarks, had I thought to bring a map and compass, all would have been fine. I did not think to do so. I did have a small radio and when I drove to the top of a mesa, I could hear chatter from the seismic line, but with my limited broadcast power, they couldn't hear calls from me. Using the sun to estimate the direction I needed to go only made the situation worse and soon I was completely lost. Once this predicament became apparent, I recalled a piece of advice Dad offered when I was ten. I had wandered for hours, lost on the Appalachian Trail, so his advice stayed with me. "When you get lost," he said, "just sit down and wait for someone to find you. The more you move, the harder you are to find." Sadly, I didn't take his advice. I had water and plenty of fuel, so I had every chance of lasting a couple of days, but pride overcomes wisdom when you're a fool. The embarrassment of having to be rescued was more than I wanted to contemplate, even when weighed against the possible consequences of desperate measures. I continued on.

My lost Jeep seen from the top of a mesa.

My first glimmer of hope was spotting an old Bedouin camel herder. I had passed him and his long line of camels twice while trying to find a track that seemed to head in a good direction. On my third pass, he came running at the Jeep, robes flowing, shaking his stick while yelling at me. *Stopping might be a sensible idea,* I thought. *Better a stick than a bullet.* I stayed in the Jeep but rolled down the window to listen to his animated lecture, for which I had not the slightest spark of understanding. He'd jabber away in Bedouin while pointing one way or another with his stick. I'd babble back in English and we'd both stare blankly at each other in between. As his side of the conversation got more agitated, his stick frequently pointing at me, I got a flash of brilliance and understood exactly what he was saying. *You stupid piece of camel dung, don't you know how to speak?*

Camel herders in the desert.

In reply, I removed my floppy field hat, shrugged my shoulders with arms held wide and shook my head an apologetic "No". With that, his face lit up, he smiled a big gap toothed smile and nodded his head in a vigorous yes of approval. Then, without another word, he took off back to his camels happy as could be. *What the hell had just happened? Did he want me to take off my hat as a show of respect?* I'll never know. I stared after him for a moment, started up the Jeep and departed as well. Geez, Saudi was weird.

No closer to rescue, I decided my best bet was to keep going in what I thought was a southerly direction until I found a real road or some sign of civilization. An hour of this got me to a small village alongside an ancient fort. Just a dozen flat roofed buildings standing in a cluster down the single street. Having baked under the furnace of a relentless sun for many years, all but one had lost all color, now bleached to the shades of the desert in which they sat. I stopped in front of the one that may have once been yellow. As soon as I got out, a handful of people ducked out of sight upon seeing my white face. A noble looking fellow, dressed in fine robes, approached from within. "Salamu alaykum," he said.

I replied "Alaykum al-salam" meaning "and peace be unto you." At least he spoke city Arabic instead of the Bedouin dialect. I knew a little Arabic. When our greeting was complete, the village elder showed me into an inner courtyard where I sat on the ground in a circle of a dozen men, shaded by a group of manicured trees. The elder called to a boy who'd been watching from inside one of the rooms surrounding the courtyard. He sent the boy running down the street on an errand of unknown intent. As my eyes became accustomed to dim light, I saw several veiled women and young girls peeking out at us from within other rooms. A slight catching of their eye caused the women to quickly pull away as the girls stared shyly and giggled.

By this point we had reached the limits of my Arabic, none of the men spoke any English, so our conversation stalled. A young man rose to his feet and approached a large clay pot where he dipped in a ladle to offer me water. At first I wasn't too sure about accepting nasty old water that had been stewing in an algae-covered pot for who knows how long, but I noticed even my slight hesitation was causing these guys to get uneasy. Offering water to a guest is the pinnacle of good desert hospitality. To refuse would have been a serious insult, so I accepted, enjoying every drop.

As I finished, the boy returned with a European looking fellow whom I soon learned to be a French doctor working a circuit throughout the region. It was my good fortune his route brought him to the village that day. With his limited English and my grade school French, I explained my predicament, and he relayed everything to the elder. A member of the council identified a villager who would know where to find our base camp and the boy ran off to fetch him. Through the doctor, I assured the elder that if their man would guide me back to our camp, I would feed him a decent meal and ensure he got a ride back to his village. All was agreed and as I prepared to depart my new friends, with great relief I thought, *Alhamd lillah, jayid jidan. Praise God, this is very good... I'm gonna get out of this blunder.* Before leaving, I retrieved a container of water from the Jeep and gave it to the elder. "Shukran. Saddiq," meaning "Thank you. Friend." All the village men smiled and nodded their heads. It seems I had done well.

Ottoman fort near my rescuers' village.

An uneventful hour's drive with little conversation took me back to base camp where my coworkers were just beginning to wonder what might have become of me. *Cool. They don't even have to realize how dumb I am.* After giving my guide fresh water, I used hand signs to ask him to wait in the engineer's trailer while I left to find help. The crew's headman, Ali, supervised our line workers and seemed well suited for fulfilling the rest of my arrangement. He was somewhat unique in that he was a native Bedouin who had left the tribes to expand his horizons by becoming more of a Saudi. I told Ali about my guide and asked that a suitable dinner be provided, along with a ride back to the man's village. Ali readily agreed. Great. All was in order, and everyone lived happily ever after. Well maybe not. Forty minutes after I left him, Ali returned to the trailer with a grave look on his face, asking to speak with me in private. When we were alone, he said that my guide was claiming I had promised him $100 worth of ryals, the local currency. Ali asked very seriously if this was true and I replied as seriously that it was not. He looked me in the eye for a moment, said thank you and left. When I found him later that evening, I asked him what had happened. Ali told me my guide had lied and brought great dishonor to his family. I asked what would happen to him? "We *explained* to him that he must not act in this way," Ali replied. "You will not see him again." I did not.

I have often wondered what became of my guide that day, especially considering I had enough money to pay him off. This was the first experience I'd had that led me to realize how solemnly these people protected their honor. Had I paid, both he and I would have lost respect. How they squared that with the rampant bribery in their country was beyond me. It seemed incongruous but "crossing the palm" (with money), to expedite bureaucratic activity, was an ancient and accepted practice.

Our staff house had a pub. Pubs needed booze, and I knew where to get it. I also had a piece-of-junk Volkswagen station wagon that took me places most of the time. With wheels, I often drove friends to local social events and occasionally got called upon to make a Siddiqui run. Close calls with the law, while running booze or driving inebriated, seemed inevitable.

On one occasion, Mark Forbeson and I were returning from a party at the Schlumberger housing complex. Mark was an American about my age from Florida where I attended college, so we had something in common. We spent lots of time together, both in country and on leave. He was usually up for anything, but had a bad habit of listening to me, which tended to lead him into trouble. The safest way back from Schlumberger, cutting through five miles of desert, kept us off more populated roads and free of official scrutiny.

That night we figured our luck had run out when we saw an army checkpoint alongside our desert path. As we drove toward armed soldiers, I looked at Mark and said "I'm not stopping, hold on," then turned off the lights, floored it and left the road. Mark bounced along beside me, screaming like a drunken cowboy.

"YEA-HA. GO FOR IT!"

There are no streetlights in the desert, so I couldn't see much, but that was the whole point. They couldn't see me either. As we raced past their checkpoint, I glanced to the left and saw four soldiers under pole lights with stunned looks of surprise on their faces. They stood there with their mouths open, too shocked to move. Mark and I tore off into the night at full speed, laughing like the drunken fools we were. "CAN

YOU SEE WHERE YOU'RE GOING?" Mark yelled as we bumped on through the dark.

"NO, I CAN'T SEE WORTH A DAMN!"

Mark rolled down his window and stuck his head out. "HEY, I CAN SEE BETTER. I'LL GIVE YOU DIRECTIONS."

That seemed like a fine idea. I had only a vague notion of what lay in our path and was afraid of hitting a boulder or something. We continued on that way for a mile or two, with Mark yelling "turn right", "right again, LEFT!", then hit a rough patch that bounced Mark's head between the top and bottom window frames. He didn't knock himself out, but as he pulled his wobbly head back in, we hit another bump which sent him into the front window. SMACK. His head cracked the windshield, then his body folded over itself in the seat. I slowed down while Mark came back to life with a moan.

"ARE YOU ALRIGHT?" I yelled.

"Yeah, I think so, but I don't want to go on any more rides with you."

The soldiers had not tried to follow our mad run through the desert. Without further conversation, Mark and I made our way back to the staff house.

For obvious reasons, the normal esprit de corp among my mates wore a little thin when it came time to make a booze run to resupply our pub. Purchase and delivery of Siddiqui was a simple, yet solitary affair. Just total up orders in five gallon increments, collect the money, go buy the booze and return. It had to be five gallons at a time because raw Siddiqui was delivered in five gallon jerry cans. Hard plastic cans are easier to handle than bottles and a lot safer. Back at the pub, we'd cut our raw liquor with water, then bottle it for use at the bar. When mixed with Coke, Siddiqui made a palatable drink. I tried a straight shot of Siddiqui only once. It tasted so bad I had to take several deep breaths to keep it down. The dangers of running booze could be great and the rewards limited. I did not volunteer often. All I got in return for the risk was a little thanks from the rest of the guys in the staff house. Still, somebody had to do it and as I'd learned as a kid camping with Dad, each guy needs to do his bit for the common good.

Running booze at night is not generally a good idea either. It tends to cause suspicion and the police are more active. I, being twenty-four, bullet proof and having survived a midnight encounter with the cops, let myself get in a situation where I was traveling after midnight with three cans of booze in my car. Within a couple of miles of our staff house, I saw two police cars patrolling side streets by illuminating any moving vehicle. *If I keep going, they're likely to light me up. That can't be good. If I make it home and they see me unloading I'm screwed for sure.* My only hope seemed to be, pull over, kill the engine, lie down, and wait. After twenty minutes of lying low, the police had moved on.

With the success of my recent trip in mind, I again made my way home with the headlights off. Unfortunately, the results mirrored my previous adventure, and I hit a large pothole. The bump sent my forehead and eye smashing into the metal strip where my front window met the roof. Have you ever had a deep cut on your forehead? It bleeds like crazy. I had blood running down my face by the time I arrived at our front gate. To make matters worse, the night locks had been set, so I couldn't open the gate, and our guard wouldn't wake up to come open it for me. I pounded on the door, then rang the bell for a few minutes, but I had no luck getting anyone up at that hour. All the rational people were sound asleep. Our garden was surrounded by a twelve foot wall that in normal circumstances was not that hard to scale. It's a little harder with blood in your eyes, but I darn sure wasn't going to wait on the sidewalk for some nosy policeman to pass by. Up I went. I had just climbed on top of the wall when Ned Bennett came out of the house to see what the racket was about. "Ned. Up here," I called to him.

Ned saw me at the top of the wall. "Holy shit Geiger, what the hell happened to you?" he asked as he came over to stand below me.

"I had a wreck, come and help me down off this wall." Ned moved a cement planter into position, climbed on top and reached up to grab ahold of my belt. He needed little help as he lowered me down the wall. Ned was strong enough to carry me like a child.

Inside our walled garden, seen from the roof.

"We better get you inside and look at your head. You look like crap."

"Yeah, I know. But wait a minute, you gotta help me get somethin' outa the car." Ned and I opened the gate from the inside so we could go to the car and retrieve fifteen gallons of Siddiqui. Once back in the house, with the liquor safely stored away, Ned gave me a very solemn look "Man, you are nuts."

"I must be. Let's go get me cleaned up."

That's how life in the Kingdom flowed. At times a little dangerous, but not too bad as long as things didn't run out of control. I'd been there over a year when control took a holiday. Our staff house lease had expired, so we were preparing to move to temporary quarters across town. In our great wisdom, we, the residents, decided it would be better to drink all our alcohol rather than transport it. We had a great party on the last night before moving. Beer, Looney Juice, Siddiqui, wine... it was obviously much safer to consume it than risk getting caught taking it to our new home. Late into the evening, some bright boy suggested putting an abandoned car in the front foyer! That would be a fun joke. Nothing funnier than a car in your hallway, right? Lots of trashed cars out on the streets and with thirty strong men it would be easy. It was easy. We carried an old Renault up the steps, through double doors and deposited it as a present for the new occupants. Hardy cheers all around and time for bed.

We didn't like the owner of the house very much. A group of four men privately decided it would be a good idea to dump twenty pounds of powdered chlorine in the pool and pump it into the garden. That would teach the old son of a pup to mess with us. With added chlorine, the water turned white as milk and sent the smell of bleach beyond our walls. Satisfied with their work, the four joined the rest of the now quiet house in well-deserved sleep.

BAM-BAM-BAM-BAM. Rapid pounding of a fist on my door woke me at first light. As I sat up in bed, I could hear shouts as others woke to a rising scene of panic. "SOLDIERS AT THE FRONT GATE. THEY'RE COMING IN!"

Oh shit, I thought, *we're screwed now*, and threw on some clothes while heading for the courtyard. I arrived as a squad of armed troopers formed up on the patio, flanking a determined looking captain, our gate guard, and a young Saudi man in expensive robes. The Saudi pointed to the car while screaming in Arabic at one of our older residents who had apparently been drafted as our spokesman.

Our man, Barry, a tall, bearded, Yorkshireman from northern England, was patiently explaining that he didn't understand our guest. "If the young gaffer would pack in his yappin' a tad, we'll be 'appy as larks to assist 'im." Barry had not been part of the car moving but he made a fine dark ale and probably had a lot to lose should the authorities make it to his room.

The Saudi gentleman didn't calm down at all and switched to accented English. "You insult my father's house. I am to move here today and you show me it is fit only for broken old automobiles. You defile my home with alcohol. Captain, search this house." After pushing Barry and the others to the side, the captain and his troops marched through our front doors. I was still standing outside with three friends. We had a particular interest in what else might happen here. The Saudi pointed to the pool and yelled "WHO HAS TRIED TO POISON MY FAMILY?" As he continued to get more violent in his shouting, the gate guard caught my eye and held it. He drew his thumb across his throat from ear to ear, while nodding his head in a promise of what was to come. In Saudi Arabia, the gesture was not an idle expression.

Inside I found all our men gathered in the common room, under guard, as the captain tried to organize a search.

That task was not as easy as you might think. All the rooms had separate locks and several residents were out of the country on leave. One of our guys had chosen a cooler as a seat. When the captain decided to inspect that cooler, the tone of the day quickly darkened as he kicked our man to the floor for not moving fast enough. The soldiers had already found a dozen empty bottles from our previous night, but incredibly, they had yet to find any actual booze. Barry, being an all-around level-headed fellow, pledged full cooperation while negotiating permission for us to continue with our moving. He pointed out that if the owner wanted us to depart, we would need to pack and be ready to move should we be released from custody. They reluctantly agreed and although the soldiers were deadly serious in their search for contraband, they weren't very good at it. We managed to hide most of our remaining stock under the guise of preparing to leave by shifting bottles from unsearched rooms to rooms that had previously been inspected. Up one flight of stairs, down another. When a soldier passed one way, we scooted the other. Our juggling played out like a living performance of an old Marx brother's movie. We got away with it by using all our guys and smuggling small quantities on each trip. They never caught on and only confiscated a few bottles of beer for their efforts.

Still, those few bottles, along with the empties, were more than enough to put us all in jail, because that's what the owner wanted. By mid-morning, word of our fiasco had reached upper management. Soon, the ranking GSI administrator in Saudi showed up on site to take over any legal requirements. Our purchasing coordinator, a man named Rod, was acting General Manager because the rest of the important men were all out of the country. By the time he arrived, the search was over, armed guards stood at our gates and we were all under arrest. The authorities huddled up, working on a list of who should face charges and how many would go straight to prison.

For the four fools who had poisoned the pool, the stakes were far higher. We'd seen the captain pulling fingerprints from an empty chlorine can. All foreign workers are printed when they enter the country, so we assumed those responsible would soon be identified. It seemed a good time for drastic action. After finding a secluded corner, we got together to discuss prospects for the near future. None of us panicked, but all knew our situation was serious in the extreme. "The way I look at it," I began "we can wait and hope for the best or try to escape. I don't see much point in just letting them chop my head off, so I'm in favor of making a go of it."

No one disagreed, but my buddy Mark replied, "Damn Geiger, I didn't much like our last ride, but I guess I'm game to try again. We survived the first time, didn't we?"

Tim Kent, with whom I had spent a night on the roof celebrating my old roommate's release from prison, then shared information that until then he'd kept confidential. "I've got an uncle who works for the US Diplomatic Corp. He lives in consulate housing down near the airport. If we can get to his place without being followed, we should be safe for a while. He'll help us if he can."

The fourth member of our team, Doug from England, saw things differently. "No," he said. "You fellows go on without me. I'm going to carry on here, but I'll cover for you once you're off."

"Doug," I replied, "we can't leave you here. This is for real. It's dangerous."

"No, I'm not much for running," and that was all he'd say.

The three of us who wanted to run decided time was more valuable than retrieving our belongings. Tim started us moving. "Grab whatever money you've got and meet me back here in five minutes. Then we'll take a look at the guards to see what they're watching." When we returned a few minutes later, Mark and I each took a quick pass by a gate, while Tim studied things from second floor windows. "They're not really looking inside the garden," Tim said when he got back, "just hanging out at the gates so nobody leaves."

"Yeah," Mark joined in, "they look pretty bored. I don't think they're expecting anyone to go over the wall."

"Ok," Tim said, "there's a spot behind those bushes on the other side of the swimming pool that's kind of secluded. I think we should be able to climb the power pole at the corner of the pump house and make it without being seen. The bushes will cover us a little."

"Well let's get going before I chicken out," I said.

With the decision made, getting out was surprisingly easy when it came to it. We walked across the garden, climbed the wall and dropped down to a side street on the outside. My beat up Volkswagen parked at the curb half a block from the front gate sat there waiting for us. We strolled up like we owned the world, got in and drove away. The "be bold" strategy I'd learned in my younger days paid off again. Fifteen minutes later we arrived at our temporary refuge.

"Yes, you boys are definitely in a world of shit," agreed Tim's Uncle John. "I don't yet know how much, but I'll try to find out without causing a ruckus." As Uncle John worked to discover the details of our situation, Tim and Mark went to a bedroom to rest, leaving me alone with my thoughts. Thoughts that led me to the conclusion I could not run further without knowing what had happened with those I'd left behind. I told Uncle John I'd be back soon and left.

Bravery is not the absence of fear; it's being afraid and doing what's necessary anyway. In that sense Doug's decision to stay at the staff house was more brave than mine, but I found my courage soon enough to avoid regret. I returned to the scene of our foolishness. My actions were no more heroic than my two friends back at Uncle John's, just more obsessive. I needed to find out if I'd have to struggle over any tough decisions about turning myself in. Once again, I'd come to a point where the only way to address my fear of what lay ahead was to face the bear by meeting my adversity head on. For me, knowing beat the stress of uncertainty every time.

I didn't have a clear plan for what I would do when I got there, aside from somehow trying to discover what was happening, so I first made a quick pass by the house. *Son of a gun*, I thought, *the guards are gone*. When I saw some of my friends loading vehicles, I pulled over to have a quiet chat. I walked up the sidewalk thinking, *Well that's a good sign, everyone seems to be happily going about their business*. Then I heard, "Hey Geiger, where you been?" coming from Ned who was loading a truck.

"I went out for a drive in the desert. No soldiers? What's going on?"

"Aw, the whole thing's over. They dropped the charges and left. We've gotta' be packed and gone by evening."

"How'd that happen?"

"Who knows? The Saudi owner, the old man, not the son, came and told the soldiers to get lost, so they did."

"Thanks, I'll catch you later. Have you seen Doug?"

"He's already moved to the new place." I hopped into my wagon and sped off for the safe house to share this wonderful turn of events. We were all soon back in the mix of moving with few people having noticed our absence.

The whole question of courage was now moot, a situation I much preferred. Was Doug braver than me? I'm not sure. HIs timing was certainly different. Later that day, when

I'd finished moving to our temporary staff house, I talked to him about what had ended the occupation. He told me that no one who knew the real story was talking publicly, but rumors claimed two of our long time field managers cornered the building owner alone for some personal negotiation. These gentlemen had been in country for years and the owner was a former employee who understood their mettle. They *explained* to him that it would be in his best interest to make this problem go away. Should one of our guys go to jail, true or not, we would testify that we got the booze from him. Apparently they were convincing, or more likely, knew where his old skeletons lay buried because the owner then had a private meeting with the Captain in charge of our demise. A fair sum of money exchanged hands and the whole thing was forgotten.

Life's like that. Things can change from disaster to triumph in a moment. Hiding on a commode seat secured my escape back in high school. One minute I'd been flowing out to the North Sea, the next I found myself safe on deck. Possible death on an African street was avoided by acting crazy. Unfortunately, the flip side of that coin is just as true. We can be rolling along all comfy and cozy when, WHAM… our life goes spinning out of control when we're hit with some personal calamity. Our character is defined by how we react to these events.

At the end of the staff house fiasco, I was feeling very fortunate to be free considering what my actions deserved.

228

Our foolish pranks in the night came within a heartbeat of irreparably damaging several lives. I didn't quit taking risks, but for me this event finished the practice of thoughtless mischief. My last act in the staff house affair was to look up Rod and apologize for my part in putting him through such a mess. He accepted my apology, and we both got on with life in Saudi Arabia.

You might think that after such a near miss we would have curbed our activities somewhat, and I can confirm we calmed down a little because there were no more incidents with cars and no more early morning raids by the police. We did not, however, discontinue our pursuit of adult beverages, progressive entertainment and some kind of social life. With his renewed contact within the State Department, Tim had a source for good whiskey. Every day, diplomatic pouches arrive at the airport from the States. Diplomatic pouches are exempt from customs inspections, so what do you think finds its way into those pouches? The good stuff cost quite a bit, about $80.00 for a fifth of Scotch, but sometimes we'd splurge. This got me thinking I could just bring in my own. I came in and out of the country every three or four months. The customs inspectors never checked me too closely and surely wouldn't make me take my boots off. I thought, *I bet that's why mickeys come in flat, curved sided bottles. They fit so well in a boot.* The next time I arrived back from leave I had one in each of mine. For added bonus, I also smuggled in two posters of half-naked women. I had them rolled up inside a throw rug. In all honesty, as I walked the long hall from the plane to the inspection station, I was having second thoughts about the wisdom of my latest escapade. *Geez, what am I doing taking such a risk for some darn booze? It's kind of exciting ... but crap.* By then it was too late to turn around. Reverting to an old standby I put on an "I own this place" attitude while Mr. Customs Man searched through my bag. He never looked in my rug or my boots.

After a few months in temporary quarters we moved again to our new staff house. A nice five story apartment building. No walled garden but a much better facility on the inside where several of us old timers got private rooms. What heaven! With a private room I had a place to bring ladies. Too bad there were no ladies. Actually there were a few, but with a ratio of about thirty eligible men for every available women, including wayward wives, the odds of finding a girlfriend didn't look good. I don't know how I managed to be the one guy picked by Allah, but much of my time in Saudi I spent in the company of a young lady named Monika from Natchitoches, Louisiana. Monika lived outside Al Khobar with her parents, so I'd been blessed with a companion as well as an adopted family. For that I was grateful. December 1976 is the only Christmas I've ever spent away from my own family. Good fortune allowed me to spend it with hers.

The new staff house also had a new pub needing drink and decoration. With more room than our previous establishment, the possibilities for enhancement were intriguing and the topic of much discussion but little action. This didn't sit well with me, so one evening over a fine jar of Siddiqui and Coke I pitched an idea to my old friend Mark. "What this place needs is a casino," I said. "We could set up tables there at the end of the bar."

"A casino?" Mark questioned. "Have you lost your mind? They arrest you for that! Besides, who's gonna run it? Who's gonna be the bank?"

"Why, we will of course."

"Not me. No way. We don't know anything about running a casino."

"I do," I replied. "I've been to lots of them. They're all pretty much the same."

"Well good, 'cause you're on your own."

Which I was, because I couldn't get anyone else interested either. *Hell*, I thought, *if I'm going to take so many chances in this crazy country, I might as well make some money doing it*. Besides, from the house point of view it's not really a game of chance at all. It's a game of odds, and all the odds are in the house's favor. I had a suspicion that running a whole casino by myself might be more than I wanted to attempt and concluded that starting with just one game would be best.

The easiest game, with the least investment in equipment, seemed to be Blackjack. With a small table, a yard of green felt, and two decks of cards, I started a nightly Blackjack game in our pub, using the same rules as the casinos. I kept the stakes low, $5.00 maximum bet, to prevent any major damage to a player's wallet and my health. Then I sat down behind my Blackjack table and entered the gambling business. Customers, mostly guys in transition to or from a field crew, arrived the first night and every night I was open thereafter. I wasn't always busy, but it was steady. Nor did I come out a winner each time I opened, but over the course of the first week my profit was amazing. With three weeks under my belt as an entrepreneur, I could see why Vegas made it so big. I was making a steady income of hundreds of dollars with just one table. That's when I got worried. *You know, with this much money coming in, sooner or later somebody's gonna get upset. When upset guys are also drunk, they can get violent. What am I going to do then? Is the money worth the consequence?* No, it was not. I guess that's why I never became a successful business owner. I always saw the potential downside. The next night I quietly shut the game down, pleading laziness in response to complaints I got from customers over the following weeks.

As I remember these days of adventure in Saudi Arabia, I'm roused to question why I've shied from the risks of business, while being tolerant of other risks that seemed like a routine part of everyday life. Just leaving home was a risk. After twenty-two continuous months without once setting foot in an English speaking country, I returned to the States for Christmas, then back to Saudi for another dose of foreign commotion. I know I didn't seek risk. It was simply an occasional complication triggered by other things I wanted to accomplish. I'd been living on my own much of the past eleven years and felt bulletproof. A legend in my own mind. Getting away with a bold move here, a foolish decision there, or a brush with death, reinforced my feelings of invincibility. I think this is a process common to many. It's not until we've suffered a few casualties that reality can worm its way into our consciousness. Then, if we're not careful, we become timid old loafers, too afraid to risk our comfort in any new adventure. The trick is to find a good balance somewhere in between.

On June 17, 1978, I left Saudi for the final time. My stay in the desert had ended, along with my three year journey through lands unknown. Like that kid on the last day of his first summer away, I was tired. I longed for the familiar comforts of home. Not the temporary places I'd been hanging my hat for three years, but the home in my heart. The home where I had roots, old friends, and memories. Even the lure of travel to exotic places had faded for me. At home, I'd be on leave every night and every weekend. At home, I'd be able to plan for the future, start a family. Today, I can still feel the joy of boarding that plane out of Saudi, knowing I was on my way home. A challenging chapter completed, a new story waiting to be written. Truly one of the happiest moments of my life.

14

August 1978

Dear Taidy,

    Let the bells ring out and the banners fly. I'm home, I'm home, I'm home. Just three years out of college and I've got stories to curl your old gray hair. I've done more, seen more and lived more than many will find in a lifetime. Thank God I'm home.

    But man I'm worn out. I need to rest, dry out from too much bad booze and mischief. Find some peace. I've been thinking back to those guys at the marina who only cared about beer, laughs and sex. Am I becoming them? I need to reconnect with the more decent aspects of my character. It's time to consider life's bigger questions. All those months overseas… I'd get homesick. I'd think about where I'd rather be and long to go off in the woods somewhere. Try finding that in a desert. I figure if I want to be alone to work things out, it's hard to beat a trip to Shark Lake. That's where I'll find water, blue sky and solitude

    My parents moved to New York after Dad finished his project in Brazil. I'll have to find a canoe and some gear, but maybe Fred has some. I wonder if Dad can come with me? Probably not. He's fifty-eight now and pretty busy at work. Besides, much as I love him, I really want to be alone.

Rog

Longing for a trip with little chance of human contact soon turned to planning and then saw me heading to Shark Lake. Dad and I had been there a dozen times and had never seen another boat on the lake, let alone other campers. All I had to do was work out how to get there. I owned no gear of my own, so I borrowed everything, including a car and canoe, from Fred and Dad. My father was not overly enthusiastic about me going off for four days on my own. I'd survived three years in the far corners of the world. A trip to the Canadian bush didn't seem like a great challenge. When I pointed this out to Dad he countered, "Yes, and there you always had people nearby to lend a hand. Up at Shark there's nobody and no way to call for help."

"Dad," I said, "I'm twenty-five, I'll be careful. I've done the trip lots of times with you. I even went once with Jeff and Steve. That might have been more dangerous than going by myself."

"Well I can't argue your point, but the backwoods is no place to mess around, especially when you're alone. At least set a time for when you'll be back. If you're late, we can send somebody looking."

"OK, I'll be on the lake four nights. When I come out, I ought to be back to the car by 3:00. I'll call as soon a I find a pay phone."

After an early start from Toronto, three hours on the highway, plus a few dirt roads, led me to the sandy parking area on the south end of Coon Lake. The day was still young and the weather fair. A cool breeze blowing in off the lake smelled like heaven and carried an aura of calm I'd been missing for years. Research proves nature is a tonic. In 2015, an article in *The Atlantic* magazine proclaimed, "Exposure to nature has been shown repeatedly to reduce stress and boost well-being." Times I've spent on a secluded lake or in the woods always seemed to strengthen my spirit.

It didn't take long to secure everything on board and head out. My canoe sat low in the water, trailing only a long V to mark our passage up the lake. Soon we were lost from view by any watching from shore. My small boat and I leaving the world behind as we merged with the surrounding forest. It felt good to be back.

With paddling and portages, it took several hours to traverse five lakes on the way to the island campsite on Shark. There's no break for slacking because once you get there you still have to set up camp, lay in some firewood and make dinner. But summer days are long up north. I had plenty of time to get settled in, with enough daylight remaining to throw a few casts and land a couple of nice bass.

Back at camp that first night, I sat beside the campfire smelling forest air and listening to the wild sounds of the woods. The lonely call of a loon, bullfrogs boasting along the shore, the song of howling wolves way off across the lake. I was happier than I'd been in months. I felt the stress of too much travel, too much work, and too much play follow the sparks of my fire up to the stars. Certain I was alone, I dug a harmonica out of my pack and did my best to add to the lively song of the night. I found some of the peace I'd come looking for as I sat there staring at the flames.

Next morning I woke bright and early to another beautiful day. The air blew cool through a clear sky, and the sun sparkled off a ripple of small waves stirred up by the breeze. I closed my eyes to listen, noting sounds and smells that I might take for granted with the normal pace of life. Water lapping against rocks, wind through leaves, a Jay boasting, coffee perking in its pot. The scent of pine, earth, water, and blueberries. I was surrounded by nature and felt a part of it. The more at one with the forest I imagined myself to be, the more I enjoyed my solitude.

Around noon, as I was surveying the beauty of the lake from my island home, I noticed something exceedingly strange. Three canoes, coming down a small river and entering the lake from the north. I vaguely recalled a portage that hit this stream from miles off in the distance, but that route was difficult. The round trip from parking to Shark Lake and back was too long to make it worthwhile. No one ever came in from the north! Then again, no one had ever come in from any direction while I was on the lake. After invading my solitude, the newcomers set up camp in a small meadow under large maples. Across the lake on my little island, I guessed they wouldn't bother me much. Without giving them more thought, I finished my day as I had the last and enjoyed another good night. Those wolves I'd listened to the evening before seemed to be closer. I was glad to be on an island.

There are only two places on Shark Lake worth fishing. One of those places is where the north stream comes into the lake, close to where my new neighbors had camped. I was curious about them anyway, so the next morning I decided that was the spot I should fish. I know I can be odd at times, but this bunch of travelers blew the top off the strange bucket. As I watched, one camper was bonking her companion on the head with a stick. Another young fellow, who was wading in the lake with his backside toward me, figured it would be a good time to drop his britches! He didn't so much moon me as a statement of disrespect, he just judged they were no longer needed and let them go. Two others were trying to stop a third from throwing everything out of their pack, and the last of their bunch was sitting in the middle of it all crying.

I'm no stranger to weird events, so I took this all in stride, but it got me wondering exactly what the hell was going on over there. I watched a little closer. There were nine campers, all of whom were young, all of whom were way too far from home and six of whom obviously had issues. The other three had to be their chaperones, which, from what I'd seen, appeared to be cause for concern.

I had to decide. Should I paddle back across the lake to the other spot that's worth fishing and hope I didn't read about this expedition in next week's paper, or should I go over to their camp and see if they needed assistance? As I was asking the fish their opinion, one leader started frantically jumping up and down, waving her arms in my direction while motioning for me to come over. Being a young fellow in good health, I couldn't help but notice how some of this cute young lady's attributes bounced appealingly as she tried to get my attention. Solitude is all well and fine, but some priorities have limits. I decided a closer look might be interesting and paddled up to a landing place on their beach. As I stepped out of the canoe, her frantic waving turned into frantic conversation. "Hi, I'm Mary. We're lost and we've lost our map. I don't know how to find where we're going. Can you help us?"

"Well," I replied with doubts nibbling at the edge of my charitable nature, "I know where I am, and I know how to get home. I guess I could help you." By this time a small crowd had gathered round us, and several pairs of eye were looking at me with a disturbing degree of hope. *Geez*, I thought, *I'm a doodlebugger not a forest ranger, and some of these kids look a lot like those boys Tom used to hire. They're a bunch of Hooples.* Recalling my experiences with state school inmates on my cousin's dairy farm, I was not all that comfortable around some of these campers. Really, I was starting to get damn nervous. I became aware of a rather insistent tug on my sleeve, so I turned to look down into two squinty eyes in a little round face. The owner of those eyes said in a crusty kind of voice, "My name Winnie. Who you?"

"Hi Winnie, my name's Roger. I'm camping on that Island over there across the lake." The top of Winnie's head didn't even make it to my chin. When we talked, she had to look up, making wisps of blond hair fly around in the breeze. With puffy cheeks, a button nose and eyes that sparkled with their own kind of smile, she was about the cutest thing I'd seen in years. "Do you like camping Winnie?"

"Ya."

"Did you see me paddle over in my canoe?"

"Ya."

"Is this your campsite Winnie?"

"Ya."

"Could I have my sleeve back now?"

"Ya."

Oh great, I thought, *just when I should be running from the "weird" kids, I kind of like one of em. Besides, anyone who's scared of this angel is nuts.*

I realized my conversation with Winnie wasn't going anywhere so, detaching myself from her attention, I returned to Mary, the evident leader of the band. "Um, how did you get lost?" I asked.

"It was Martin's fault," she replied, pointing to the short, round faced, squinty eyed lad who looked an awful lot like Winnie. "He lost the map. At least we guess he did because it was in his pack and now it's not. Yesterday, as we were hiking between lakes, Martin was about three quarters of the way up a big rock hill when he decided he no longer required a pack. He took it off. RIGHT THERE ON THE SIDE OF THE HILL! He kept going up, and the pack rolled back down, on its own, with things falling out all the way. We found Martin walking along the trail without a pack, and we found his pack at the bottom of the hill with our belongings strewn everywhere. I'd imagine the map never got picked up to be returned to the pack. We came in over several lakes up North and we're supposed to meet our ride south of here somewhere."

"I lost my pa-ack. I lost my pa-ack. I lost my pa-ack," Martin sang as he marched in circles around us.

"ALEX, can you gather them up and move them along for me? Um, me and..."

"Roger."

"Roger and I need to chat."

I noticed that no one was going anywhere, including the camp counselors, so I asked "Do you remember if you were supposed to end up at Coon Lake? That's where I came in, and it's the only other way to get here."

Mary took my arm and walked us away from the group far enough for a more private conversation. "I don't know, damn it. The others are starting to think I'm a complete incompetent. Do you have a map?"

"No, but I know the way well enough that I don't need one."

"When were you planning to leave?" she asked with a smile.

"In a couple of days."

"AUGH, that's no good. We have to meet our ride tomorrow. Could you possibly give me directions?"

"Well," I replied, "it's not too difficult if you've done it before, but it would be kind of hard to describe." I guess my answer was not too helpful because she looked at me like I was a real dip.

Our conversation withered on the vine at that point, but one of the other leaders, Louis, walked over to join in. "So, like, that was you we saw camped on the island last night? We saw your fire too, eh."

I nodded my head.

"Yeah, we picked up on your harp too, man. Pretty cool. But we thought we heard dogs howling, ya know? Did 'ya hear em?"

I nodded my head again, "I heard them both nights I've been here. I suspect they're wolves."

With that, Mary gave Louis a good 'Told you so' look, so I added, "I wouldn't worry much. Ontario wolves are sort of small. More like coyotes. I've never heard of anyone being hurt by them." I don't think I was much encouragement because they all moved off toward their tents, which presented me with an excellent opportunity to make an exit. I considered just walking over to my canoe and wishing them good luck as I paddled away, but decided that would be bad form. I mean, what kind of guy would leave a bunch of novices alone to fend for themselves when they're lost? Not this one; so I followed them back to their camping area. Besides, I liked it when Mary held onto my arm. Apparently, I'd stayed in Saudi, the place with few women, too long.

It was a nice campsite, although a little buggy, and I'm not sure why we had never stayed there. Dad looked at it the first time we found Shark Lake, but then moved on to our island. Habit I guess; less bugs and the island was closer to the best fishing hole. Dad and I used to call that spot Hugey Bay because we caught huge bass there. Once, I landed two seventeen inch bass on one lure, at the same time. That's the beauty of fishing, you never know what the next cast will bring, and I've always loved it. Psychology calls it the principle of intermittent reinforcement. You're not successful every time, but the more often you are, the more you want to make it happen again. As far back as I can remember, fishing has meant satisfaction and joy. It's all tied up with good times spent with Dad, my love of the outdoors, and the immediate reward of achieving a simple goal. I understand some people are bored by it, and I admit time can pass slowly when the fish aren't biting. I do my best to avoid that.

The campsite my new neighbors had chosen was nice, with flat, sandy ground and a few logs set up like benches around a large fire pit. It was on these logs that the counselors and I sat to continue our conversation.

"So, what are you going to do now?" I asked, hoping to encourage them to work it out for themselves. Mary gave self-help a good try.

They looked at each other, looked at me and Mary said, "If you can tell us how to get out, we can write it down on something and try to make our way tomorrow."

I blew out a sigh and thought about how difficult that would be. The portages were poorly marked, and I remembered how turned around Dad and I got the first time we came in this far. With this group of day camp counselors, it could be a disaster. Not to mention their six protégées. While sitting contemplating how to get out of this, I noticed Martin take a big two-footed jump over by the shore. As I watched, he'd jump, stand there a few seconds looking at the ground and then jump again, all the while laughing. I stood up and walked over to him, to ask, "What'ya doin Martin?"

He looked at me with his little eyes wide open and whispered, "Frog".

"You're a frog?" I asked confused, "or do you see a frog?"

"Frog," he repeated much louder and made another great jump, splashing into the wet sand along their little beach. I watched for a while longer with great amusement, considering how much I enjoyed the two kids I'd just met, then returned to Mary and the others. About then my other new friend, Winnie, sat down beside me and said, "Hi. Time for lunch? You like lunch?" Her round little face was without a care and full of smiles, but it was too much for me. These kids had personalities; they were interesting and not at all scary. Best of all, I liked them. Winnie, Martin and the other kids were obviously somewhat helpless. Their leaders didn't have the knowledge to guide them safely, and I couldn't leave my new friends to the wolves so to speak.

"Ok," I said, "I'll guide you back to the Coon Lake parking area." That seemed to generate excitement, and soon everyone was having a small celebration there around a cold fire pit. Mary was particularly relieved and thanked me several times for coming to their rescue. I noticed that Louis didn't seem too thrilled by the attention she was giving me. Maybe he and Mary had something going, or he wished it were so. I didn't give him much thought. I did think about Mary a little, hoping a hug or something from her might be in order, but all I got was a polite pat on the back. Not to worry, I wasn't doing this to inspire her affection anyway. With the day half spent, and figuring it would take them a while to break camp and pack up, I suggested we aim at leaving first thing the following day. The three leaders agreed that would be fine. Our plan was settled. I stepped into my canoe and pushed off, promising to meet them there at about 7:00 the next morning.

After a quick lunch back on the island, I thought about what to do on the last afternoon of a shortened trip. *You know,* I said to myself, *you might try chatting up the pretty girl, or you could go off chasing fish.* My priorities may have gotten distracted from time to time, but they were well established. I chose fishing. My thoughts then turned to what I had committed to do. I was a little disappointed about leaving early, but fairly inspired about being able to do a good deed. Reward seemed unlikely, and that was fine with me. I didn't want a reward and had one been offered, I would have had to refuse. Sometimes doing what's right is its own reward. Anything I received from others would cheapen the experience.

At my campfire that evening, I pondered why I was afraid of people with mental problems and felt discomfort about my attitude prior to this trip. With such limited involvement in the area, I had little to go on, but suspected Raymond from the state school had soured my opinion of the whole group. Besides, I seemed to fear any strangers who were different from me. *Funny how that's worked in my life. Once I become acquainted with a few individuals from a new circle of people, the rest are less scary. Then I learn to enjoy the company of many others I might never have known. Only in ignorance have I chosen to avoid the experience.* After that bit of philosophical revelation, I needed a rest. Later, while crawling into my sleeping bag for the night, I thanked God for continued good weather, asked Him to please keep it nice for at least another day and went to sleep.

The next morning again broke clear and bright. I was pleasantly surprised to find everyone ready and waiting across the lake. Mary, Winnie and Martin greeted my arrival. "Good morning," I called from the canoe, then pointed west. "We'll be going that way till we reach the end. You'll be faster than me, so take it easy." With two paddling in each of their craft, I figured I'd have to hustle to stay with them. Au contraire mon ami. They zig-zagged down the lake like water bugs chased by a duck. I constantly had to slow down to wait for them. Admittedly, their bow-men didn't have the best of attention spans, but it was hard for the counselors to keep their canoes straight because they had little notion of how to steer and paddle at the same time. My reputation as a woodsman ticked up a notch when they saw I didn't change sides when I paddled, yet kept a straight course. Basic instructions on paddling and steering improved our progress considerably. We soon made it to the end of the lake and the first of our portages.

Shark Lake is the fifth lake in a string starting at Coon. That meant we'd have to cross four portages. Two are short, but the others are over half a mile. This first one out of Shark was a long one. The trail head looked small for four canoes and ten people. With large helpings of patience, we got everything on shore where we could load up to start hiking. The portage path varied from packed dirt to rock covered slopes with a few crossings of large granite outcroppings the size of a house. When camping at Shark Lake I used just two packs. One large and one small. That way I finished the portage in two trips. The first time with the small pack and the canoe, and the second with the other pack plus any extra hand carried items. As I was preparing to head out, Mary looked at me with a puzzled expression and asked, "Um, how do you get all your stuff to the next lake?"

"Well," I said, "I carry it. How do you get yours to the next lake?"

"Oh, we carry it too, but there's three of us who can carry a canoe. Two of us carry one canoe and we make three trips. The kids carry most of the packs and bags. How do you do it by yourself?"

"I just put the canoe on my shoulders and carry it. Pretty easy unless there's a wind. Wind will blow you around a bit. I guess you carry yours right side up like you paddle it?"

"Ah, yeah."

"That's the hard way. Let's see if one of you can carry it by yourself." I showed them how to lash up a yoke with their paddles and use a towel for a shoulder pad. After doing the same with my canoe, I rested the bow upside down on a tree branch and easily ducked under with my head between the paddles. "Lift the canoe with your shoulders and move it off the branch when you get your balance worked out. Once everything feels right, start walking." Only Louis was confident enough to try carrying a canoe solo. Everyone shouldered their gear and off we went with me in the lead, leaving the rest of our supplies in a stack near the trailhead. Our progress so far had been limited, and I tried to set a fast pace. It was not to be. These folks were slow, especially Alex and Mary who carried a canoe together. I called to Louis behind me, "I'm moving on to the next lake. I'll catch you on the way back."

After laying my canoe along shore at the far trailhead and taking a quick drink from the lake, I headed back up the path to retrieve more baggage. Our little parade stretched out along most of the trail. Louis was doing well enough with his canoe, but the two counselors carrying a canoe together had only made it half way. It seems backwards, but carrying a canoe with arm strength alone really is more difficult, even with two people. In the interest of getting to our final destination before dark, I volunteered to carry their third canoe on my return trip.

My next encounter on this trail of comedy was Martin, the young fellow who had lost their map to begin with. He was plodding along up the face of a steep rock slope at a turtle's pace, and no wonder! Martin was about five feet tall and his pack had to weigh sixty pounds. The stocky little guy, bent over, carrying a big green canvas pack, was not only as slow as a turtle, he kind of looked like one. No surprise he had dumped it earlier on their trip. He made it to the top of the hill but as he did, he slipped on a patch of loose pebbles and fell down, rolling onto his back. The weight of his pack took over, lifting him off the ground, while his arm and legs clawed at the air. Sure enough, just like a turtle he couldn't get himself righted again. I should have given him aid a little quicker, but I failed. The image in my mind of Martin the turtle was too darn funny. After a couple of moments, I got myself under control and walked over to help him. As he tried to flip over I said, "Martin, yesterday you were playing frog, today you're playing turtle. Let's get you back on your feet." We had to work his arms out of the pack straps to get him upright again, then dust him off and load the pack onto his back. Martin wasn't as happy with his current situation as he had been with the frog so we didn't discuss the incident further. He looked at me out of the corners of his eyes and mumbled what I took to be a thank you.

After that, I completed two more trips across the portage. One with their canoe and another with my remaining supplies. In order to save time, I refused their offers of help on the last trip so I was the last to show up at the end of the trail. All our gear was securely stowed in canoes, sitting in the water, with bows resting on shore. They were learning. My troop of friends, however, were not yet willing to go. All of them, counselors and kids, wanted to welcome me, shake my hand, and pat my back. I've got to admit this was one of the proudest moments of my life. While waiting for me to arrive, the gang had been talking about all the things I seemed to be capable of out in the woods. My status as an outdoorsman was elevated to frontier mountain man. They raised my reputation to be on par with legends like Daniel Boone and Davy Crockett and I loved it. Still no hugs from Mary though.

The rest of the day was much the same as it had started. Paddling, portages and beautiful weather. Late in the afternoon, we made it to the parking area on Coon Lake where their transportation was waiting for them. Everyone again thanked me. As we loaded our gear into cars, I only had a few moments to say goodbye. Mary assured me she had an interest in meeting again soon, then all of us were on our way back to Toronto. The last I saw of Martin and Winnie, they were waving goodbye through the rear seat window of a big station wagon. Sadly, my fame as a guide was fleeting, and I never heard from Mary, nor saw any of her group of campers again.

My sister once commented that I'd made a habit of aiding women in distress. The sales lady at Canadian Tire, an English nurse on a Mediterranean island, and now a trip leader lost in the Ontario wilderness. "Do you think your actions in some way relate back to the woman you didn't help?" She asked. "That woman who you saw raped in the back seat of a car?"

"I don't know," I replied. "I'm sure I didn't consciously have her in mind when I helped the others. I guess I've never considered it until now. If coming to the aid of anyone, man, woman or child, is an opportunity thrust before me, I hope I'll do what's needed if I can. Wouldn't everyone?"

15

February 24th, 1980

Dear Taidy

You won't believe it, but I'm skiing way down south in New Mexico. No kidding! I'm in a place called Red River, at a great little ski resort. Sure, it's not the Alps or Vermont, but not too shabby for being a short trip from Dallas. A friend of mine, who worked for GSI in Saudi, invited me to come with him on a excursion put on by Dallas Snowchasers ski charters. Gary and I flew from Dallas to Amarillo, then took a bus from there to Red River. Get this… they had a keg of beer on the bus! Don't guess you'd find that in Canada. Down here, they measure distance in beers. When I asked a buddy how far it was to Oklahoma, he said, "Oh, about a six-pack I reckon." I've even seen cops drinking a beer with lunch at a hamburger drive-in named Keller's.

Gary mentioned the last guy who skied with him met a girl and ended up getting married. Not to worry. That'll never happen to me. I did meet a girl on the bus though. She and her friend Sandra sat in the seats behind Gary and me. Her first name is Jerre, but I keep forgetting that so I call her by her last name, Parker. Only in Texas would they name a girl Jerre. She's a fox and can drink more beer than I can! It's a long ride from Amarillo to Red River, so after about five hours of talking and drinking, Parker and I were becoming really friendly. Then I sort of had to take a nap. My nap lasted until we got to our ski lodge and when I woke up, she was already off the bus. I lost her.

A little thing like not knowing her room number didn't stop me. The hotel had outside walkways in front of all the rooms. I strolled along through the snow on the walk yelling, "PARKER! PARKER! WHERE THE HELL ARE YA, PARKER?" After a while, just as I passed a door on the third floor, it opened behind me. A long arm reached out of the room, grabbed me by my coat collar and yanked me inside. It was Parker, and she wasn't exactly happy about her name being screamed throughout the hotel. I, on the other hand, love it when a plan works out so well. Guess she got over it pretty quick. When I asked her to dinner, she accepted. Too bad for me that's all our evening amounted to. A meal and see ya later, cowboy.

By dumb luck, Gary and I ate breakfast at the same restaurant as Parker and Sandra. They let us join them, so I figured I was on a roll. I'd eaten two meals in a row with the same beautiful lady. Parker claims I also invited her to dinner last night but stood her up. I reckon confusion, brought on by wishful thinking, got to her. To work my way back into her good graces, I bought us drinks at the hotel bar and promised to take her to breakfast. Parker must be some kind of puritan or something. I've tried my charming best to get romantic, but all we do together is eat and talk. No encouragement for making out from this woman.

When I went to her room this morning, she was just finishing up putting her clothes on. I found her lying flat on her back *across the bed, trying to zip her tight jeans. "I don't get what the deal is here," she said, "but I'm havin' a real hard time getting into these pants."*

My face broke into a wide grin as I cocked my head to look her in the eyes. "I know what you mean," I replied, "I'm having the same problem." I think she kind of liked my little joke. Maybe I'll see her again back in Dallas.

Rog

By the end of August, 1978, I'd packed up my few possessions and moved to Texas. I never dreamed it would become my home for the rest of my life. Fortunately, I learned Texans are a friendly bunch. Good, sensible people, who welcomed strangers. Some of them, like Parker, I got to know well. When I arrived, I thought it was just another state. Kind of like Florida, but with more cowboy hats. Several locals set me straight. The state of Texas is an independent republic that agreed to "partner up" with all the other states, in 1845. Although fiercely American, many native Texans owe allegiance to Texas before all else. My first year or two, I occasionally found it to be as foreign a country as any I'd visited overseas.

Employment waited for me at GSI's headquarters in Dallas where I had accepted a position in their marine data processing center. My job was to make maps from all the navigation details sent in from seismic vessels. For the first time in my life, I rented a place of my own rather than living in accommodations provided by family, school or my employer.

The apartment stood within a loosely defined neighborhood known as "Single City." The whole area teemed with young people, falling in and out of lust, as they rode waves of success through the late 1970's. With pleasant landscaping, a play pool and clubhouse, my new home boasted all the amenities desired by unattached professionals. Holly Hills' claim to fame grew out of providing lodging for rookie Dallas Cowboys. These residents stayed around until they got cut from the team or finished building their million dollar homes.

My first encounter with a professional football player came during an open party at the clubhouse. After excusing myself from a place at the bar to visit the restroom, I returned to find a very large man occupying my chair. I could no longer reach my drink, so I politely said, "Excuse me, but I think you're sitting in my seat."

"Oh, sorry guy," the friendly fellow replied as he stood. "Here, you siddown. I can stan'."

I thanked him and resumed my spot at the bar. Prior to coming to Dallas, football and I were only casual acquaintances. I'd watched some Super Bowl games during college, but had lost track of the game while at sea and in Saudi. As I sat there sipping my drink, I noticed everyone at the party seemed impressed with the Goliath who'd just vacated my chair. As soon as the surrounding fuss died down a little, I caught his attention. "Wow, you seem to be fairly popular here. What's your name?"

"Well, I'm Larry Bethea," he smiled proudly.

"Well, I'm Roger Geiger. Glad to meet ya." We shook hands while I asked, "Where do you work?"

"Ah, I play ball. With the Cowboys. Where you from man?"

Texas summers are hot. They're not nearly as hot as Saudi Arabia. To save money, I bought a car without air conditioning. It wasn't all that bad until the temperature passed my body temperature. Above ninety-eight degrees, open windows didn't help. In compensation for summer's heat, most of the time winters are marvelous. On New Year's Eve 1978, it was not. We got hit by the worst ice storm in thirty years. Cracking booms woke me the first morning of 1979 as tree branches crashed to the ground. From my balcony I looked out onto a winter wonderland surpassing anything I'd ever seen. An inch of ice covered everything. With almost no traffic, the normal noise of the city turned silent. It even smelled like winter. Raw air blew in the door, all crisp and new. I enjoyed the scene for several minutes before the sounds of icy wreckage tweaked my brain. *Should I check my car?*

What a mess! My little blue hatchback, encased in ice, sat under a thick limb. The branch had done no real damage because it remained attached high in the tree. Boughs large and small acted like a giant cage trapping the car. Only a few of the smaller branches broke loose when I pulled on them. *How am I gonna' move the whole thing? Cut it into little pieces?*

I worked to break branches out of the ice for several minutes. Soon, one of the football players walked out of our building complex and came over to take a look. "You know anyone with a chainsaw?" I asked.

"Unh-uh. Les' see if we can heft it." We put our backs under the limb and strained to lift. It didn't budge. The whole mess remained glued to the ground with ice. "Me an' a bunch uh ma' buddies are fixin' to watch the Irish wup up on Houston in the Cotton Bowl. They got in las' night an' stayed over. Hold up a space an' I'll round em up."

As my new friend hustled back to the building, I chipped enough ice to crack the door open and squeeze inside. The car started like it enjoyed icy mornings. I gunned the engine to get heat while waiting for my rescuer to return. When I saw him in the mirror, I got out. He was not alone. Behind him, a dozen athletes followed to help. They had me climb back into the car while the team ducked under various branches and lifted. The limb shook, ice shattered and in one mighty heave, the whole mess came off the ground. Once they had raised it to the full extent of their arms, my friend yelled, "BACK IT UP." I backed out from under the tree and through the huddle of players without doing damage to anyone. After I was safely out, they dropped the broken part of the tree, then gave a little cheer. You won't read about it the record books, but on New Year's' morning, 1979, the Cowboys beat the Ice.

"Can I buy you guys a coffee or something?" I asked in amazement.

"Nah, we're cool," one of them replied. "Happy New Year!"

The following spring, I bought a house in Plano, a suburb north of Dallas. Donn Eyman had given up grad school and signed on with GSI, so he and Dave Clarke joined me as boarders. Our reunion didn't last long. Donnie and Clarkie spent most of their time traveling the world. Three weeks after moving in, GSI asked me to take a temporary assignment in Calgary. Temporary lasted until late October.

In both Texas and Canada, finding female companionship, for a night or a handful of weeks, was more difficult than I'd hoped, but I often prospered. Few of them struck me as likely partners for the future. My relationships with two exceptions, a Canadian woman and a German fraulein, ended badly. The others didn't resonate with those aspects of good character I'd sought on an island on Shark Lake. When I met Parker the following February, I already had two casual girlfriends in Dallas. I never saw either of them again. The day after our return from skiing, Jerre and I started dating regularly. Within three weeks we were together almost daily. I'd never met anyone with whom I felt so close. One evening, while sitting on my back porch, I asked her, "Parker, do you suppose it's possible to love someone after knowing them just three weeks?" Her amorous response suggested she agreed it could happen.

Jerre Lynn Parker, is a sixth generation Texan from Hughes Springs, a small town so far east it's almost in Louisiana. Her father, "Big George" Parker, wanted to learn more about the boy she was dating. They called him Big George for good reason. He was a large, no-nonsense kind of guy. Sitting at the formica-topped table in a kitchen paneled with old knotty pine, he asked her, "Now Sister, just what does this fella do for a livin'?"

"I don't recall he ever told me what he does, Daddy. I think he must deal drugs or somethin'. He's always travelin' around the world, skiing and partyin' and stuff." Parker enjoyed messing with her father. She never set the record straight, but I'm sure he knew she was teasing. I can be confident in this assumption because when I finally visited the Parker home, George didn't shoot me. He kept a shotgun behind the kitchen door and a small pistol in his pocket. Once I got used to Jerre's tough Texan father, I liked him.

Mrs. Parker, a quiet woman with a ready smile, rarely uttered a harsh word. She was the opposite of George. People used to say, "If you want to see how a woman will act after she's married, look to her mother." Jerre's mother took care of her home and family with the heart of a willing servant.

By mid-summer, I was arguing with myself. *Don't bring up marriage, things are fine as they stand."*

Yeah, but what about the future? What about those intentions of evolving and growing?

Forget it… getting married is a big risk.

What about kids? I love kids. I'd be a great father. Kids are what life's all about.

No! It's too scary! Once you're in, that's it. No turning back.

Face the bear, coward. I'm gonna' do it.

Jerre's parents had become used to the idea of me as a potential son-in-law. George even introduced me as his daughter's fiancé a few times until I asked him to stop. "George! You can't call me that until I ask her. We talked about it once, but we're not ready yet. As soon as we get there, I'll let you know." Several weeks later, the Parkers decided to come to Dallas for a visit. My mind refused to leave me in peace. *You love Jerre, and she loves you. Go for it.* The opportunity to make our relationship official inspired me to action.

Dave and Donn were both out of the country, so I invited the Parkers to come to my house. Three bedrooms allowed sleeping arrangements even a Baptist would approve. George didn't like to stray from Hughes Springs for long. As he walked in the front door, he told Jerre they could only stay one night. "We got to get home for church Sunday mornin'."

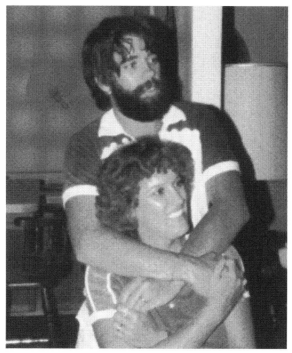
Roger & Jerre, circa 1981.

Alrighty then… tonight I ask her.

By the time Mr. and Mrs. Parker went to bed, panic had all but eliminated my ability to speak. If I'd tried to propose by going down on one knee and looking lovingly into Jerre's eyes, I would have seized up completely. Instead, I offered her a back rub. I realize straddling your intended's back with her lying face down beneath you is not the traditional position for such an important question. At least I was on my knees. Slipping a small box containing a large diamond out of my pocket, I lay it on the floor in front of her and mumbled, "Wanna' marry me?" Ten minutes later, her parents were awake and joining us in a toast of champagne.

Although the Parkers seemed pleased with the idea, word of our plans caused Jerre's father sharp questions from his co-workers at Lone Star Steel. "George, what the hell you doin' lettin' your daughter marry a damn Yankee?"

"Yankee?" He'd reply happily. "He's a durn foreigner!"

Two days after Christmas, Jerre and I married. Steve, Donnie, Clarkie, and Taid stood with me to make sure I made it through the ceremony. Big George bet me ten dollars he would show up at the wedding rehearsal in overalls. I lost. The bill I used to pay him off went into a frame with his daughter's graduation picture. It rested there, displayed on the mantle over his fireplace, until the day he died.

16

July 2, 1983

Dear Taidy,

    Security guards are such a pain. Some doofus rent-a-cop tried to stop me from parking in a space reserved for emergency vehicles only. What'd he think I was doing at the hospital, having a picnic? Before we left home, the doctor had told Jerre to come to this hospital instead of the one we'd planned on because, "Your baby is coming like it or not. Presby's the best facility anywhere for preemies. Go NOW! I'll meet you down there." I let the old guard yell at me and left my truck where it was.

    Although the outside help didn't hear about it, apparently we were expected inside because Jerre got set up in a labor room without a lot of fuss and delay. I tried to stay out of the way. One nurse, who had been in three times, clearly became a little put out with me. "Why aren't you helping her?" she demanded, with Jerre moaning and groaning on the gurney behind her.

    "Ah, help her do what?" I asked.

    "You need to be doing what they taught you in baby school!"

    "Oh… well, our first class is next Tuesday."

    After that she approached me with more sympathy. "Look, just get her to concentrate on something on the wall and make her keep breathing. That's about all there is to it." I tried to do as instructed. Jerre grew louder, and staff scurried all over the place.

When Jerre's doctor came, they kicked me out while he got down to business. A couple minutes later, the doors burst open as they rushed her off to delivery. The nurse refused to let me go with her because I never took baby classes. "Sorry, no classes, no delivery room," she said. "That's the rule."

Good thing the doctor gets to veto that rule. When he spoke up saying, "No, allow him to come in. He needs to be there." I was given a gown and shown how to sanitize my hands. Still waiting to get into delivery, I thought about what he'd said. "Now why was the doctor so quick to say I need to be in there? Why did those nurses look at me and change their attitude so fast? What the hell are they waiting for?" Then I felt my limbs turn cold as a seed of fear tried to blossom into panic. "Oh jeez... They think maybe this will be my only chance. They think our baby might not make it! We lost our first one before he got started and now this one too? Jerre won't survive if we lose another."

A nurse poked her head out the door and waved for me. "Mr. Geiger, we're ready. You can join us now."

I'd worried myself sick, but I couldn't very well leave Jerre on her own. I darn sure wanted to be part of my child's life no matter how long that life survived. The staff pointed to a place behind my wife's shoulder where she'd be able to see me smile. I tried to look confident. Fear could wait. I had to face the bear. At least Jerre knew I was there. I assume they'd kept me outside until the job was about done because once I arrived she endured only a few more minutes of pushing and groaning. The doctor said, "That's it. Stop pushin," and out came the tiniest little girl I'd ever seen.

The word joy does not do justice to how I felt as they let me hold her. She fit in the palm of one hand. Both hands shook with excitement as I held Katie for the first time. "This is what I was put here to do," I thought. "Be a dad." Then as quick as bad news, things got really urgent. The nurses gave us no time for goodbyes. They took our baby, furiously working on her as they laid her in an incubator and rushed out of sight. "She's going to the ICU," one of them told me. "You can find them there." With a brief kiss for Jerre I barreled out the door, tore off my scrubs, and charged down bright halls, looking to follow them. Before long, someone guided me to a viewing window where I could see the staff treating her. When it's your child in danger, nothing else matters.

From outside I watched Katie receive critical care. Our poor baby girl had quit breathing. A respirator tube hung out of her mouth. She had no muscles for sucking milk, so a different tube snaked down her throat and into her tummy. To deliver medications, her limbs had been taped to sandbags and IV tubes stuck out of her little arms. Her skin blushed dark red like an apple. We named her Katie Elizabeth. God help us, Taidy, she's barely eight minutes old, she isn't due for another eight weeks, and I don't know if she'll live another eight hours.

I have to go now. I haven't seen Jerre since I left delivery, and I want to make sure the nurses let her into the ICU to see Katie. We're going to need each other to get through this. Ain't it a wonder? I'm a Dad.

Daddy

Nov. 30, 1985

Dear Taidy,

    Call the media, this just in. I'm a dad again. This delivery was a lot less stressful than the first. Jerre's doctor stitched her up like stuffing in a turkey so everything would stay in place till the time was right. I told the man we expected the baby would come spitting out like a watermelon seed as soon as they released the stitches. It didn't happen. We enjoyed a normal delivery of a healthy, giant sized, baby girl. I'm glad I got to go to baby school this time. We're naming her Caroline Kristine, but plan on calling her Carly.

    Oh, wait a bit, we have an update. I'm not supposed to call her giant because it might give her complexes and she's no bigger than most babies. Well excuse me, but she's more than twice the size that Katie was! She came out sporting a black mop of hair, with big dark eyes peeking over her chubby little cheeks. Besides, she screams big. I'd say this kid's a giant. Good job I love giants.

Daddy

For some of us, the reckless exploits of our teenage youth might carry on into adulthood. Sooner or later, we have to grow up. I started asking myself questions about the meaning of life while working at the marina. It took me years to figure out my purpose had to embody notions more enduring than a collection of t-shirts and pictures from faraway places. *Children,* I decided. *To nurture my children. That's why I exist.* Two little girls gave deep value to my life.

Katie and Carly. I've called those names together so often, they want to roll off my tongue as one like peaches and cream. How can genes from the same parents create daughters so different? Katie, the gentle follower, always struggled with her social skills. Carly, the determined leader. She'd rather fight than follow. Katie earned state honors with singing and piano. Carly did the same through academics and karate. I love them both dearly.

After Katie's birth, she breathed on her own for only a few minutes, then relied on a respirator for her first few days of a long stay in the Neonatal Intensive Care Unit. Day after day for six weeks, Jerre or I spent every waking hour in the unit to sit with her. Only during shift changes did the staff ask us to leave. Katie was so tiny they ran out of veins to hold IV needles in her arms or legs and tried to stick them in her temples. When that didn't work, the nurses had to give up, hoping she no longer needed whatever the tubes provided. On the glorious day they released her to our care, we had to dress her in doll clothes. At home we laid her in the bay window where sunlight would help cure her jaundice.

"Give her a bath? In what, a soup bowl? She's so tiny I'm afraid I'll break her."

Katie "Cuddle Fish" Geiger

"In the sink, dumb butt," Jerre replied. "You're her dad. You better get used to it." In spite of exhaustion and fear, our first months as parents were a joy I'll never forget. During my own childhood, I'd learned I could overcome most things if I doggedly kept going. That lesson gave us simple guidance. We gained daily renewal through drawing strength from each other. We overcame our struggle through perseverance. Jerre and I grew in confidence as parents, and by Christmas our little Katie was as healthy as any other baby.

In contrast to our first birth, Carly's arrival was tame. Most of the details from that day are lost to me. I'm sure the event lives on in greater detail in her mother's memory, but all I remember is that delivery took longer and she arrived home sooner. There is no truth to the rumor Carly came out smoking a cigarette and drinking a beer.

Their diverse entries into the world gave our two children distinctly different approaches to living. Katie had a tough time getting here, so she didn't dare push many limits in her life. She sensed that beyond those limits lay danger and wanted no part of it. She was a daddy's girl from the start and knew, no matter what, I would be there to care for her.

Carly, on the other hand, kept pushing until she found the limits, then pushed a little more. She was neither a mommy's girl nor a daddy's girl. Despite being her own girl first, Carly never acted more confident than just after we had established a limit, reinforced with corporal persuasion if necessary. Katie seemed content with the simple joy of sunflowers, fireflies, and babies. Carly wanted to understand how, why, and where. "How do I fix sunflower seeds so I can eat them?"

"Why can't I stay up late to catch the bugs with their own lights?"

When Carly was just five years old, she asked a question that never entered Katie's mind. "Dad, where do babies come from?"

We didn't shy away from such things so I replied, "Remember what Mom told you Carly? They come from their mommy's tummy."

"I know THAT," she said, looking at me like I needed remedial education. "But how do they get in there? HOW DOES IT WORK?"

Jeez-Louise, why me?

"Well, first the mommy has to grow an egg, you know like we eat for breakfast. Mommies do that all the time but they don't grow into babies until the daddy puts in his fertilizer. Kind of like when I put fertilizer on the tomatoes to make them grow. Once he's done that, and things work out right, the baby grows inside the mommy," I said with a smile.

"Oh," she acknowledged, "I guess that's OK, but I still don't know how."

"How what, Kiddo?"

"DON'T CALL ME KIDDO!"

"Sorry. What don't you understand?"

"Where does the baby come out?"

Please take note that the anatomical term used by the Geiger girls to describe a woman's vagina came from East Texas, not Canada. They called it a scooter. The only man in the house had no say in the matter. When the girls got to elementary school PE, and the teacher told the class to go to the gym and play with their scooters, you can understand their confusion.

I considered her question, *Where does the baby come out?*

Carly "Ducky Bob" Geiger

"Oh. Well, once it gets big enough and is ready to be born, it comes out it's mommy's scooter," I said.

A look of serious concern crossed Carly's face before she cried out, "WOW, that's gotta' hurt!"

Before Carly turned seven, a friend of ours asked his daughter, my two girls, and another little friend what they wanted to do when they grew up. Two of the girls wanted to be teachers, and one wanted to own a store. When he looked to Carly for her answer, she said, "I want to be the leader of a motorcycle gang!"

As Carly grew, she habitually confronted adversity with unflappable grit. Carly once had her jaw dislocated while fighting in karate. She didn't even whimper when instructors popped it back in place. This girl was tough! Her inquisitive nature and competitive disposition allowed Carly to interact well with peers and adults alike.

Being less sure of herself around others, Katie learned to be more comfortable with her dreams, her music and her faith. After she grew too old to wake up and crawl into our bed, I had to be careful when getting up at night. Many times I found Katie lying asleep on the floor beside me. That's where she felt safe. Right up until she left home for college, the things she didn't understand, the people who treated her differently, the fears of the night, all became anxieties with which she could cope as long as she was within reach of my hand.

As the girls entered into their teens, Jerre and I decided to let Katie spend her high school years at Garland Christian Academy. When compared against public school, GCA seemed to suit Katie's tender heart well. At church and school, Katie grew strong in her relationship with God.

GCA's tempered environment offered far too little for Carly's active mind and feisty spirit. She flourished in public school. Her high school years were filled with academic achievement, leadership, and determination. In a reversal of roles during their final year together at home, she emerged as a mature sister for Katie. After completing undergraduate studies at Texas A&M, Carly earned her master's degree at the top of her class from the University of Texas at Dallas. Today, she owns her own home, is thriving in her profession, and making plans to enhance her career through greater challenges. Carly's many accomplishments allowed her to achieve success beyond anything I would have dared hope. I am proud of her in many ways, but the thing I enjoy most is this. As Carly continues through her adult years, her personality is more obviously and more often similar to my own. She would wish it otherwise, but she can't help it. It's in her DNA.

Katie took a different path. "What looks good for college Kate? What would you like to do?"

"I like to sing, Daddy. I like to sing in church."

"You like kids too. Did you ever think about teaching kids to sing?"

Three Christian colleges offered Katie scholarships before she chose to study music education at Baptist Bible College in Springfield, Missouri. Her choice of a college so far from home surprised me. Separation and increased independence helped Katie mature in ways she could never have achieved had she stayed in Texas. Still, being apart from September through November was hard on us all.

Thanksgiving at Lake Catherine, Arkansas, had become a family tradition. Every fall we traveled north to enjoy crisp air, vibrant colors and hikes through mountain woods. Lake Catherine is also not terribly far from Springfield. Katie arrived early in the evening as I worked at the grill behind our cabin. She slipped in unnoticed by parking her car in the front driveway. All her newfound maturity evaporated. When Katie saw me, she took off like a four-year-old who just spotted a lost toy. I didn't notice her until I heard a screamed, "DAAADDYYY," right before she threw her arms around me, hugging with all her strength. The joy of our reunion gripped my heart with delight.

Carly and Katie, Lake Catherine, Ar. Thanksgiving, 2001.

"What'd you learn at Bible college Kate?" I asked, after we got her settled into the cabin.

"Lots of things. Mostly what I want to do with God."

"What would that be?"

"I'm gonna' be a missionary and work with kids."

"Well good for you Kate. I'm proud of you."

Maybe it was the fall leaves or maybe it was seeing our children outgrow childhood; however, it was probably just all of us being together. I remember 2001 as our best Thanksgiving ever.

Here is an excerpt from a letter Katie sent from college in Feb., 2002:

"Dear Dad... You have taught me so much throughout the whole eighteen years of my life and I am so appreciative that you went out of your way to show me what's right and just to keep me on the right track as I go through my life. Words cannot express how much I love you. I will always remember all the times that we spent together and the dates that we went on just me and you, alone. Thank you so much for all the lessons you have taught me so far in my life."

Raising children is difficult. A thousand gurus will teach you how it's done, but I'm convinced it boils down to healthy doses of love, attention, discipline and respect. Although I was not a perfect practitioner of the art, rarely was I a parent who would abdicate his responsibility in favor of convenience. Good parenting costs lots of time. It also involves creative efforts that offer alternatives to other sources of entertainment poised to hold your child captive. Not just occasionally but consistently. They are worth the sacrifice.

Work with your kids. Play with them. Talk to them and teach them how to live well. Your children come into your life; you turn around a couple of times and they're gone. Spend the time you get with them wisely.

17

March, 1986.

Dear Taidy,

My relationship with God is not what you would call a complicated affair. Back when I was a kid, Mom dragged me to church. I stopped going as soon as I was old enough to make up my own mind. I like to stay in touch with the Guy on a personal level. It seems a good way to be sure we're still friends.

To be polite, I've gone to First Baptist Church in Hughes Springs a few times when we visit Jerre's parents. Their clergy are way too concerned about southern traditions that are lost on me. A few weeks ago, Jerre asked me to come with her to a church just down the road from us in Sachse. I didn't want to, but I agreed. I'm thinking my girls ought to have religion in their lives. Park Lake Baptist Church is a dinky little place. Their services are in an old house. Still, I like Pastor Mark well enough. He wants to talk with me about Jesus someday. I told Jerre that would be fine as long as the man doesn't expect me to keep my opinions to myself. The only experience I've had with God came back at HTI. It's a good story. Should I tell it to the preacher or stay quiet? This is what happened:

Anglican Sunday School taught me that God cares about how we act and what we say. By the time I got to college, I had a habit of consulting with Him on small things like the weather and asking for minor favors. I'd long since quit enjoying a weekly visit to His house. The idea of God coming to mine never crossed my mind.

At HTI, our lives centered on the beach, a few classes, rock music and poker. Occasionally, we'd even study. I tried surfing a couple of times, but couldn't quite get the hang of using a surfboard. For me and my buddy Donn, body surfing turned out to be the next best thing. Surfers told us the waves on Cocoa Beach were better than anywhere else on the East Coast. The really good rollers hit when a hurricane passed by our coast. As long as the storm didn't get too close, we loved it.

For this story, you'll have to understand our dorm building had been built to withstand hurricanes. We lived on the second floor and outside our windows, a narrow catwalk surrounded the rooms. On the outside of that, a full wall of decorative cinder blocks allowed air to pass through while keeping wind out. Air could flow around the dorm rooms, but the blocks didn't allow storms in to tear things up inside. We hated those walls because they messed with our view.

Donn and I liked to play poker almost as much as we liked to body surf. I'm not sure who taught him, but Dad showed me how to play before I was big enough to hold the cards. He made wooden holders for

Amy and me, then cut poker chips out of an old broom handle. On special occasions like New Year's Eve, we'd get to stay up playing till midnight.

In the dorm, our games started in the early evening and lasted until morning. All night long, the sounds of plastic chips, laughter and cursing drifted out the door beside smoke from odd-smelling cigarettes. When we finished, everyone headed to the Camelot Inn for breakfast. If one of us had a bad night, a winner usually donated a few bucks to spring for our omelet and hash browns.

My luck has always been awful. I struggled to win even though I didn't consider myself a bad poker player. Donn was the luckiest guy in the world. That bothered me. One day when we were standing in his room, I asked him, "You ever notice you have amazing good luck? I'm never delt what I'm looking for. How do you manage to get good cards every time?"

His answer shocked me. "Cause I pray to the devil to give me luck."

Donn knew I believed in God, and I suspect he was just saying that to needle me, but I couldn't let it go. "Don't say that man. God'll get you."

"Come on God. Come and GET ME." Donn laughed, holding up his arms and looking to the ceiling.

As soon as he uttered his challenge, roaring noise filled our ears and a great wind blew into the room. It went 'round and 'round, lifting ceiling tiles off their grid, while throwing books and papers off shelves. Posters flew off the walls. His window screen sailed right out of its frame and into a corner. The commotion lasted several seconds then disappeared as quickly as it came. The place was a mess.

In the middle of the room Donn had a table built from a cable spool. On top of the table sat a large sea shell ashtray. "Hodj, look at the table. That demon poster was on my wall. Now it's laying on the table… but it's UNDER THE ASHTRAY!"

We looked at each other, screamed like little kids and ran out of the building to see what had happened outside. Nothing. Just a regular, sunny, Florida day with no wind. Stopping in at the room next to Donn's we saw no destruction at all. "Hey, did you guys get a wind in here?" I asked.

"No. Wind don't blow indoors. What are you boys smokin'?"

Back in Donn's room, debris still lay all over the floor. For several moments, my heart raced and hairs stood up on the back of my neck. "Holy shit. God heard you."

After I helped Donn pick things up, neither of us felt much like talking about what had happened. I didn't think an "I told you so" would be very useful, and Donn didn't mention what he was thinking. We agreed that it would be best to keep the event to ourselves.

Since that day, I've occasionally pondered if it was really God coming to my place for a visit or simply an odd wind. At the time, I thanked Him for backing me up, just in case. I wonder how Donn's luck's been running?

Rog

My walk with God got more complicated as I grew older. After the excitement of Carly's birth died down, I found myself dwelling on an emptiness I'd felt since Katie came home from the hospital. I'd come a long way in my search for deeper meaning in life, but I couldn't shake the notion I needed to do more. "You have a hole in your spirit," the pastor of Park Lake told me. "It's a God shaped hole and only He can fill it. You need Jesus in your life." Acknowledging the truth in what Brother Mark said led me to the realization I should fix that spiritual hole. I welcomed the restoration God was offering.

Looking back on my religious journey, I think I could form an ecumenical council all by myself. I've been christened in a Methodist church, confirmed in the Anglican Church, and ordained in a Baptist Church. My spiritual walk began as a believer, wandered away as an agnostic, got born-again, then fell to a state of frustrated limbo. Today, I'm hoping to return to a place where God and I have a simple, happy relationship.

One basic principle of all religions is the need to have faith if you want to walk with God. In June of 1986, having recently accepted Christ in fellowship with wonderful evangelical Christians, I had serious faith. We saw little serious faith in the Anglican church of my youth. The style of faith that guides a person's minute-by-minute actions seemed to be much more common to denominations like the Baptists. Jerre's parents were faithful Baptists to their core. The Parkers lived by the word of God and raised my wife in the "nurture and admonition of the Lord." Although they welcomed me, knowing I was not initially a believer as they defined the term, they rarely failed to share God's love when they had a chance to do so without offense. After all, one of the abiding tenets of fundamental Christianity is the imperative Christ taught for sharing one's faith along with its source. That is, to evangelize.

I can remember meeting a few Jesus freaks who engaged in evangelism back when I lived in Toronto. Although I could admire their zeal, their methods left a lot to be desired. The group of Christians with whom I associated were not like that at all. They were a reasonable, thoughtful community who took a literal view of what the Bible had to say. Their message of salvation filled that void I had felt for some time. I believe God works through people of faith when He has a mind to do so. During the summer of 1986, He worked through me.

Jeff Simon and I first met in the mid-sixties because he was a neighbor of my friend, Steve Finlayson. The three of us spent hours together, hanging out in Jeff's home and indulging teenage curiosities, largely free of adult supervision. My conversations with him often went like this.

"Jeff, let me bum a smoke man. I'm all out and don't get paid till Saturday."

"Ok… but only if you say please."

"Please."

"Now say Jeff's the best."

"Jeff's the best. The best dickhead."

During one of those sessions, Jeff showed me a book he'd been reading. "Hey, look at this. It's about a guru guy from Tibet named Lobsang Rampa. It tells you how to let your spirit leave your body so you can fly all over the world, man. He calls it astral projection. Ya' wanna' give it a try?" We tried it. The experience was so spooky we scared ourselves and swore never to do it again. After that, our experiments drifted back to things we could smoke.

A multi-million dollar trust fund ensured financial security within Jeff's family while alcohol issues left his father unemployed for many years. In the seventies, his parents divorced. Later, his father died. The terms of Jeff's trust limited its use to education purposes only. As a highly intelligent teen with unlimited money, Jeff attended the most prestigious private school in Toronto. There he studied topics most of us never see. He also displayed legitimate talent as a painter. I got to meet a few of his school mates. Their level of wealth bought butlers, Bentleys and Piccassos. One of his courses required students to read the Bible and other sacred texts as part of their curriculum. None seemed to bolster his faith, nor did they help him overcome the family problems that left him firmly opposed to religion.

Jeff and I almost lost touch after I worked overseas. In Texas, I'd occasionally receive drunken, midnight phone calls from my friend. He'd let me know he was still alive, then ramble on about life's injustice. When I moved to Wylie in 1984, my phone number changed. Jeff never kept a steady number so we were cut off for good.

In 1985, my employers decided I needed to work a convention scheduled for June, 1986, in Toronto. Jerre and I jumped at the chance to combine business with an extended vacation up North. Later, after meeting Jesus so to speak, my priorities in life made a turn toward the divine. A compulsion to find Jeff gripped my soul. *If a deeper relationship with God can provide peace for me, surely the same bond can help Jeff.* Introducing him to my source of comfort took on all the power, purpose and excitement of a mission from God. *You and me God. Let's do this!*

While I prepared to travel to Canada, Jeff worked the loading dock of a warehouse proud to have lasted in the job three years. In addition to funds he couldn't spend, Jeff had inherited his father's problems with alcohol. His high-priced education, high-priced friends and notable skills all slipped away as he followed a destructive course of poor choices. One evening in May, 1986, he borrowed a coworker's car, had a wreck causing significant damage, and was taking money from each pay packet to cover repairs.

On May 29th I arrived in Toronto believing with clear certainty I would have a chance to speak to Jeff. During the first week of June, the show kept me tied down with work. I had no spare time for trying to find him. Jeff's situation got worse. In an attempt to extort more money, his "friend" inflated repair costs. The guy claimed he had friends who would help him give Jeff a beating if he didn't pay up soon. To save himself, Jeff quit his job and went into hiding.

According to his account of the story, Jeff sat alone on the night of June 8th in a rundown boarding house. His whole world reduced to a bed, dresser and chair. Jeff considered the extent to which he had fallen. A house phone hung from the wall in the hallway outside his room. Who was he going to call? He had no one. The wreckage of Jeff's life bore down upon his ruined spirit, and he contemplated suicide. Then, for the first time in fifteen years, he prayed. He prayed that God would send someone to help. With that prayer fresh in his heart, Jeff decided to wait until the next day before he would take his own life. My conference ended that same day.

The next morning, still under a strong conviction to find Jeff, I had no idea where he currently lived, and no grasp of his situation. While I sat at breakfast in the hotel, thinking about how best to search for him, Jeff sat in his room, writing a suicide note. I spent the rest of my morning hunting down old acquaintances who might know how to contact him. By late afternoon, I spoke with a mutual friend, Blake Ross, who had recently talked to Jeff. During our conversation, I heard for the first time about some of Jeff's problems. Neither of us were aware of his immediate danger. After talking to Blake, I prayed for Jeff's safety, and that God would help me find him soon. Late in the day, as I talked with another friend, Jeff had prepared rat poison for a deadly drink. He hesitated, then changed his mind, keeping the mixture ready beside him. For the remainder of the evening as Jeff wavered between life and death, I tried to reach him through every means I could imagine. I failed.

By 9:00 pm, I felt I'd done everything in my own power I could do. Alone in my hotel room, I kneeled at the coffee table and prayed. "Lord, I've tried all I can to find Jeff. If you want it to happen, please let Jeff find me." My quest was in God's hands.

At 10:00 I grabbed the phone before its second ring. "Hello, this is Roger".

"Roger? It's Jeff. I'm calling from a restaurant. How soon can you get here?"

My thoughts screamed, *YES! Thank you!* To Jeff I said, "I'm leaving now. I'll be there in ten minutes."

Stale grease and pesticides fought for fragrant dominance as I stood in the doorway of an old cafe. I looked over worn tables with few patrons as my eye adjusted to dim light. Jeff, sitting near the back, watched me make my way toward him. With our eyes locked, I sat down and declared, "God sent me."

Jeff's mouth opened and his hands shook as he stared at me in disbelief. A watery sheen filled his eyes. He whispered, "I asked Him to send someone! I was ready to drink poison, and I asked God to send someone to help." Jeff then described his problems from the previous few weeks. Defeat wrapped his tale of the extortionist hunting him and how fear forced him to quit his job. Before he finished, Jeff related more about his near suicide.

I shared how my life had evolved since becoming a father and how my attitudes had changed. I explained my source of peace. We talked for hours. Later, as we prepared to go our separate ways, I gave Jeff a small Bible. "Read the Psalms if you get close to the edge again. They will help."

I left thinking, *You did it God. You rescued Jeff. This is amazing!*

Jeff didn't sleep that night nor the next day. Around midnight, he called, and we again met to talk through the darkness. We sat in my car in the pouring rain. Jeff described his day. "For the first time in ages, I wasn't afraid," he said. "What can they do that I wasn't ready to do to myself? How can I make this last? Like, how do I get to be a Christian?" My Bible lay on the console between us as we read through passages describing what it means to be a believer. In the middle of the night, in the middle of a storm, in the middle of a wrecked life, Jeff became a Christian. He then told me, "Man, you are the only person in the world I would have listened to about this stuff. How did God know and send you to help me?"

"He knows everything," I replied.

Was it God or good fortune that let Jeff run into someone who'd heard I was in town? Did God steer Jeff to my hotel, or did simple word of mouth allow me to connect with him? I've come to the conclusion that that's the way it goes when we work with an omnipotent God. You never know for sure. That quandary of belief is by design. Those quoting scripture say, "Faith is the substance of things hoped for, the evidence of things not seen." If I profess to believe God guides circumstances directly, I'm required to accept those actions through faith.

The morning after our second meeting, I had to leave for my parent's home many miles west of Toronto. "I'll check on you a few times before I go back to Texas," I told him. "Find a church you like and get involved. People there will care about you." A week later we talked on the phone. Jeff was doing well. He no longer lived in fear and had told his tormentor he would repay according to the original plan and that was it. We agreed to meet again the following Thursday.

Late Wednesday evening, I got a call from the GSI office in Dallas. An emergency in one of their South American branches required someone to go to a lawyer in Toronto, pick up legal papers and immediately deliver them to Lima, Peru. As the only employee available in southern Ontario, they chose me to make the trip. I was frantic.

No one picked up the rooming house phone when I called Jeff to tell him I wouldn't be there. Each time I tried, the call ended in unanswered ringing. I had to break my commitment without letting him know why. Upon returning a couple days later, I still had no luck contacting Jeff before my family and I departed for Texas. Thirty minutes after arriving home from the airport I got a call from Blake Ross. On Saturday evening, two days after we'd planned to meet, Jeff got drunk, took an overdose of prescription medication and died. *At least he found God before he died,* I thought. *At least I'll see him again in heaven. Right?... RIGHT?* I hung up the phone as tears slowly rolled down my cheeks.

I have often considered the events leading up to finding Jeff and cannot comprehend them through mundane explanations alone. It seems God must have taken an active hand in those circumstances. Did He also take an active hand in pulling me out of the situation while I could still have had a positive effect? Could I have been more diligent in trying to contact Jeff? Should I have tried to find his room and left a note? I don't know. People have had these questions since they first believed in higher powers. Perhaps all religion is merely humankind's attempt to come to grips with suffering and death. The higher power I'd experienced did not appear obligated to answer my questions. Almost three thousand years ago, a prophet named Isaiah reported that God explained it this way, "For My thoughts are not your thoughts, nor are your ways My ways..."

I've noticed my Christian friends are quick to credit God for the good events in our lives, but loath to consider He may have had a hand in the less pleasant. To me, it seems clear we can't be so selective. God doesn't always choose to get involved in a way we recognize. When He does, sometimes we enjoy it and sometimes we don't. We seldom get to understand why. A believer has to accept His will as it comes. Doing so after Jeff's death was like having a thorn stuck in my thumb. Not painful enough to interrupt daily activities, just a reminder of something I wished was not there. I accepted that thorn and got on with life.

In March of 1988, Taid died. My grandfather lived ninety-three years and managed to reside at home until a short time before his death. Four years later, Dad died on Katie's birthday. I have missed Dad and Taid dearly, but losing them fell within my expectations for the natural order of things. All of us experience the passing of earlier generations. Unlike the crisis my family faced near the end of 1988, they were not events for which I would question God.

Three weeks before Christmas, I again experienced Him in action. At that time of year, everyone within the Geiger home stayed busy on Saturdays. Jerre had left for the mall, Katie was with her Sunday school class, and I worked at putting up decorations with help from three-year-old Carly. Late in the morning, as Carly and I stood in the kitchen going through boxes, the phone rang. "Hello?"

"This is the Smith County Sheriff's Department in Tyler Texas. Is Jerre Lynn Geiger home?"

"No," I replied. "This is her husband Roger. Can I help you?"

"Yes sir. I'm sorry, but her mother, Jerre Parker, has been killed in a car accident and her father George is not expected to live out the day."

"Oh no. No."

"Yes sir. They were coming out of the Sam's on the loop and got broadsided. They have Mr. Parker at Mother Frances."

"OK, thank you. Is there anything else you can tell me?"

"No sir, that's about it."

"Thank you. Goodbye." I said, then sunk to my knees, moaning in shock.

Carly knew at once that something was wrong. She came to my side, patting my back saying, "It be OK Daddy. It be OK."

I looked at her and smiled. "That's right Ducky Bob. It will be OK. We've got to find Mama."

After pulling myself off the floor, I made several phone calls. First to Jerre's brothers, letting them know Big George and Granny had been in a wreck. Then I called friends from our church. They were fantastic. There's nothing like a tragedy to send church ladies into action. Before I had time to panic, a whole house full of people arrived. They watched over Carly, packed clothes for Jerre, and tried to get hold of Katie's teacher so we could bring her home.

We had leave for Tyler soon if we hoped to see George alive, but finding one woman in a giant mall on a Saturday before Christmas? "It's not possible," they said. "You'll just have to wait till she gets back."

I wouldn't be put off. "I've asked God for some help. Trust Him. I know I'll find her."

Against everyone's better judgment, three of us headed for the mall. One to drive Jerre's car, one to drive mine and me to hold my wife on the way home. As expected, every space of mall parking appeared full. I was not deterred. Entering the nearest lane to look for a space, I said. "There's her van." We parked in a vacant spot four cars away. Inside, I walked to the main concourse and searched with my eyes through the glittering bustle of Christmas shoppers. Within ten seconds I pointed down the corridor to the entrance of a Christian bookstore. "There she is."

We hurried over to the store, entered and found her alone in the back. Jerre looked at the three of us. "What...?" was all she got out. I braced my heart for a terrible chore.

Taking her in my arms I said, "Jerre, your mother's been killed in a wreck. Your father is in the hospital in critical condition. We have to go to Tyler now."

She stared at me in disbelief, and in a faint whimper asked, "Mama? My Mama? My Mama's... dead?" Half carrying and half guiding, I helped her out of the mall, into the car and home.

The church ladies took over helping Jerre. Others had gone to pick up Katie, and someone kept Carly occupied while I packed. Soon, the four of us were racing down the highway to be with Big George. As I drove, Jerre talked about her parents, preparing herself for the ordeal to come. Thinking back to her first pregnancy that never made it to full term, then the anxiety of Katie's birth, I tried to offer hope. "Hey, we've faced hard times before Ma. As long as we have each other... we can handle this."

"Yes we have Daddy. Yes we can."

Jerre and I arrived at the hospital in time to find George alive but badly broken. His bruised body lay on a bed in the ICU. He was full of tubes and on a respirator. Jerre stayed by his side for a month. Big George Parker must have been a tough old bird. He lived another seven years before succumbing to cancer in 1996.

As with my other encounters while He worked, I am unable to explain my ability to find Jerre so directly, without giving credit to God. I had trusted Him when others did not. He chose to get involved. I believe He led me to Jerre in a time of great need.

Although this belief bolstered my faith, I again found it difficult to understand God's will. If He had good reason to take part in helping me find Jerre, why would He let an accident happen in the first place? In answer, I concluded God doesn't always control every leaf falling from every tree. He usually lets life progress as it will. In doing so, unpleasant events are sure to occur. I am certain our faith offered Jerre and me strength to face our bear. We accepted that strength. Still, enduring Granny Parker's death left more thorns in our spirits. Thorns like I'd suffered after Jeff died. With two girls to care for, Jerre and I had little choice but to yet again put one foot in front of the other in order to carry on living.

18

March 10, 2002.

Dear Taidy,

It's nice that Katie calls us most weeks. I like to learn all about what she's up to in college. Last week she was talking about something called a barn swing. As I understand it, barn swings are a big deal in Missouri, especially for kids at BBC. Their social activities appear to occupy a higher plane of virtue than those in which I participated. I'm just glad she's fitting in so well. Katie hasn't said much directly, but from hints I've picked up on, I think she has a boyfriend!

This week she wanted to tell us she'd been sick and had to skip her classes. A sister of one of our church members lives in Springfield and is checking on Katie while she rests in bed. That's somewhat hard to do in a dorm. Next week is spring break, so we figured it would be quiet enough for her to recover. Jerre's school is out as well. She left yesterday, headed for BBC with her friends Kathy and Linda. They went up to be Katie's nurses while all the students disappear for vacations and were hoping to make it a caregiver's holiday.

Bad luck for them. When I talked to Jerre today, she said they took Katie to a doctor. She's got mono, the sickness old folks call the kissing disease. I'll have to talk to the boy about that, if I ever meet him. Doesn't everybody get mono in college? I did. It was no fun, but I got over it after a few weeks. We decided to move her home until she gets well. Jerre and her crew have worked out how to transport Katie without tiring her out. Cathy and Linda will drive Jerre's Mustang and Jerre will drive Katie's Escort. The patient can lie down in the back seat with pillows and blankets to keep her comfortable. I wish Katie wasn't so sick, but I'm glad she'll be home to visit. I miss her.

Daddy

Katie rested at home for several days before she was able to stay out of bed for an hour. On Friday evening, we sat quietly on our couch simply enjoying each other's company. "You look way healthier today Kate. I bet you'll be as good as new in a week or two."

With her head on my shoulder, she put her hand in mine. "I like sitting here with you. It makes me feel better. I love you Daddy."

"I love you too Cuddlefish. Sit by me a little longer, then back to bed. Just 'cause you seem a bit more lively, doesn't mean you get to stay up all night. I'll see you when you wake up tomorrow."

The next morning I woke early to Katie's call.

"Da… DAEE?"

I'm a light sleeper. In a few seconds I stood inside her door. "Mornin' Kate, how ya doin' today?"

"Ne sa watr."

Layers of dried mucus crusting over her mouth and nose made speech difficult. "Let me get a washcloth from the bathroom." Back in Katie's room, I sat beside her on the bed, wiping off crud with the damp cloth. I gave her a bottle of water and she took two long swallows. "How about we give cleaning your face another go? OK?"

"K."

A minute of gentle rubbing washed away most of the mucus. "Is that better?"

"Yeah."

"Now try some more water… Katie? Kate?"

Katie's eyes opened wide. She stared up, past my face at nothing, then violently crushed the half empty bottle in her hand.

"DADDY I CAN'T HEAR YOU…"

"DADDY I CAN'T SEE YOU…"

Katie is falling on her side, dropping the crumpled bottle to the floor.

"Kate?"   "KATIE!"   "KAATTIEEEE!!"

I check for breathing… nothing.

I listen to her chest for a heartbeat… NOTHING!

I pull her from the bed and give mouth to mouth.

Jerre calls from the door… "Should I call 911?!"

"YES!"

Thoughts scramble for attention within my brain. *Just do what they taught you in lifeguard school. Blow the air in, let it out. The ambulance will be here soon. The hospital is close. Blow the air in, let it out. Hospitals always save people.* My efforts seem meager. *Oh God, save our Kate. Please save our Katie.*

Carly sticks her head through the door, a stricken expression of fear twisting her face. "Dad? What can I do? Is she gonna be OK?"

"WATCH FOR THE AMBULANCE. THEY'RE COMING ANY MINUTE. AND PRAY!"

Outside, she passes in front of the window, running through the yard with arms stretched wide. I catch a glimpse of her eyes. They're fierce. *Carly's searching for a miracle to save her sister.*

I continue to work on Katie. *Blow the air in, let it out.*

Breathe Katie, breathe. Your color looks good. Am I helping you? Real help is coming. Oh God, don't let her die. How long has it been? Ten minutes, twenty?

Blow the air in, let it out.

"I'll keep breathing for you as long as it takes. Don't leave me Kate."

Outside, Carly is yelling to people.

Blow the air in, let it out.

Jerre's at the door. "They're here."

Blow the air in, let it out.

Blue uniforms are all around me. I see equipment, medical bags.

Blow the air in, let it out.

A hand on my shoulder. "We'll take over now, sir." His eyes hold mine until I let go of Katie.

Jerre is waiting in the hall. We face each other for the first time. "Will she be alright?" Jerre asks.

"I hope so. They can do anything at hospitals these days. Let's pray before we go."

"God, if it be your will, save our daughter. In Jesus' name, Amen."

"Amen."

Paramedics are pushing a stretcher carrying Katie out the front door. She's full of tubes and breathing support. The scene slaps me with a memory of the first time I saw her that way, then I run for my truck. Jerre will come with Carly in the car. As I wait to follow the ambulance, our neighbor hurries to the fence, "Roger, what happened?"

"It's Katie."

"Will she be all right?"

"It doesn't look good." I reply, while moving down the driveway to follow the ambulance.

We're in a mad rush to the hospital. I'm tailgating with caution lights flashing. People in scrubs and white coats burst through the doors and take Katie. I follow. They push her into a large room full of bright lights and electronics, leaving me behind. For a moment I'm alone with my fears. My mind is crumbling. *NO! Not yet.* Now I'm outside making a tearful call to Jerre's brother. "Bentley… Katie's dying. We're at Lake Point. Come quick."

Again inside, I find Jerre and Carly standing in the operating room where they've laid Katie. It's cold in here, and bright. She rests on a stainless steel table, covered in blankets. She's alone. Medical staff have given up trying. One of Katie's arms sticks out from under a blanket and hangs over the edge of the table. Death bruises at her elbows and wrists confirm what I already know. Katie has left us. Maybe someone tells me but I don't know. I don't hear. A young doctor is sitting by himself on a stool in a corner. His head buried in his hands. *Who comforts the doctor at times like this?* I wonder. Jerre, Carly and I grab ahold of each other, too grief-stricken to let go. "We've been through so many tough days already," I sob. "Together we can survive this one too." We cry.

Jerre has made calls to friends. Our church family is arriving. I see Kathy Countryman enter the nurses' area where others have already gathered. Kathy looks at them, and into Jerre's eyes. She knows. Her face is melting in horror and grief. A few minutes later, Bentley arrives. "Can I see Katie?" he asks quietly.

"NO. She's already gone."

"I still need to look."

Like me, he has to see her to be sure. "She's in there." I point to the cold room where a cold table holds Katie's cold body. Bentley folds a knee onto the floor, kneeling in silent prayer. *He's asking God to give courage for what comes next.* More people fill Lake Point's emergency room. We circle together, hand in hand, to thank God for His will. Leaning on His stability, I make heartbroken calls to my mother and sister. Pain dims perception; I remember no more.

The following morning, I dragged myself out of a tortured night to a world changed forever. My first conscious thoughts gnawed at the realities I'd have to overcome to get through the day. *Start yourself moving or you'll slide down into the pit. Misery will suck you in and never let go.* It was 6:00 am. I tried to rise without waking Jerre while getting ready for an early prayer group at church. She rolled over, resting her head in the pillows while she spoke.

"Did you sleep?"

"Some. Not much. How 'bout you?"

"Not much. Where are you going?"

"To church. I always go early on Sunday. Why should today be different? What am I supposed to do? Lie here crying all day?"

"You don't have to go."

"Yes. I do." I had to move, make plans, take control of a life gone wrong. If I slowed down for a second, grief would grab me and hold me. I remembered a lesson from long ago. *I know I'll make it, if I just… keep… going.*

At Park Lake, a few members had already arrived to ask God's blessing on the day's services and pray for people in need. People like me. When I walked into the sanctuary, shocked faces turned to greet me. One said "Brother Roger? You didn't have to come. How…?"

"I don't know. Life goes on. Where better to get started than in God's house?" We prayed, searching for joy in His strength. Later, my fellow deacons and Pastor Max began planning funeral arrangements. I fought to hold onto my faith.

The weekend before Katie died, I had attended a men's retreat put on by a local Methodist church. Part of the program included letters to each man from dozens of friends and family. None of us knew they were coming. The surprise filled us with joy and the notes from friends inspired our hearts. Although I enjoyed all the letters and did my best to answer them, my favorites came from Katie, Carly and Jerre.

Katie's reply wasn't delivered while she lived. On the afternoon before her funeral, I visited her body at the funeral home. Just the two of us, alone in a small viewing room. "I got the letter you wrote me Kate. It's like God let you say goodbye before you had to leave. Here's the one I wrote back. Wish I'd delivered it a few nights ago." Wiping tears from my eyes, I patted her shoulder and slipped my letter under a small pillow supporting her head.

Our church family was wonderful. They cared for Jerre, Carly and me, in body and spirit, throughout the days surrounding Katie's funeral. On the day of her service, the scent of flowers greeted us as we entered the church. Soft music drifted in background to the murmur of quiet voices. The service celebrating Katie's life encompassed an outpouring of support for our family. Several hundred friends and relatives honored us with their presence. After the songs had been sung, and the words had been spoken, all those people queued up to wish us well. The procession lasted for more than an hour. Despite encouragement from the funeral home to hurry the process, I refused to leave until everyone had a chance to express their sorrow. A few of our close friends waited as the last mourner hugged our necks. We watched attendants prepare Katie's casket for the long drive to a cemetery not far away.

My thoughts drifted while I stared unseeing at houses passing our limousine's windows. *What a wonderful thing. People from all the places and times of our lives came here to join us.* Our motorcade rounded a wide corner, slowly rolling to the bottom of a long hill. I turned to gaze back over a line of cars stretching well over a mile. Every vehicle contained a memory; a time in my life, going back to childhood. Those in the distance, dim and hard to make out, just as the memories they carried would become dim and hard to recall. *Each one of them has their own trail of lives following unseen behind them.* I watched for a long moment trying to hold onto my trail of lives. Then we arrived. With more words and more prayers, we let go of Katie's days amongst us. The parade ended. One life gone, another breaking apart like the long procession of cars.

The time had come for our friends to return to their own concerns. Only my extended family remained, each of us dealing with our sorrow. When they departed, I escaped to my bed but peace eluded me. *All those times I saved myself from life's calamities. Now this. I couldn't even save my own daughter. To hell with the bear! God, it's fine with me if I go to sleep and never wake up. Let the bear do what he wants. I'll face him no more.*

Dear Taidy,

I feel the thorns; I know the thorns. They pierce my heart. They've torn my mind. Where is faith? Where is life?

Brother Roger

Jesus said "Behold, the sower went out to sow; and as he sowed, some seeds fell beside the road, and the birds came and ate them up. Others fell on the rocky places, where they did not have much soil; and immediately they sprang up, because they had no depth of soil. But when the sun had risen, they were scorched; and because they had no root, they withered away. Others fell among the thorns, and the thorns came up and choked them out. And others fell on the good soil and yielded a crop, some a hundredfold, some sixty, and some thirty. He who has ears, let him hear."

19

July 5, 2002

Dear Taidy,

If you ever want to see a lavish display of home-grown fireworks, come to Cocoa Beach on the fourth of July. Last night we watched sparkling colors explode up and down the beach for miles. Our condo is amazing. We're on the third floor, with one balcony facing east over the Atlantic and another facing north to Canaveral Pier. The building where I survived HTI is still there, across the street and up a block. Ron Jon's surf shop is a couple of blocks in the other direction. It's the size of a supermarket now. When I lived here, Ron Jon's was just a tiny shack. They sold board wax out front and built surfboards in the back.

A week on the beach has been great for all of us. There's something healing about getting up in the morning and looking out over water. Rich salt air and the sound of waves crashing the shore washes away any remaining dross from unruly dreams. I like to sit on the balcony watching pelicans fly in formation, inches off the water. The "dawn patrol" never fails to raise a smile. Later, kids playing in the sand below remind me of happier days.

Jerre spends her day lying by the ocean and I do lots of body surfing. I'm not as good at it as I was thirty years ago. Do you suppose that has anything to do with weight? I've grown to over two hundred and sixty pounds. Carly and her friend Rachel like to hang out at the pier. That's where all the action is. I enjoy watching Carly cut her strings to wander off without Jerre and me looking over her shoulder. A bit of panic sets in when I think about the summer I was her age. At sixteen, I lived on my own for a while. Residue from the marina bothered me for a long time, but I can't shelter Carly forever. Besides, she can take care of herself just fine.

When I'm not in the water, I'm staring at it, and thinking. Thinking about Katie. Sometimes my mind drifts off like I'm dreaming. Awake and asleep, events from her life come back as if they're happening over again. I miss her every minute of every day. Most of the time I'm able to keep moving forward. Occasionally, I manage to smile. The pain never goes away.

This morning I drove down to Satellite Beach and watched the lifeguard races. Ocean rescue teams competed in rowing and swimming events out in the surf. One contestant, a thin, white haired dude, had to be pushing eighty. What he lacked in speed and agility, he made up for in spirit. That man has got it going on. An old timer in great shape who won't let anything slow him down. Least of all age. He's gonna' keep moving till he drops.

After the old lifeguard finished his events, I lost interest in the competition. Other than fishing, nothing holds my attention long these days. I sat listening to gulls argue over a scrap of food and watching waves run up the sand to erase footprints left by beach walkers. Soon all record of their passing disappeared like they never existed. I saw myself in that imagery. My own mortality written in the sand.

When I consider the fleeting years until all record of my passing disappears, I don't so much want to end my life, as get on with it. It's like any unpleasant task. I want to get it over with sooner rather than later. No matter how I measure the rest of my days, my time will end before I know it. Do I care? I'm not sure I do. For the moment it's enough to sip my beer and enjoy the ocean.

Roger

In the weeks after Katie died, my plans for lying in bed with grief as my partner only succeeded during the short hours I slept. When God proved Himself indifferent to my requests for eternal slumber, body aches and boredom forced me back to a world without choices. No choice but to get out of bed. No choice but to interact with the world. No choice but to put one foot in front of the other and go on. Five days after the funeral, I returned to work. There, focused distraction allowed me to function as if heartbreak didn't hold me captive. Although real improvement evaded my grasp for years, daily habits of participation, conversation, and laughter recovered within weeks. Diversion became my best ally in the pursuit of mental stability.

Months passed with little change in my routine. I'd get up, go to work, come home and retreat to my bed. Books offered more distraction until sleep brought intervals of fitful escape. In the wee hours of the night I often awoke to tired clichés chasing doubts through my mind.

What doesn't kill you, makes you stronger... Stronger for what? A life of pain?

Life gives back what you put into it... So these deaths are my fault?

It's the journey that counts... Screw that! How long before this ride's over?

If you're not growing, you're dying... If you're not growing, you're dying.

Echoes of past trauma returned unbidden to my dreams. *"KAATIEE? KAATIEE? Katie, where are you?"* We're at a motel. Katie and Carly are missing. Fear grips my heart. *The girls are gone! Call the manager! They were right there in the playground just a second ago.* My body sails high over buildings and cars as I search for them. I hear Carly crying and banging on a metal door, then find them in a locked stairwell. Katie dissolves. She's no longer there. *"Kaatiee. Where are you?"* This time I was asleep when the nightmare hit. Many times, I am not.

Three months after Katie died, my cousin Bill invited me to join his family for a week in the Adirondack Mountains of New York. I hadn't been to the Adirondacks since Dad and I got snowed in at Lewey Lake over Easter weekend in 1965. I'd always loved the Adirondacks, and trout-fishing was in my blood. Of course I wanted to go.

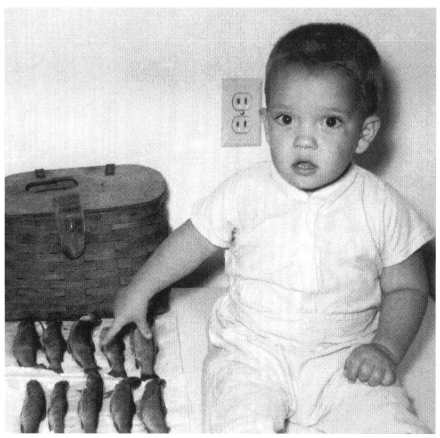

Roger, age 1 year, with trout

Stalking brook trout through mountain streams proved to be a wellspring of preoccupation. It rekindled a passion that first arose alongside my father and will continue until I breathe my last breath. Some of us enjoy fishing yet others do not. Why do I love fishing so much? The obvious answers are nostalgia, camaraderie and recreation. Every time I go, I am reminded of simpler, carefree times. Wilderness areas that haven't changed since I first fished them; great trips with a troupe of trout fishing buddies who have become my closest friends; traditions passed on through third and fourth generations.

There are also more complex explanations for why I fish. Motives like the principle of intermittent reinforcement, and the stress relieving properties of nature. For how long would fishing remain attractive if I caught fish on every cast? Obviously, not long. With fishermen, intermittent success is the bait that keeps us coming back. Likewise, do you think fishing from a swimming pool in the city might offer the same joy as a stream in the mountains? Of course not.

In the middle of mental chaos, trout fishing became a soothing endeavor over which I could exercise a small amount of personal control. The cares of my life seemed to drift away with the current as I schemed to outwit shrewd Mr. Trout. Nothing to worry about but the next nibble. If I failed on one cast, there was always another. If I failed all day, wasn't the forest air refreshing? Aren't the white birch beautiful against the green of that mountain? Didn't I enjoy the song of a sparrow singing harmony with my gurgling brook? To paraphrase an old saying, "A bad day fishing always beats a good day grieving."

Over ensuing years, I discovered greater challenges returned greater satisfaction. During one outing, Bill and I fished the Jessup River near Indian Lake, New York. We had to bushwhack all day through beaver swamps and alder trees along the river bank as we fished. Our fishing ended when we reached the lake. "Bill, let's take a look at your topo map. Maybe we can find our way back over higher ground. I don't wanna' slog through those alders again."

Thousands of mosquitos and black flies swarmed our heads as Bill pulled a map and compass out of his fishing vest. We retreated uphill to where they weren't so thick and laid the map over a fallen log. "It's a couple of miles back to the road," he said. "Looks like we can keep climbing this hill, then follow a ridge going west. If everything goes according to plan, we should make it out in an hour or so."

It is too bad topo maps show little about trees. A short way along the ridge we ran into a dense spruce thicket. Small, young evergreens grew so close together we had trouble getting past them. We tried to go around, but that led us off in the wrong direction. Working our way back to the river seemed a poor option, so we pushed on into the forest. Bill typically led the way when we followed a compass course, but he's not a large fellow. We were soon brought to a standstill by saplings. "Let me lead," I suggested. "Maybe I can break a trail and you can hug my back." After a hundred yards, the thicket stopped me as well.

Small trees don't spring up in the forest by accident. They have to have light. Light coming through the holes where old trees have fallen dead to make space. *There must have been a heck of a storm in these mountains to cause enough deadfalls for this thicket.* Nearby, one of the large dead trunks lay on its side. "Hey, let's see if we can walk on that deadfall."

I moved over to the moss-covered tree, climbed on top and took a few tentative steps. "The spruce tops only come to my knees. I've got a pretty good path up here. Come on up!" Before we got to the end of that log, another crossed it at an angle. I stepped over to the new trunk and continued on along our elevated trail. It was not exactly a hike on the sidewalk, but there were plenty of trees going in more or less the right direction. We trekked along a bark-covered, zigzag pathway until the spruce thicket ended.

Bill Davis, age 71. "Because he still can."

Thinking about our retreat from the forest stirs more vivid memories of that day than the fish we caught. As I grow older, extreme trout fishing has become my personal confirmation of vibrant longevity. "Why do you do it?" friends ask me. "Why do you endure long hikes, bugs and discomfort, when you could fish from a boat in the lake?"

My answer is always the same, "Because I still can."

In June of 2002, I couldn't make that claim. Lack of exercise and ballooning weight left me exhausted after three days in the mountains. While the others enjoyed their final day of fishing, I sat alone at a picnic table drinking beer and thinking. *If I don't make some changes, depression will be irrelevant. I'll die of a heart attack.* Three weeks later, my encounter with a geriatric lifeguard in Florida led me another step toward recovery.

When faced with the stark truth of my own mortality, I was forced to examine vague notions of death as an escape. The consequences of an early demise became clear in my mind. *What am I going to do, leave my family behind with an extra helping of grief? That's pretty selfish. If I can't overcome sorrow, I'll just have to stick around until I outlast it.* Experience reminded me that given time, even grief would evolve. Eventually, I'd get used to it.

Back in 1995, while working the self-help course that identified my three important male influences, I was instructed to guess how long I would live. I predicted eighty-four, which meant I had thirty-something years to go. Passage of time compresses as we age. Years that dragged on forever when we are ten, fly by like weeks when we're sixty. *Thirty years will pass before I know it. If that's all I have left, I ought to live them well. I want to lose weight, indulge my curiosity, create things. To waste what's left of my life as a boring bump on a log would be like coming to this condo and spending all my time indoors watching TV. I wonder if a guy who's overweight and old can really get into shape?*

Apathy had other ideas. I procrastinated though three more months with little sign of improvement. By November, I'd had enough. *That's it! Something good needs to happen in my life. Ain't nothin' gonna' stop me from reachin' one-eighty before next summer.* My goal to get fit became a vessel into which I could pour all the mania of depression.

While signing me up at the gym, a sales associate asked, "And what are your fitness goals sir?"

"I'm fifty years old and I want to live to be fifty-five." Soon I was working out six days a week. A mile swim at 5:00 am, then thirty minutes of stretching. Aerobic kickboxing two evenings a week. Ninety minutes of machine-work during off nights and weekends. I became the crazy man for fitness.

I also joined a renowned weight-loss program, attended all their meeting and counted all their points. After nine months of effort, I reached one hundred seventy-seven pounds. I'd lost eighty-five pounds and ten inches off my waist. Friends asked if I had cancer. A pretty young reporter even wrote an article about me for the Wylie paper. The following summer, when I stepped out of my car at a cabin in the Adirondacks, Bill took one look and asked, "Where's the rest of you?"

Longing to keep a spark of devotion alive, I continued to attend Park Lake Baptist Church for two years after Katie's death. Church services left me sad and uncomfortable. Try as I might, I failed to find joy in the Sunday spectacle of Christian life. I was not then, and am not now, angry with God. Stuff happens and God is not pulling the strings. When Katie died, much of my Christian faith and cheer died with her. Despite my best efforts, I found I could no longer accept church doctrine and tradition at the expense of reason. Years later, a counselor I talked to asked, "So you fired your God?"

"No," I replied. "When His joy left my heart, I left His church."

As with parenting, a host of books and experts are available to share valuable lessons on the subject of grief. Months grew to years, and none of those lessons proved equal to lifting my sorrow or calming the deranged surge of thoughts that tormented my nights. Goals of a life well lived remained out of reach. Still, the distractions that added value to my days were having a positive effect. A baby born in November of 2004 helped as well.

When Abbie Bell Parker entered our world, I felt a spark of sunshine arrive with her. Tink, as I call her, is the first child of Jerre's brother Bentley and his wife Trish. Since the day

Abbie joined us, I have loved her and later her younger brothers, William and Wyatt, like grandchildren. They ARE my grandchildren. Jerre and I adopted them as such, without the hassle of paperwork. Shortly before Tink's birth, we discussed what the next generation should call us. We needed to work out our grandparent names.

"Well nobody better call me Granny," Jerre declared. "I like Toot." The rest of us thought Toot was silly, but the name stuck. "What about you Daddy? What can we call you?"

"I've always heard that Taid is Welsh for grandfather. My mother called her grandfather Taid, and I called mine Taid. As Taid got older, his great grandchildren called him Taidy."

"So you want us to call you Taid?"

"No. You can call me Taidy."

My new name has proven to be a good one. Today, even children born to Carly's friends call me Taidy. At first, Carly appeared flustered about people thinking our new granddaughter was hers. I hoped she understood, but had no way of knowing for sure. After Katie died, Carly and I didn't talk intimately for years. She never seemed eager, and I didn't try very hard. I was immersed in my grief for Katie; how could Carly compete with that? As a child, she had always proven herself to be resilient. Rationalization allowed me to assume her strength would get her through the aftermath of her sister's death without help. Grandfathers learn a lot about what they should have done while apprenticing for the position. Dads don't always notice the world around them.

But now I am Taidy and writing about my journeys of discovery is almost done. I have enjoyed reading these letters sent forward from my youth. Were it possible to do so, I would return the favor and send letters back to my younger self as I complete this story of renewal. I'd like to let him know he will survive. Only in a memoir do I get to share the words he should hear.

20

Oct. 2010

Dear Rog,

I still like doing jigsaw puzzles. I can work them for short stretches or long. Friends can join in. Puzzles are good exercise for my aging brain. If the years since tragedy took over my life were a puzzle, maybe it would be the picture of a bear. The trials I've weathered while working my puzzle will not be forgotten. Pieces I knew had to go here, eventually found their way to a proper fit there. Others I thought lost for ever have returned. I have struggled while contemplating each interlocking segment, and now circumstances are fitting together like the last few pieces lying on my table. I enjoy a great sense of harmony with only three holes left to be filled. Now two. Now one. I am not finished with puzzles, but this one is done.

Taidy

Adversity did not withdraw from my life once I became Taidy. In late 2006, my sister called from our mother's home in Florida. "Well, it's bad news, Rog. Mom's doctor says she has abdominal cancer. She's going to refuse any kind of therapy." My mother was eighty-five years old. She realized aggressive treatment offered little hope of success and wanted to spend her remaining days without enduring useless discomfort. Hospice rules allowed help for patients with less than six months to live. Mom was eligible. Over the following half-year, Amy, Fred, and I took turns as her caregiver.

The weeks I spent with Mom passed quickly. She wasn't very demanding, and we had daily help from Hospice assistants. While they looked after her, I could take a break. Enough time to gain temporary relief from new stress I didn't yet comprehend. My mother endured her fate in good spirits with little complaint until she died. Her final lesson for her children was to show us how to go with dignity. I accepted the fitting end to her long life and am grateful for having participated.

Mom kept a copy of the serenity prayer taped to her refrigerator. The one about accepting things we can't change, changing things we can, and knowing the difference between the two. I remember that prayer because one does not spend six months watching one's mother die without cost. Long absences from my job, plus diminished concentration when I returned, combined to bring my position as Director of Technology for Forney Independent School District into question. When a security breach opened the district website to attack, our superintendent felt the need to take action and started the process of hiring my replacement. Calamity surrounded my psyche like wolves circling the slowest elk. With guarded desperation, I agreed to attend an assessment interview at Richardson Regional Medical Center.

The RRMC psychiatric unit provides "crisis stabilization service for mental health disorders and addiction." If on some future morning a nice lady asks you, "Sir, have you ever considered suicide?" don't answer until you are certain of the consequences. When I did so honestly, I might as well have hit a big red panic button. Their crisis management system sprang into action. Before I had time to come to grips with my immediate future, I had agreed to treatment and the medical staff deposited me in the ward where they confiscate your shoe laces. Three of the other patients still had bandages on their wrists. As an outpatient client, I didn't have to spend the night, but during the day I remained locked up with the rest of the unhinged. The crisis team had overreacted.

Near the end of my first day, I met with a resident psychiatrist. "Obviously, you do not belong in our psych ward," he said. "Unfortunately, hospital protocol requires you to schedule appointments with an outside psychiatrist and counselor before you can be released. You're suffering from acute clinical depression and post-traumatic stress disorder. Even though you don't belong here, you need to get help somewhere." I spent another day and a half in the ward while organizing my own discharge.

That was not the first nor the last time I'd hear that diagnosis. Over the next two years, a handful of doctors told me I had PTSD and severe depression. One seemed most interested in prescribing medication and dishing out cookie cutter solutions. Another provoked interesting, insightful conversation. Visits with the more fascinating counselor were like receiving a forty-five minute mental massage. I enjoyed his sessions while they lasted, but failed to realize much change. I do not discount the value of professional help, nor the positive effect of modern medication. Both are wonderful tools that help countless patients throughout their lives. In my experience, however, those remedies proved less effective than advertised.

Most nights I slept three or four hours then woke with my mind racing along currents of contemplation like water rushing over river rocks. Odd notions of existence collided with personal experience to form existential philosophies. In one of these episodes, memories of Nikos and concepts from his math class led me to consider the nature of now. *What are the dimensions of the present? The past is an infinite series of ever decreasing units in time on the minus side of a chart. The future is the same infinite series on the plus side. The present is merely a plane of transition from minus to plus. It has no dimension. It is no more substantive than the plane of transition between east and west, today and tomorrow, life and death. Now does not exist. If the present does not exist, pain does not exist. Only the memory of pain, or the fear of pain to come. Can I choose to ignore it?* I understood these eccentric ideas had first emerged long ago. Great thinkers of centuries past probably named my notions and argued over them in essays.

But attitude CAN be a choice. I've met people who choose to be offended at every opportunity and spend their lives angry. Others choose to be cheerful, even during seasons of prolonged misfortune. People can choose to be angry or not. My father worked his way out of poverty so Amy and I would enjoy lives with options. Can I choose to be depressed or not?

In a fantasy novel titled *The Orc King*, by R.A. Salvatore, I found a passage asserting that fearful people resent any change to their inflexible vision of themselves and their world. The lead character argued for change. He said change did not always result in growth, but growth surely started with change. *If you're not growing, you're dying... Is that what killed Jeff? Did he fail to grow? Can I grow or will I die as well?* My grief remained unimpressed by trivial philosophy.

Two years after Mom died, circumstance again ambushed the Geiger home. In an unexpected moment of revelation, Carly told us that she is gay. My first response was, "It never ends! One more shitty day in my rotten, screwed up life." The pain of another big thorn in my heart almost crushed me. Then I thought about a friend of mine. She'd been homosexual in the South during an era when it could have exposed her to violence. Even as an evangelical Christian, I'd always liked and respected her for the strength of her character, without considering her sexuality. If I could accept her, how could I do less with Carly? During a heartfelt discussion about her being gay, Carly explained it is not the type of thing people get to choose. It is who they are.

The trials I'd faced since Jeff's death altered my perspective on everything, including Carly's revelation. *I've already lost one daughter, and I'll be damned if I'll lose another. I don't care that she's a lesbian. At least nobody died. I'm not even convinced her situation is a sin for which she needs forgiveness. How can I judge her as if being gay is her choice? In many aspects of life, our fate is thrust upon us. It is in our response to that fate that we discover our character.* My choice to love Carly and accept her unconditionally came with instinctive certainty. Her road has proved no less difficult than my own. Despite grief, intolerance and heartbreak, Carly is doing well. Today, we are closer than ever.

Another year passed while thoughts I shared with no one continued to invade my mind. *For eight years, everyone has been telling me I need to deal with depression. What the hell does deal with depression mean?* To some it meant getting back to an arbitrary condition called normal. Was a kid making pipe bombs, or a man escaping thugs by acting crazy, normal? I had never been normal, nor was normal a condition I cared to pursue. *If healing means no longer noticing the loss of those I miss, I don't want to heal.* Was I supposed to turn off my brain and forget Katie and the others? During one moment of utter despair, I discovered a person cannot dissolve their own mind by force of will alone.

Medication left me feeling as inspired as an old piece of wood, and the behavioral therapy employed by my therapists did not appear to be going anywhere. *I'm tired of people telling me I'm depressed. How is recovery stimulated by persistent emphasis on the problem?* I sensed a self-fulfilling prophecy. Defiance urged me to face depression as I had faced other situations that required me to make a decision, overcome fear, and take decisive action. In an attempt to regain control of my place in the world, I took the only bold action available. I ditched my doctors.

Since my initial forays away from home, I had been on a quest for a joy-filled life. First through curiosity and adventure, later by adding the deeper fulfillment of family, religion, and character. *If I want to live, I've got to grow. To grow, I've got to place sad memories on a shelf. Not forgotten, but neatly put away where they won't muddle my mind. Yes, I have experienced pain. Pain will visit again. Will I continue to let it bind my life, or cut those strings?*

I realized my quest had not failed. *I've seen more, done more, and loved more than any man has the right to expect. How do I recapture the imagination that started me on the road to adventure to begin with? Well DUH... I have to focus my energy on new interests and experiences.* My understanding of dealing with depression made a U-turn as I grasped the futility of looking back to face the bear dancing behind me. That bear would always be there and I didn't want him to leave. Clearly, my only worthwhile goal should be that of living the rest of my life well. *Let the bear find fun on his own. I've got a future to open. Starting today, I'll be depressed no longer!*

I enjoy it when an unpopular plan succeeds. Like walking the tops of downed trees to escape a spruce thicket, my unconventional path to recovery worked well for me. After choosing to dwell on the future, life improved quickly. The following year, fate must have decided I'd had enough. Charlie Jackson, our new Executive Director of Technology at Forney ISD, valued my experience. I suspect he resisted suggestions to show me the door. We became a good team and worked well together for several years. When Charlie left Forney for a better opportunity, Forney's new superintendent asked me to reclaim my past position as director. I happily accepted her offer.

Jerre retired from teaching at the end of May, 2010. The subject of where we would live once I retired came up often. "I don't know if I'll be able to leave this house," I told her. "Too many memories rest here. I'm afraid of leaving them behind." With plenty of time to narrow down potential locales, Jerre and I agreed to explore likely sites for our future home. That night, I thought about all the best places I'd lived and visited in my life. *Maybe the best way to accept moving away from my memories is to choose someplace so much better I'll be glad to move?* There was that word again. Choices. *What a wonderful thing it would be, to choose to live by the water.*

"Denise says there's a place near Hughes Springs that has houses on a lake. Can we go look at it?"

Jerre seemed pretty excited about the prospect of moving home, but Hughes Springs? Toronto, the city I grew up in, was over a thousand times bigger. *There are three things I'll never do in this life. I'll never wear cowboy boots; I'll never get one of those belts with my name on the back; and I'll never move to Hughes Springs.*

"Sure Ma. When would you like to go?"

Simpson Lake sits nestled in the middle of the East Texas piney woods about ten miles south of Hughes Springs. As Jerre and I rolled down the highway toward Avinger, every mile seemed to add more greenery, wildflowers and pastures. Rolling hills covered in forest soon stretched as far as we could see outside our windows. At the entrance to the lakeside community of Eagle Landing, we parked under a thick canopy of trees to rendezvous with a pair of local realtors. Frank and Norma lived on the lake and would be our guides for the afternoon. Frank drove a meandering route through the forest. Deer stopped on the road to question our intrusion into their domain. As his car topped the crest of a hill, a beautiful lake came into view below us. The scene looked remarkably similar to a poster I used to gaze at in my room in Saudi Arabia. It hung on the wall between two showing half-naked women standing in fields of wildflowers.

"Jerre, this looks like the lakes in Ontario. It reminds me of Camp Comak. If I didn't know better, I'd think we were in Muskoka."

The first house we viewed was a small log cabin on the east side of the lake. I stopped outside a weathered screen door to inhale forest air and noticed tree shade had lowered June's heat by a few degrees. Down a gentle slope, I could see a dock stretching out over silver ripples. *Cool! I'm gonna check out the water.* While the others toured inside, I walked a path leading toward the lake. At the end of the dock, I stood transfixed while gazing at bottom weeds under several feet of water. In a moment, I rushed back up the hill and into the cabin. Excitement made coherent speech difficult. "JERRE! The lake. Come and see the lake! Quick. Come on. It's looks like up North. It's not all muddy like Texas lakes. The water is clear!"

Two weeks later we made an offer to buy a beautiful home on the shores of Simpson Lake. Lake houses should have a name. We named ours "Fin De La Rue." Both literally and figuratively, it's the End Of The Road. Jerre and I moved here permanently right after I retired.

Fin De La Rue has a big front porch where I can sit while keeping an eye on the forest, and a back deck overlooking the lake. Our small community is full of active old folks like us who all have great stories. The scars of my past no longer slow me down. Here I can concentrate on living well. Not with a spirit of self-gratification, but an attitude of curiosity and service. On the day I retired, I rushed east to the Piney Woods and began training as a Texas Master Naturalist. Every day on Simpson Lake is an adventure filled with imagination, nature, and volunteer activities throughout the region. Living in the forest, far from the turmoil of a modern world, is not for everyone, but I am as happy today as I have ever been. I am growing. If circumstances allow, I will remain at Fin De La Rue until choices about Taidy become Carly's problem.

Dear Rog,

Today I rise early. Crisp air welcomes as I lift my canoe, laying it alongside the dock. Knees, grown stiff with age, complain when asked to forgo a seat, yet settle down as my blade touches water. I back slowly from shore. Now on the lake, a shift of balance places the gunnel just inches above the surface. Strong stokes carry me swiftly as I race whirlwinds of mist illuminated by the dawn. I am stubborn in my refusal to switch sides, reveling instead in my capacity to steer a straight course. Continue on, longer, deeper, faster; then slowing as reality trumps reminiscence. Retreating to the dock my mind chants a forgotten camp song. It is a good morning. It is my best morning.

Taidy

Morning at Fin De La Rue

Made in the USA
Columbia, SC
02 July 2017